Tezcatlipoca

Tezcatlipoca

Trickster and Supreme Deity

EDITED BY
Elizabeth Baquedano

UNIVERSITY PRESS OF COLORADO
Louisville

© 2014 by University Press of Colorado

Published by University Press of Colorado
245 Century Circle, Suite 202
Louisville, Colorado 80027

All rights reserved
First paperback edition 2020

 The University Press of Colorado is a proud member of
the Association of University Presses.

The University Press of Colorado is a cooperative publishing enterprise supported, in part, by Adams State University, Colorado State University, Fort Lewis College, Metropolitan State University of Denver, Regis University, University of Colorado, University of Northern Colorado, University of Wyoming, Utah State University, and Western Colorado University.

ISBN: 978-1-60732-287-0 (cloth)
ISBN: 978-1-64642-113-8 (paperback)
ISBN: 978-1-60732-288-7 (ebook)

Library of Congress Cataloging-in-Publication Data

Tezcatlipoca : trickster and supreme deity / [edited by] Elizabeth Baquedano.
    pages cm
  ISBN 978-1-60732-287-0 (hardback) — ISBN 978-1-64642-113-8 (pbk: alk. paper) — ISBN 978-1-60732-288-7 (ebook)
  1. Tezcatlipoca (Aztec deity) 2. Aztecs—Religion. 3. Aztec mythology. I. Baquedano, Elizabeth.
    F1219.75.R45T49 2014
    299.7'138—dc23
                    2013035024

Cover illustration: Tezcatlipoca holding two flint knives, from the Codex Laud.

To the memory of my beloved father and sister.

To the memory of our dear friends and mentors
Beatriz de la Fuente, Doris Heyden, and H. B. Nicholson

Contents

List of Contributors ix

Acknowledgments xi

INTRODUCTION: SYMBOLIZING TEZCATLIPOCA
   Nicholas J. Saunders and Elizabeth Baquedano   1

1. THE ARCHAEOLOGY OF TEZCATLIPOCA
   Michael E. Smith   7

2. ICONOGRAPHIC CHARACTERISTICS OF TEZCATLIPOCA IN THE REPRESENTATIONS OF CENTRAL MEXICO: THE EZPITZAL CASE
   Juan José Batalla Rosado   41

3. ENEMY BROTHERS OR DIVINE TWINS? A COMPARATIVE APPROACH BETWEEN TEZCATLIPOCA AND QUETZALCOATL, TWO MAJOR DEITIES FROM ANCIENT MEXICO
   Guilhem Olivier, translated by Michel Besson   59

4. Tezcatlipoca and Huitzilopochtli: Political Dimensions
   of Aztec Deities
   Emily Umberger   83

5. Tezcatlipoca as a Warrior: Wealth and Bells
   Elizabeth Baquedano   113

6. Gender Ambiguity and the Toxcatl Sacrifice
   Cecelia F. Klein   135

7. The Maya Lord of the Smoking Mirror
   Susan Milbrath   163

   References   197

   Index   231

Contributors

Elizabeth Baquedano

Juan José Batalla Rosado

Cecelia F. Klein

Susan Milbrath

Guilhem Olivier

Nicholas J. Saunders

Michael E. Smith

Emily Umberger

Acknowledgments

Many people provided different types of assistance in the preparation of this book. In the first instance, the Tezcatlipoca Symposium that provided the basis of the present publication, I thank the Mexican Embassy in the United Kingdom, especially Ambassador Juan José Bremer and Minister Ignacio Durán, who helped in various ways. I thank the present Mexican Ambassador to the United Kingdom Diego Gómez Pickering, Deputy Head of Mission Alejandro Estivill, and Education Attaché Evelyn Vera. My sincere thanks to Chris Winter, who helped with the Tezcatlipoca Symposium, making my life easier. I also thank Alison Taylor-Smith for the design of the poster. I owe special thanks to Brooke Mealey, who read the entire manuscript. Her great attention to detail made the volume appear flawless. Last but by no means least, I thank the staff of the University Press of Colorado, particularly Darrin Pratt and especially Jessica d'Arbonne, who provided help at every stage of publication. Her assistance has been invaluable.

Tezcatlipoca

Introduction

Symbolizing Tezcatlipoca

NICHOLAS J. SAUNDERS AND ELIZABETH BAQUEDANO

A presence of absence defines the ambivalent nature of Tezcatlipoca, the supreme deity of the Late Postclassic Aztec pantheon. In the dark ephemeral reflection of his obsidian mirror and the transient sound of his ceramic flower pipes lies the sensuous nature of a god who mediates materiality and invisibility with omniscience and omnipresence. These qualities are evident not only for the Aztecs but also for scholars today. As Michael Smith (this volume) points out, only recently have we begun to move beyond the written words and painted images of the codices to assess a different kind of Tezcatlipoca's material traces—the objects in which the numinous becomes tangible.

In one sense, Tezcatlipoca was a reification of age-old Mesoamerican patterns of symbolic thought, which abstracted supernatural connotations from the natural world. Specifically, Tezcatlipoca emerged as a supernatural embodiment of cultural attributes inspired by, and bestowed upon, aspects of regional geography/geology and local fauna by the Late Postclassic, pre-Aztec cultures of the Valley of Mexico that were shaped by analogical symbolic reasoning and political exigencies (see Umberger, this volume). Perhaps nowhere is this more evident than in the deity's relationship with obsidian (*itztli*) and the jaguar (*ocelotl*)—two natural kinds imbued with ideational significance across Mesoamerica, recombined in metaphysics, and given physical expression in a distinctive kind of material culture: obsidian mirrors (Smith, this volume).

These reflective devices were powerfully ambiguous, not least because they shone with a "dark light." They partook of what has been called a pan-Amerindian "aesthetic of brilliance," which accorded sacredness and power to a multimedia assemblage of shiny objects—the material metaphors of access to and control of the glowing spirit realm from whence status and political power flowed (Saunders 1998). Baquedano's (this volume) analysis of Tezcatlipoca's golden ornamentation, where brilliance and the sounds of bells (symbolic of warfare) reinforce this conceptual association, is epitomized by Durán's description.

Tezcatlipoca was thus a product of both a conceptual landscape that drew upon the physical environment (and what was made of it metaphorically) and a cultural landscape composed of the ever-changing political milieu in which he operated, from the Late Postclassic to the Early Colonial period (Saunders 2001, 225–27).

Hitherto, with the exception of Guilhem Olivier (2003), a sustained analysis of Tezcatlipoca has been long overdue. This volume begins to redress the balance and focuses on a wide variety of approaches to one of the most intriguing and complex deities of the Mesoamerican world. In this brief introductory essay, we attempt an interdisciplinary overview, building on the volume's specialist contributions but extending into the realm of what is often called "material culture studies" (e.g., Buchli 2002; Tilley et al. 2006). Our focus is on the relationships among landscape, deity, and constructions of worldview as mediated by objects and their role in ideological enforcement.

A GOD IN THE LANDSCAPE

Obsidian mirrors, like Tezcatlipoca himself, are ambiguous (see Klein, this volume). Their raw material is mined from the earth and shaped by people, and, if we believe ethnohistorical sources, they appear to give their owner access to the intangible world of reflections, where souls, spirits, and the immanent forces of the cosmos dwell. From this perspective, it is hardly surprising, though in no way predictable, that Tezcatlipoca is a potent combination of such power imagery whose name is a linguistic apotheosis of Aztec conceptual thought—the "Lord of the Smoking Mirror" (Nicholson 1971, 412).

Tezcatlipoca's omnipresence was commented upon by Sahagún (1950–82, book III: 11), who said "his abode was everywhere—in the land of the dead, on earth, [and] in heaven." Like the wind he is invisible, and like a shadow he moves across the land (ibid., book I: 5). In other words, Tezcatlipoca crosses spatial and mythical boundaries with impunity, as a truly shaman-like transformative figure (Saunders 1990, 166–67). This shamanic quality, albeit lifted to the level of an imperial state divinity, was also expressed by his omniscience and represented by the wielding of his eponymous magical obsidian mirror (*tezcatl*), itself a metaphor for rulership and power (Heyden 1991, 195), with which he "knows everything" and is able to see into the hearts of men (Sahagún 1950–82, book III: 11).

Such was the semantic proximity of material and deity that obsidian was considered a manifestation of Tezcatlipoca (Ruiz de Alarcón 1984, 229). Fray Diego Durán (1971, 98) observed that the god's temple image was of a lustrous stone, black as jet, from which sharp blades and knives were made (cf. Heyden 1988, 222). The relationship of Tezcatlipoca and the overlapping physical and supernatural associations of obsidian illustrate Alfred Gell's (1992, 44) point that "the *technology of enchantment* is founded on the *enchantment of technology*" (original emphasis).

The associations between Tezcatlipoca and obsidian (in its various cultural forms) were extended into the realm of animal symbolism as represented by the god's relationship with the jaguar (*Panthera onca* [ocelotl]). Across Mesoamerica and South America, the jaguar was the salient predator of the natural world, a prototype for cultural categories of agonistic activities such as hunting, warfare, and sacrifice and as the spirit familiar par excellence of shamans, priests, and political leaders (Benson 1998; Roe 1998; Saunders 1991). Aztec jaguar symbolism shared this wider conceptual categorization of the feline, finding expression, for example, in its ocelotl warrior cadre and the nocturnal predatory nature of Tezcatlipoca himself (Saunders 1990; also see Sahagún 1950–82, book XI: 1).

A dramatic example of Tezcatlipoca's feline associations is his transformational manifestation as the jaguar Tepeyollotl (Jiménez Moreno 1979, 28), sometimes represented as such in the codices (e.g., Codex Borbonicus, Seler 1904, figure 28a). In the Codex Telleriano-Remensis, Tezcatlipoca's face emerges from the jaws of a large feline, and on the carved-stone "Hackmack Box," Cecelia Klein (1987, 334) identifies the individual engaging in auto-sacrificial bloodletting as Tezcatlipoca, in his guise as Tepeyollotl, because of his spotted-feline apparel.

The identification of Tezcatlipoca with the feline is enshrined in Aztec mythology, where he is described as a nocturnal deity whose alter ego was the jaguar (Caso 1958, 14–15). In a typically shamanic association, he was also the patron of sorcerers who manipulated the animal's claws, pelt, and heart in their magical activities (Sahagún 1950–82, book XI: 3).

The conceptualization of the jaguar in Aztec natural philosophy penetrated many levels of everyday life, not least astronomical phenomena, where he was associated with the moon and the constellation Ursa Major and his omniscience was perhaps connected to his identification with the planet Jupiter, which appeared to dominate the night sky (Olivier, this volume). Those individuals born under the sign of the month called Ocelotl were regarded as possessing the attributes of strength and aggressiveness signified by the jaguar (Durán 1971, 402) and thus as particularly suitable to lead a warrior's life. Similarly, terms with ocelotl as their root were applied adjectivally to individuals who displayed the appropriate qualities: thus, *ocelopetlatl* and *oceloyotl* were considered particularly appropriate terms to describe valiant warriors and the qualities of valor and bravery in general (Siméon 1988 [1885], 352).

A concentration of jaguar imagery was, perhaps inevitably, associated with the clothing and paraphernalia of Aztec royalty. Sahagún (1950–82, book VIII: 23–25) relates that Aztec emperors adorned themselves with jaguar/ocelotl capes, breech clouts, and sandals made of the animal's pelt and that they wore an insignia of ocelotl skin into battle (Siméon 1988 [1885], 352). This symbolic identification is also revealed in royalty's privileged access to ocelotl-skin thrones, mats, and cushions (Sahagún 1950–82, book VIII: 31) as an expression of authority and rulership (Dibble 1971, 324). This tripartite association of Tezcatlipoca, the jaguar, and rulership characterizes the deity's role as patron of royalty and his appearance in rituals of royal accession, in which mirror symbolism is also prominent (Saunders 1990, 167–68). This elite association has pan-Mesoamerican resonance as, among the Maya, Kawil was a "royal" god linked with ruling lineages (Milbrath, this volume) and many Maya rulers incorporated the deity into their personal names, particularly at Tikal (Martin and Grube 2000).

Tezcatlipoca brings together and creatively recombines obsidian, mirrors, elite status, sacrifice, and age-old ideas concerning the jaguar. Late Postclassic codices preserve the iconographic evidence for this symbolic equation in representations of Tezcatlipoca with his left foot replaced by a "smoking mirror" and a jaguar head (Seler 1904, figure 28a) and displaying his stream of blood: *ezpitzal* (Batalla Rosado, this volume). The smoking mirror symbol (which replaces the left foot)—the *atl tlachinolli* glyph—might refer to the billowing smoke and dust of a battlefield, as the term *tlachinolli* appears to be associated with battlefield cremations of dead warriors (Brundage 1979, 247), those who have made the ultimate blood sacrifice for the Aztec state and cosmos.

The co-identification of Tezcatlipoca and Tepeyollotl—at least in part—further elaborates such ideas. Tepeyollotl means "Heart of the Mountain," and according to Heyden (1981, 25), obsidian is the "heart of the earth." *Yollotl* signifies "heart"— the human heart being the most precious offering humans could make to the gods (López Austin 1973, 60).

It can be argued that the chthonic associations of both Tezcatlipoca and his jaguar familiar, Tepeyollotl, are related to the geological origins of obsidian, drawing on Aztec (and wider Mesoamerican) beliefs concerning the "sacred earth," caves as portals to the spirit world, and the notion of the earth as the progenitor of fertility for humans, animals, and flora (Saunders 2004).

The use of obsidian blades in acts of human blood sacrifice (including auto-sacrifice), whose spiritual and ideological purpose is to reinforce, maintain, and induce fertility and thereby guarantee physical and cosmic survival, might be considered an integral part of a Tezcatlipoca cult (Saunders 1994, 178–80).

The symbolic complexities of Tezcatlipoca's relationship with the earth and obsidian, and their etymological combination and representation in the name "Lord of the Smoking Mirror," may embrace elements of the pre-Aztec and Aztec observation and classification of their distinctive physical environment. The Aztec capital of Tenochtitlan was built on an island in the center of Lake Texcoco in the tectonically active central highlands of Mexico. This was (and remains) a landscape of fuming geological vents, smoking volcanoes, and snow-covered peaks, around which fog, mist, and rain clouds gathered (see Townsend 1987, 373).

The prominent volcano Popocatepetl is represented in the Codex Mendoza with four volutes of smoke and identified as "the mountain which smokes"; smoke is the "word" of the volcano, signifying its presence as a spiritually alive entity, and its fumes express premonitions and oracles (Roiz 1997, 90). Beneath its peak lies Lake Texcoco, which steams in the morning and at dusk. This was a region from which many different kinds of smoke and fumes emanated, each kind possessing its own metaphysical qualities and associations and whose interrelationships defined the Aztec (and wider Mesoamerican) view of the world (Saunders, in press).

The association of smoke and shadows in Aztec metaphysics extends these associations with Tezcatlipoca further still. An individual's cosmic identity is signified as his or her *tonalli*, recognized as "life force," associated linguistically with a person's shadow (López Austin 1988, 205–6). Tezcatlipoca played an important role in this respect, as he brought illness, misfortune, and death by casting his shadow (Sahagún 1950–82, book I: 5): "he was . . . like the night, like the wind. On the occasions when he called to someone, he spoke like a shadow" (López Austin 1988, 218). More widely, he was believed to be a master of transformation, a trickster, who had the power to cheat and betray individuals (Olivier 2003, 30, 270). In prayers designed to appease him, the Aztec intoned "O master . . . May thy smoke, the cloud [of thy ire] cease; may the fire, the blaze [of thy rage] be extinguished" (Sahagún 1950–82, book VI: 4–5).

These interlocking complexities of Tezcatlipoca's nature, multiple roles, and metaphorical attributes illustrate (albeit briefly here) the extent to which his influence penetrated Aztec belief and social action across all levels of Late Postclassic central Mexican culture. Once the interpretive framework was in place, everyday life reinforced it. Seeing one's reflection in water, encountering (or even dreaming of encountering) a feline in the night, watching mist blown by the wind from atop Popocatepetl or smoke curling up from a copal censer or a burned-blood offering—all could be signs of Tezcatlipoca's presence in the world.

Such attitudes, of course, were not an Aztec invention; they were part of an ancient and distinctive Mesoamerican engagement with the world (Houston and Taube 2000), a product of symbolic analogical reasoning. Yet while this worldview was an ancestral legacy, it was actively reconfigured by a pre-Aztec, then Aztec, political reality in the Valley of Mexico, from which emerged an ideological imperative couched in terms of an all-seeing, all-controlling, and ever-present god.

1

The Archaeology of Tezcatlipoca

MICHAEL E. SMITH

From the seminal nineteenth-century works of Eduard Seler (1990–98) through the present day, scholars have emphasized the works of the chroniclers (primarily Sahagún and Durán) as primary sources on Aztec gods, myths, and ceremonies, coupled with ample use of the ritual or divinatory codices to illustrate religious themes and activities. This body of scholarship can be considered the standard or dominant approach to Aztec religion. Although intellectual perspectives and paradigms have changed through the decades, scholars return again and again to this same small set of primary sources. As a result, ethnohistorians and art historians now pose questions far more sophisticated and detailed than their predecessors of a few decades ago. Fortunately, the primary material is quite rich, and we are far from exhausting its potential to add to our understanding of Aztec religion.

The continuing reliance on a small number of sources by scholars working in the dominant scholarly approach to Aztec religion comes at a cost, however. Although our understanding of the details of Aztec iconography and symbolism has advanced greatly, we still know very little about many important topics that—for whatever reason—are not featured in the works of the chroniclers or the codices. Unless scholars can begin to incorporate other kinds of information, research on Aztec religion could become so detailed, involuted, and esoteric that it ceases to contribute to the wider task of illuminating the Prehispanic past. Fortunately, a nascent trend suggests that scholars are beginning to move beyond the confines of the chroniclers and codices to produce important new insights into Aztec religious beliefs and practices. The chapters in this book are part of that trend.

It is no accident that the new scholarly trend focuses on the deity Tezcatlipoca. Not only is the Lord of the Smoking Mirror one of the most important Aztec deities, but he is the god whose scholarship has clearly surpassed that of his siblings in quantity and quality. Although a number of significant studies of Tezcatlipoca have appeared in recent years (e.g., Carrasco 1991; Heyden 1989; Matos Moctezuma 1997; Olivier 2002; Saunders 1990; Valencia Rivera 2006), the majority of the credit for advancing scholarship on this deity must go to Guilhem Olivier. His detailed book-length examination of Tezcatlipoca is an important breakthrough in many ways (Olivier 1997); subsequent citations to this work will be to the English translation (Olivier 2003). Strange as it may seem, Olivier's book is the first comprehensive book-length treatment of an Aztec deity.[1]

Among the significant accomplishments of Olivier's book are its systematic comparisons among sources (e.g., tables of attributes of the deity images of Tezcatlipoca in the codices), the breadth of written sources consulted, the judicious analyses and evaluations of data and interpretations, and a serious regard for the material manifestations of the Tezcatlipoca cult. Olivier treats cult objects not just as objects that may contain iconographic texts but as important sources of material and contextual data in their own right. Although his approach to such objects is not as systematic or comprehensive as an archaeologist might hope, Olivier does demonstrate the very real advances in scholarship that can come when new kinds of data—beyond the chroniclers and codices—are brought to bear systematically on a topic in Aztec religion.

The chapters in this book build on the foundation of Olivier's book, and they illustrate diverse ways of expanding traditional emphases on the standard sources. Olivier's own chapter expands the perspective to incorporate another major deity, Quetzalcoatl. Careful comparative analysis is always a productive way to increase understanding of a topic, and the juxtaposition of these two deities is a productive approach. Susan Milbrath also applies a comparative framework in her comparison between Tezcatlipoca and the Maya deity Kawil. Her analyses encompass a much broader range of symbols and associations, and this is both a strength and a weakness. On the positive side, her study provides wider contextualization of the deities and their symbolism than the other chapters do, but on the negative side, this broad perspective makes specific comparisons more difficult to evaluate.

Juan José Batalla Rosado works within the framework of the standard sources—codices—but his work departs from past studies in its minute attention to visual detail in a highly systematic framework. He has shown the value of this approach in a variety of publications (Batalla Rosado 1997, 2002a, 2002b, 2007), and that tradition continues in the present chapter. The systematic comparisons and analyses carried out by Olivier (2003) and Batalla Rosado (this volume) represent a valuable method for continuing to derive insights from the standard sources. Elizabeth Baquedano's chapter confirms the notion that the codices and chroniclers are far from exhausted as sources of continuing insight. The military and warfare associations of Tezcatlipoca have long been recognized in the literature, but numerous iconographic and symbolic details have remained unclear. By focusing on gold and bells, Baquedano extends our knowledge of an important aspect of Tezcatlipoca's domain.

Two chapters move far beyond the standard documentary sources on Tezcatlipoca. Emily Umberger focuses on large stone public monuments, many of which have some sort of Tezcatlipoca imagery. She shows that these depictions relate less to the Tezcatlipoca cult than to the political rhetoric and propaganda that employed Tezcatlipoca as an icon of imperial power. The simple presence of images or attributes of this deity cannot therefore be assumed to relate to religion or ritual per se. This insight comes only by analyzing these monuments in their spatial and visual contexts. Cecelia Klein moves so far beyond the standard sources that her chapter is not really about the Aztec period at all but rather concerns the relevance of Tezcatlipoca for Christian representations in the Colonial period.

THE MATERIAL CULTURE OF AZTEC RELIGION

One of the limitations of the standard approach to Aztec religion as outlined above is many scholars' seeming avoidance of archaeological evidence—objects and their context. The big exception, of course, centers on research at the Templo Mayor of Tenochtitlan since 1978 (Boone 1987; López Luján 2005 [1994]; Matos Moctezuma 1982, 1995). This project has clarified many aspects of Mexica ritual and religion, and the resulting archaeological data have been embraced and used extensively by non-archaeologists (e.g., Aveni, Calnek, and Hartung 1988; Broda 1987; Carrasco 1987; Graulich 2001; Umberger 1987a). Unfortunately for the purposes of this volume, Tezcatlipoca is poorly represented in the offerings and other finds of the Templo Mayor project. A few images of the deity are found on objects (see discussion below), and some of the excavated cult items could well derive from rituals dedicated to Tezcatlipoca, but overall, research at the Templo Mayor has taught us little about this important deity.[2]

In this chapter I examine several archaeological aspects of the Tezcatlipoca cult. I focus on obsidian mirrors, ceramic flutes, and *momoztli* altars and on the archaeological evidence for the antiquity and extent of Tezcatlipoca and his cult. My treatment of the archaeology of Tezcatlipoca must be seen as preliminary because I run up against some of the basic problems that plague the analysis of Aztec material culture. In considering the lack of archaeological input to research in the dominant tradition of Aztec religious studies (beyond the Templo Mayor project), one is initially tempted to argue that ethnohistorians, art historians, and religious studies scholars simply need to take sites and artifacts into greater account in their analyses. But even a cursory glance at the archaeological literature reveals that few of the relevant objects and sites are analyzed or published in a format that can be used by other scholars. It is simply not reasonable to expect the contributors to this volume, or other scholars of Aztec religion, to root around in the dusty storage collections of museums or to find all of the relevant archaeological reports—typically published in obscure places, if at all—to see whether obsidian mirrors or flutes have been excavated at Aztec sites. As archaeologists, art historians, and museum curators, we have not done our jobs compiling and analyzing information on Aztec material culture, and this hinders our understanding of Aztec religion.

This chapter is an exploratory essay to see what kind of insights might be gained from a more systematic consideration of the materiality and context of the elements of Tezcatlipoca's cult. Although my coverage of obsidian mirrors, ceramic flutes, and altars is far from complete, it is still possible to advance our understanding of some aspects of Aztec ritual practice simply by looking at a wide range of items instead of focusing solely on the best-known and finest examples. I discuss this approach in more general terms in Smith (2011). In some ways, this chapter can be considered an extension of Olivier's monograph on Tezcatlipoca. I provide a few more examples than he considers, and I take a closer look at some of the material objects of the Tezcatlipoca cult.

The problems that limit the contribution of material culture to research on Aztec religion are (1) an art historical focus on a few of the finest objects instead of study of a wider range of less fine examples, (2) a lack of information on museum holdings, and (3) a lack of publication of key archaeological projects and collections.

Problem 1: The Art Historical Focus on Only a Few of the Finest Objects

Most art historians and museum curators focus their analysis on a small number of the finest objects, ignoring the range of variation within categories of material culture. For example, there are probably thousands of Aztec stone sculptures in museums in Mexico, the United States, and Europe, yet only a small subset of these are included over and over in museum exhibits and catalogs (e.g., Eggebrecht 1987; Matos Moctezuma and Solís Olguín 2002; Solís Olguín 2004; Solís Olguín and Leyenaar 2002). From such works, one cannot get any idea of the variation that exists within the corpus of Aztec sculptures; for this, one needs complete catalogs and documentation of individual museum collections. Unfortunately, only a few examples exist. Felipe Solís Olguín cataloged sculptures in the museum at Santa Cecilia Acatitlan (Solís Olguín 1976), and he also published a catalog of sculptures from Castillo de Teayo (Solís Olguín 1981). The recent catalog of sculptures in the new Musée du quai Branly in Paris (López Luján and Fauvet-Berthelot 2005) is another very useful work in this tradition. From this work we can begin to suggest that most sculptures of deities housed in temples throughout Postclassic central Mexico were cruder and far more variable than the finely made examples we see in all the books (Smith n.d.b).

Another example of this phenomenon is the Tlaloc jar. The small number of fine Tlaloc jars excavated at the Templo Mayor is reproduced and analyzed endlessly in books and articles, and one might easily think these were typical of Aztec ceramic vessels depicting this deity. Far more common in museum storerooms, however, is a very different type of vessel with crude Tlaloc features. Examples have been excavated at Nahualac and Tenenepango (Charnay 1888; Lorenzo 1957), Cerro Tlaloc (Wicke and Horcasitas 1957), Calixtlahuaca (Smith, Wharton, and McCarron 2003), and other sites. Leonardo López Luján (2006, 1: 140–43; 2: 454–55) has published illustrations and discussions of the variety of Tlaloc vessels used throughout Mesoamerica, including both the fancy and the crude Aztec forms. Prior to the publication of that work, however, one would never know that the crude vases are the most typical form of Aztec Tlaloc effigy because of the two other problems with Aztec material culture research: lack of information on museum collections and lack of publication.

Problem 2: The Hidden Treasure of Museum Collections

Fine Aztec objects were among the first Mesoamerican items brought from Mexico to Europe after the Spanish conquest, and Aztec objects remained popular with museums in Europe and the United States during the heyday of artifact collecting in the nineteenth century (Boone 1993). Needless to say, Mexican museums have many more examples in their storerooms. With a few exceptions, however (Baer 1996; Baer and Bankmann 1990; Carrandi, Granados Vázquez, and Garduño Ramírez 1990; Solís Olguín 1976; Solís Olguín and Morales Gómez 1991), museum holdings remain largely undocumented. A few years ago I contacted curators at a number of museums, looking for possible collections from Calixtlahuaca. Some were able to supply information, but most replied that they simply didn't know what they might have and had no convenient way to find out (given current staffing and budgets).

I have discussed the problem of undocumented museum collections in other papers (Smith 2004, n.d.b). In those papers I focus on the importance of whole objects (in museums) for interpreting the fragments excavated by archaeologists. Here, I am emphasizing the related issue of understanding the range of variation within key categories of objects. One consequence of the lack of knowledge of museum collections is the absence of a systematic catalog (or corpus) of any category of Aztec object. In Classical and Mediterranean archaeology, many categories of material objects—from Greek vases to Persian stamps to Byzantine coins—have a published corpus. Such works make many dispersed objects known and provide a standardized reference for scholars in many disciplines.

PROBLEM 3: THE LACK OF PUBLICATION

The lack of publication of both museum collections and excavations is another obstacle to using material objects in the analysis of Aztec religion. Complete publication of key collections can open up new interpretive windows and advance our understanding of Aztec religion and society. One example is the so-called volador offering, a collection of many hundreds of ceramic vessels and other objects excavated in downtown Mexico City in the 1930s. Solís Olguín and Morales Gómez (1991) published all of the volador objects in the Museo Nacional (unfortunately, they did not include numerous other objects from the volador that had been exchanged with other museums around the world). By examining the composition of the offering in terms of vessel forms, my colleagues and I were able to offer a new social interpretation of the deposit (Smith, Wharton, and Olson 2003) that would have been impossible without a systemic accounting of the several hundred objects. The situation with respect to many key Aztec sites is even worse. For example, there is simply no documentation of the early excavations at Teopanzolco and Santa Cecilia Acatitlan, and many other sites remain poorly published (see discussion in Smith 2008). We need far more richly illustrated systematic works like López Luján (2006) if we are to begin to understand the forms and variation in Aztec material culture.

One positive development in the analysis of the material component of Aztec religion is a trend toward the systematic analysis of material culture items from the codices. Jacqueline de Durand-Forest, in particular, has carried out very useful analyses of cult items in the trecenas (Durand-Forest 1998; Durand-Forest et al. 2000). Other scholars have taken systematic looks at the depictions of a number of different kinds of material culture in the codices (Batalla Rosado 1997; Durand-Forest and Eisinger 1998; Heyden 2005; Matos Moctezuma 1996), and Frances Berdan (2007) considers the economic implications of the nature and diversity of material culture used in Aztec rituals. For the Tezcatlipoca cult, of course, Olivier's (2003) book should be mentioned here.

THE MATERIALITY OF THE TEZCATLIPOCA CULT

Olivier (2003) discusses the various items associated with the cult of Tezcatlipoca. These items include sculptures of the deity, obsidian mirrors, precious stones, human femurs, staffs, shields, arrows, flutes, momoztli altars, and a variety of specific items and attributes of jewelry, costume, and body paint. To these, Han Roskamp (2010) adds metallurgy in west Mexico. Of these I single out obsidian mirrors, ceramic flutes, and momoztli altars for discussion, based on two criteria: (1) they seem to have strong associations with the deity (based on the codices and writings of the chroniclers), and (2) they are relatively well represented in archaeological excavations and museum collections of Aztec material. These objects illustrate the limitations discussed in the previous section, but they also suggest the potential to transcend those limitations through systematic and comprehensive analysis.

Obsidian Mirrors

The obsidian mirror might be considered the most important object in the Tezcatlipoca cult. This judgment is based on several factors, including the most commonly accepted etymology of Tezcatlipoca, which means "smoking mirror" (Olivier 2003, 14–15); the distinctive attribute of a black smoking mirror that replaces Tezcatlipoca's foot in numerous codex images; and the abundance of additional black mirrors as costume elements of the deity in the codices (they appear as pendants, back devices, and headdress elements). The association between mirrors and Tezcatlipoca is not an exclusive one, however—the divinatory codices contain images of mirrors associated with Huitzilopochtli and other deities. Nevertheless, their depiction with Tezcatlipoca predominates, and it seems safe to say that circular obsidian mirrors suggest the presence of the cult of Tezcatlipoca.

To my knowledge, no obsidian mirror has ever been excavated in a documented and approved professional archaeological excavation. There are numerous examples in museums, however, and they form the basis for the following discussion. Figure 1.1 shows the two typical forms of Aztec obsidian mirror, circular and rectangular. These objects, now curated in museums in the care of the Instituto Mexiquense de Cultura, do not have secure proveniences. They were both part of the collection of the Museo Regional de Toluca when it was cataloged and moved to new quarters in the 1970s (Castillo Tejero 1991). That collection originated with José García Payón's (1936) material from Calixtlahuaca, to which various donations and purchases were added over the years. Poor recordkeeping by García Payón (who directed the museum initially) and subsequent museum directors often prevents a secure separation of the Calixtlahuaca material from the later additions (Smith, Wharton, and McCarron 2003). García Payón, however, typically mentions important and

14   THE ARCHAEOLOGY OF TEZCATLIPOCA

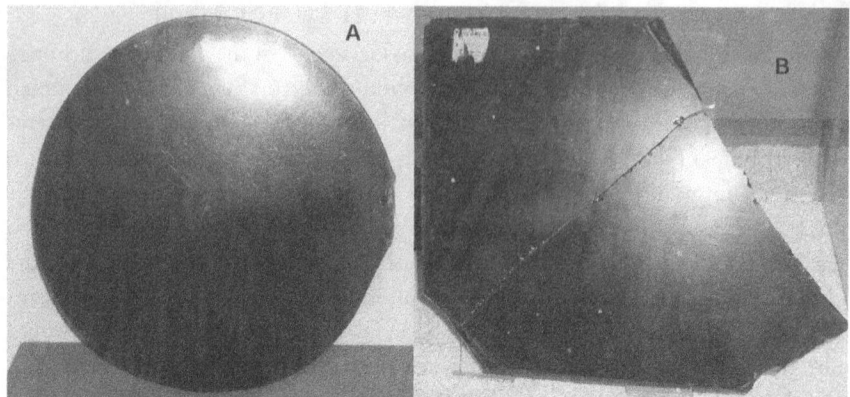

FIGURE 1.1. Obsidian mirrors from museums in the Toluca area. A: circular mirror (no.1) in the Museo Román Piña Chán at the site of Teotenango; B: fragmentary rectangular mirror in the Museo de Antropología e Historia, Centro Cultural Mexiquense, Toluca. Photographs by Michael E. Smith; courtesy, Instituto Mexiquense de Cultura.

distinctive finds in his unillustrated narrative of the excavation and finds (García Payón 1979), yet he fails to include any discussion of obsidian mirrors. This suggests that these objects were not from his fieldwork but were donations or purchases sometime between the 1930s and the 1970s.

A number of authors have suggested that rectangular obsidian mirrors were innovations of the Spanish Colonial period in central Mexico (Meslay 2001; Saunders 1997), although they fail to provide much evidence in support of this idea. The lack of rectangular mirrors from known excavations cannot be used in favor of a colonial dating, since none of the (almost certainly Prehispanic) circular mirrors have secure provenience either. But I will not consider the rectangular variety further here, for two reasons: (1) there seems to be a good possibility that they are not Prehispanic in origin, and (2) Nicholas Saunders has undertaken a study of the rectangular mirrors (personal communication, June 2007; see also Saunders 1997), which one hopes will be available shortly.

There is abundant evidence in the codices that mirrors in Aztec central Mexico—both those associated with Tezcatlipoca and other mirrors—were black and circular in form. Figure 1.2 shows a variety of examples of mirrors in the codices; all are circular and most are black. The most common image is Tezcatlipoca's foot (figure 1.2A). A mirror is part of the toponym of Tezcatepec (figure 1.2B) in both the Codex Mendoza (Berdan and Anawalt 1992, f. 27r) and the Codex Azcatitlan (Barlow and Graulich 1995, 7); it also occurs in the personal name of Atezcatl (figure 1.2C). Sahagún's mirror-stone (*tezcatl*; figure 1.2D) is round and black (Sahagún

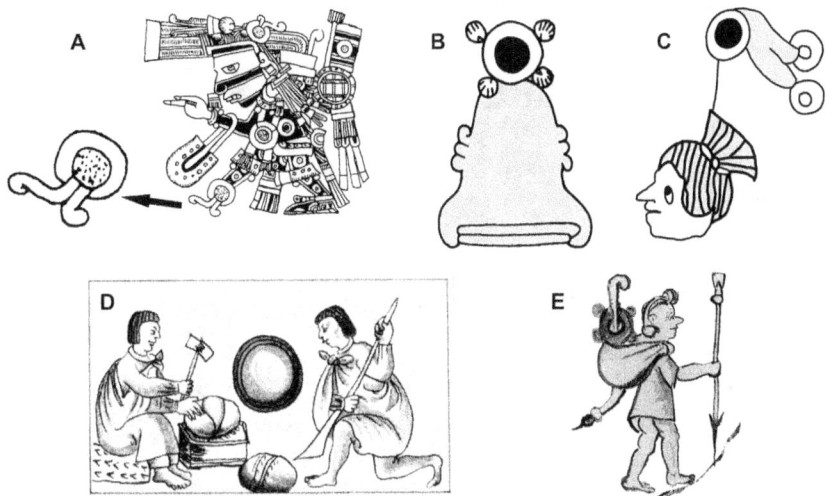

FIGURE 1.2. Black (obsidian) circular mirrors in the Aztec codices. A: Tezcatlipoca's foot from the Codex Borgia (modified after Seler 1963, f. 21); B: toponym for Tezcatepec from the Codex Mendoza (redrawn from Berdan and Anawalt 1992, f. 27r); C: personal name of Atezcatl from the Mapa de Sigüenza (redrawn from Castañeda de la Paz 2006, 154); D: mirror-stone ("tezcatl") in Sahagún (modified after Sahagún 1950–82, book XI: figure 783); E: carrier of the sacred bundle of Tezcatlipoca in the Codex Azcatitlan (modified after Barlow and Graulich 1995, 7).

1950–82, book XI: 228–29); see also his discussion of the mirror-stone seller, "tezcanamacac" (ibid., book X: 87).

The Codex Azcatitlan (Barlow and Graulich 1995, 7) shows one of the Aztlan migrants leaving Huehuetoca with a bundle that includes a smoking mirror (figure 1.2E). Barlow's interpretation of this scene is as follows: "Desde aquí parte el camino con los portadores del dios, uno de los cuales lleva a cuestas el espejo humeante de Tezcatlipoca" (Barlow 1995, 70). As is often the case in the codices, it is difficult to determine whether this image was meant to depict an actual obsidian mirror or whether the smoking mirror is a sign for Tezcatlipoca, for his sacred bundle (Olivier 1995), or perhaps for his worship and cult in general. Overall, the images in figure 1.2 make it clear that the standard depiction of mirrors in the Aztec codices was a circular black object, sometimes with plumes for smoke and sometimes with balls of down. I am not aware of any images of rectangular mirrors in the Aztec codices.

I have been able to locate secure references to sixteen circular obsidian mirrors in museum collections; they are listed in table 1.1. I exclude from consideration a number of small circular ornaments of obsidian that are probably more usefully

TABLE 1.1. Catalog of obsidian mirrors discussed in this chapter.

	Location	Catalog no.	Publications	Dimensions		
				diameter	thickness	source[a]
1	Museo Román Piña Chán, Teotenango			28.0	3.1	1
2	American Museum of Natural History, New York	30.0/6253	Keleman 1969, plate 298A; Saville 1925, plate LI	26.0		1
3	British Museum, London	OBJ 112376	Tait 1967, figure 4	18.4	1.3	1
4	British Museum, London	AM 1825, 1210.16		26.0	1.5	1
5	British Museum, London	AM 1907, 0608.2		24.0	1.6	1
6	Museo Nacional de Antropología, Mexico City		Day 1992, 46	18.8		2
7	Museo de América, Madrid	Inv. 9996, Room 4		21.5		1
8	Nasher Museum, Duke University, Durham, NC		Website	19.7	1.9	1
9	Museum National d'Histoire Naturelle, Paris		Meslay 2001, 78	25.2		2
10	Private collection		Meslay 2001, 79	28.9		2
11	Museo Nacional de Ciencias Naturales, Madrid	18611		30.0		1
12	Museo Nacional de Antropología, Mexico City		Serra Puche and Solís Olguín 1994, 50, 193, 194	18.5		2
13	Museo Nacional de Antropología, Mexico City		(display)			
14	Museum of the American Indian, Suitland, MD	163380		21.8	1.8	3

continued on next page

TABLE 1.1—*continued*

	Location	Catalog no.	Publications	Dimensions		
				diameter	*thickness*	*source*[a]
15	Musée du quai Branly	71.1882.17.568		21.8	1.5	4
16	Auguste Génin collection		Société des Américanistes 1922, 259	26.0		2

Note for Table 1.1: [a] Dimensions in cm; source for dimensions: (1) personal communication from museum staff, (2) publication, (3) direct measurement, (4) museum web page.

characterized as jewelry pendants rather than mirrors. Two such ornaments in the Peabody Museum of Natural History at Yale University (catalog nos. YPM 137867 and YPM 260565) differ from the mirrors discussed here in two ways: they are much smaller (diameters of ca. 5 cm, compared with 18–30 cm for the mirrors), and their edges are crudely flaked and not smoothed like mirrors. Similar objects, excavated at Teotihuacan by Sigvald Linné (1934), are called mirrors by Karl Taube (1992b, 169). I have not conducted anything resembling a systematic study of obsidian mirrors, and the following remarks are intended only to suggest a few patterns and to illustrate the potential of systematic research on museum collections.[3] My sample comes from the published literature, with personal inquiries to a number of museums, and it is almost certain that additional unpublished examples are found in other museums.[4] I have seen only two of these mirrors firsthand (nos. 1 and 6). A systematic study would require careful examination and measurement of each object, coupled with some technical studies (e.g., chemical characterization to determine the geological sources of the obsidian).

All, or most, of these mirrors are of the form of object number 3 (figure 1.3), the famous "magical speculum of Dr. Dee" (Ackermann and Devoy 2012; Anonymous 1968; Tait 1967). The mirrors are close to circular in form, with a single projection pierced by a hole. The likely purpose of the hole is for wearing the mirror as an ornament on the chest or in another position, a common trait in representations of Tezcatlipoca in the codices (Olivier 2003, 54–55). On object 1 (figure 1.1A) the projection has clearly broken off, and it is possible that this is the case for some of the other mirrors—for example, object 2—whose published images do not show a clear projection. The mirrors all appear to be finely polished, with smooth but distinct edges (figure 1.3). Some examples (mirrors nos. 2 and 12) are encased in wood frames; I would guess that the frames are post-conquest additions.

No secure provenience information is available for any of these thirteen mirrors. Some authors have published speculations of the general region of origin for

FIGURE 1.3. Circular obsidian mirror (no. 3) in the British Museum. This is the famous mirror used for divination by Dr. Dee. © Trustees of the British Museum; reproduced with permission.

some examples; for example, Pál Keleman (1969, 2: 361) says that mirror number 2 "is said to come from Veracruz." Olivier (2003, 331) reviews this and other such attributions, few or none of which can be given much credence in my view. Two historical citations of obsidian mirrors from Michoacán (ibid.) do suggest that these objects were probably used in the Tarascan empire. Of the three mirrors in the Museo Nacional de Antropología in Mexico City, one (no. 6) is from central Mexico and two (nos. 12 and 13) are from west Mexico (Felipe Solís, personal communication, July 2007).

There appears to be some degree of standardization in the size and form of the circular obsidian mirrors in my sample. All, or nearly all, have the perforated projection discussed above. The diameters of the mirrors have a range of 18.4 cm to 30.0 cm (table 1.1). A frequency plot of the diameters (figure 1.4) suggests a bimodal distribution (i.e., two distinct peaks of size frequency). Seven mirrors are between 18 and 22 cm in diameter, and eight are between 24 and 30 cm. The group of smaller mirrors has a mean diameter of 20.1 cm and a standard deviation of 1.58; those in the group of larger mirrors have a mean diameter of 26.8 cm and a standard deviation of 2.01.

In general, this kind of bimodal size distribution of manufactured objects suggests that producers were aiming to create two distinct sizes of objects; otherwise one would expect something closer to a normal distribution with a single mode of size (DeBoer and Lathrap 1979; Lathrap 1976). Aztec and other Mesoamerican

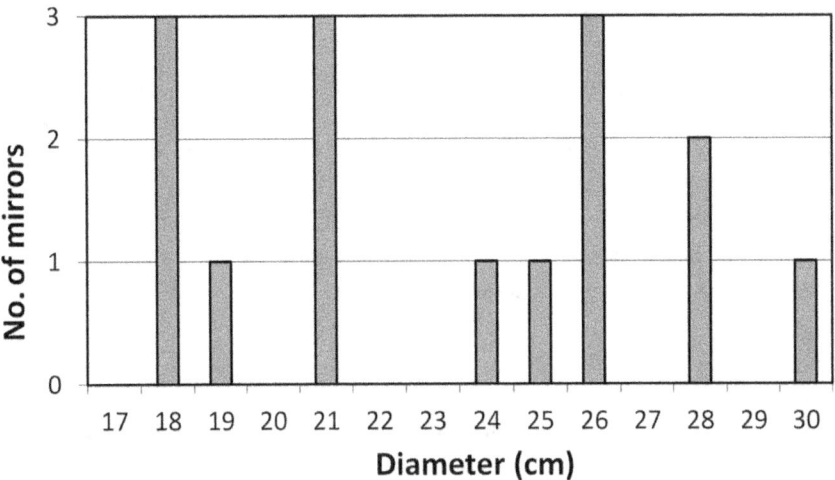

FIGURE 1.4. Frequency distribution of diameters of the obsidian mirrors listed in table 1.1.

obsidian producers were quite expert in working with the volcanic glass and could have produced mirrors of any size they wanted. Sahagún's (1950–82, book X: 87) discussion of the mirror-stone maker (*tezcachiuhqui*) indicates that mirrors were made by specialists (see also ibid., book XI: 228–29). John Clark (1994) points out that although Sahagún lists some of the steps in the production process (e.g., abrading with sand, carving, polishing with a cane), we actually know very little about how mirrors were made. But the bimodal size distribution does suggest deliberate choices on the part of Aztec mirror makers.

The inference that Aztec mirror makers deliberately produced two sizes of mirrors, in turn, suggests that there were probably cultural reasons for the existence of two different size categories. One possibility is that there were different uses for the two types; perhaps one type was to adorn sculptures or *ixiptla* (deity) of Tezcatlipoca, whereas the other was for priests to carry around to use in divination. Another possibility is that the two size types were made and used by different cultural groups—perhaps mirrors were of one size in central Mexico and another size in the Tarascan area or in the outer imperial provinces. Alternatively, the norms of size could have changed through time. These speculative interpretations are intended only to illustrate some possible implications of the data in table 1.1 and figure 1.4. Although we cannot specify the uses or meanings of different types of circular obsidian mirrors at this point, the size data do suggest a level of complexity in the uses of obsidian mirrors that would be invisible if one only examined a small number of the finest objects. The addition of more cases to those listed in table 1.1

will permit my hypothesis of a bimodal distribution to be more firmly evaluated and might lead to additional useful inferences.

Another promising line of analysis for obsidian mirrors in museum collections is chemical source analysis. Obsidian objects are relatively easy to assign to geological sources, and several of the available techniques are non-destructive. Two rectangular obsidian mirrors Murillo used for paintings (Meslay 2001) have been subjected to source analysis using the PIXE technique, along with four other mirrors in Paris museums (Calligaro et al. 2005), and the results suggest that the obsidian was from the Ucareo and/or Zinapecuaro sources in Michoacán.[5]

CERAMIC FLUTES

Compared to obsidian mirrors, ceramic flutes in general have a weaker association with Tezcatlipoca, but they are far better represented in both museum collections and documented archaeological excavations. As analyzed by a number of authors (e.g., Both 2002; Martí 1953, 1968, 117–23; Olivier 2003, 194–95, 215–18), flutes played crucial roles in the Tezcatlipoca cult, particularly during the veintena festival of Toxcatl. During the month of Toxcatl, the ixiptla of Tezcatlipoca processed through the streets of Tenochtitlan playing the flute (figure 1.5a), whose sound was viewed as the voice of Tezcatlipoca. When he mounted the steps of the pyramid for his sacrifice, he is said to have broken a flute on each stair (figure 1.5b).

Arnd Adje Both (2002) has compared ethnohistoric evidence to the physical, acoustic, and iconographic attributes of Aztec ceramic flutes. He shows that a particular kind of flute—the flower-flute—was strongly associated with the Tezcatlipoca cult. Two such flutes and a schematic cross-section are shown in figure 1.6. While all Aztec flutes have a tube with finger holes, these instruments also have a long duct leading to the aperture and a bell shaped like a flower blossom. On some examples, the flower decoration on the bell is divided into four parts. Both (ibid., 281) links the symbolism of the flower bell and its four-part symmetry to several realms, including the Aztec concept of music as "flowery song" and a number of components of the cult and symbolism of Tezcatlipoca. For example, on one occasion Tezcatlipoca's ixiptla emerged from the temple and played his flute to each of the four cardinal directions in turn (Durán 1967, 1: 39–40; see also Both 2005b, 2006).

Both has suggested to me that "specific musical instruments were closely related to specific religious complexes and probably were used only in ritual contexts related to these complexes" (Adje Both, personal communication, July 2007). The implication of this hypothesis is that whereas the flower-flutes were associated with Tezcatlipoca, other types of Aztec flutes (Both 2005a; Kollmann 1895;

FIGURE 1.5. The use of flutes during the festival of Toxcatl in the Florentine Codex. A: priest of ixiptla playing flute during a procession (Sahagún 1950–82, book III: figure 7); drawing by Arnd Adje Both, reproduced with permission. B: broken flutes at the temple during the sacrifice; image from Olivier (2003, 285); drawing by Rodolfo Avila, based on Sahagún (1950–82, book II: figure 17); reproduced with permission.

Martí 1968) may have been associated with other deities. Figure 1.7 illustrates a series of broken flutes excavated in burials from the Middle or Late Postclassic period at Teotenango in the Toluca Valley. These flutes, none of which is of the flower-flute variety, illustrate several other kinds of Aztec flute. There is no published information on the specific archaeological contexts of the Teotenango flutes (beyond the fact that they are from burials), and thus it is not clear whether they might indicate a Tezcatlipoca-related deposit.

I have excavated a number of small fragments of ceramic flutes from domestic trash deposits at Aztec period sites in central Mexico. Figure 1.8 shows ten of the thirteen identified tubular flute pieces from Yautepec, an urban center in north-central Morelos (Smith n.d.c); I also recovered two fragments at Cuexcomate and Capilco, rural sites in western Morelos (Smith n.d.a). My 2007 excavations at the Late Postclassic city of Calixtlahuaca in the Toluca Valley also turned up a small number of flute fragments. From the small size of these fragments, it is usually impossible to classify them into known Aztec flute types. Of the ten pieces in figure 1.8, all I can venture to say is that item C is not a flower-flute; it has an

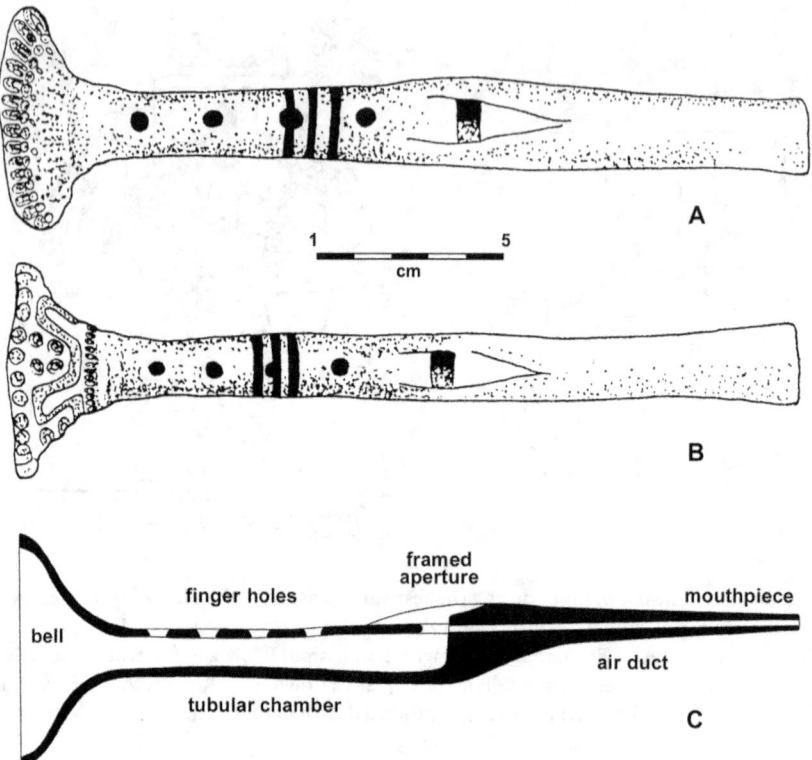

FIGURE 1.6. Aztec ceramic flower-flutes. A, B: flutes in the Ethnological Museum, Berlin. A: SMB PK, Inv. IV Ca 2548; B: SMB PK, Inv. IV Ca 2553. C: schematic cross-section of an Aztec tubular duct flute, drawing by Arnd Adje Both. From Both (2002, figures 2, 3); courtesy, Arnd Adje Both.

anthropomorphic head at the distal end, like one of the flutes from Teotenango (figure 1.7).[6]

It is difficult to reconstruct the significance of musical instruments in domestic contexts, in part because music was part of ritual, and the ethnohistoric sources contain very little information on domestic rituals (Burkhart 1997; Smith 2002). Both (2007) discusses two types of Aztec music culture: temple music performed by specialized priests, and court music performed by professional musicians. Most references to musical instruments in the chroniclers and codices pertain to these two contexts (Both 2005b, 2007; Martí 1968). In addition to flutes, the Aztec period residential contexts I have excavated also contained whistles and rattles,

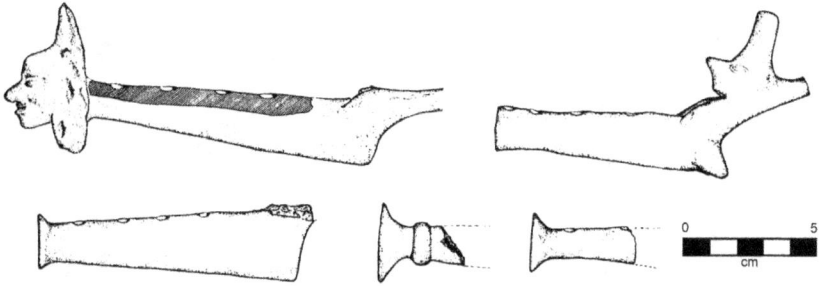

FIGURE 1.7. Fragments of ceramic flutes, not of the flower-flute variety, excavated in Postclassic burials at Teotenango (modified after Velázquez 1975, 321).

and a New Fire ritual dump at Cuexcomate (Elson and Smith 2001) contained a ceramic drum (Smith n.d.a). I have suggested that such instruments might have been used, along with ceramic figurines and censers, for domestic rituals such as divination, curing, and fertility rites (Smith 2002). An alternative possibility is that they were used when people participated in specific public ritual activities that were part of the monthly veintena ceremonies (Smith 2008, chapter 4). A recent find of a bone flute in Oaxaca (Barber, Sánchez, and Olvera 2009) extends our knowledge of flutes from domestic contexts.

In summary, the simple presence of ceramic flutes is insufficient to link an archaeological context or objects to the cult of Tezcatlipoca. Nevertheless, one specific type—the flower-flute—does seem to have a strong association with this deity. Furthermore, the presence of one or more broken flutes in buried offerings may suggest the presence of the Tezcatlipoca cult. The significance of ceramic flutes in domestic contexts is far from clear, but these objects do not seem to suggest an association with Tezcatlipoca. In fact, little or no evidence suggests that Tezcatlipoca was venerated at the domestic level. Ceramic figurines, a major component of domestic rites, sometimes depict deities (e.g., Tlaloc, Quetzalcoatl, or Xochiquetzal), but apparently not Tezcatlipoca (Kaplan 2006).

Momoztli Shrines

Small stone shrines or platforms are further along the continuum identified above for obsidian mirrors and ceramic flutes: shrines are more abundant and better documented archaeologically, but their association with Tezcatlipoca is weaker. Unfortunately, for these features there seems to be a serious disjunction between the ethnohistorical data (descriptions and depictions of momoztli) and archaeological

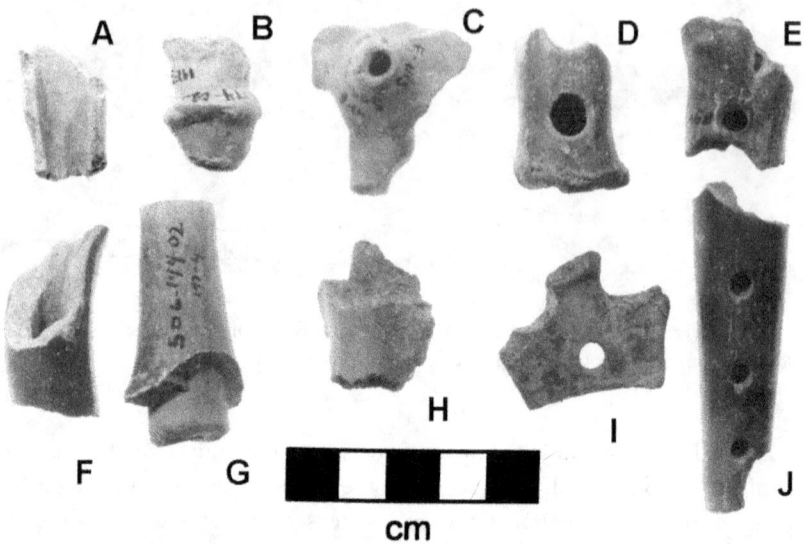

FIGURE 1.8. Flute fragments excavated from domestic contexts in Yautepec, Morelos. Photograph by Michael E. Smith; from Smith (n.d.c).

data (stone structures at sites). In a section labeled "The Problem of the Momoztli," Olivier (2003, 172–82) reviews ethnohistoric data on momoztli. These structures bear a strong association with Tezcatlipoca, but they seem to be highly variable in form and context. Olivier states, "Thus the word *momoztli* can designate several kinds of buildings, from a temple to an altar or a small oratory" (ibid., 174).

As reviewed by Olivier (ibid., 175–82), scholars from Eduard Seler's time to the present have identified a number of specific stone objects with the momoztli of the chroniclers (see also Umberger 1984). Many of these are stone boxes and other portable rectangular objects with some kind of explicit Tezcatlipoca iconography (Gutiérrez Solana Rickards 1983, lams. 03, 109, 147, 202). To my mind, these small portable objects do not match very closely the temples, altars, or oratories the chroniclers seem to associate with the label *momoztli* (although their association with Tezcatlipoca is usually clear enough). Umberger (ibid.) interprets the "teocalli de la Guerra sagrada" monument as a momoztli.

Archaeologists have excavated numerous small stone altars or platforms at Aztec sites, but it has not been possible to associate them clearly with the category momoztli or with other aspects of the Tezcatlipoca cult. A strong emphasis on small platforms built in the centers of cities was a key innovation of Aztec urban planning

(Smith 2008, chapters 4, 5). Such small platforms, of course, are found at nearly all Mesoamerican cities, from Olmec times through the Late Postclassic. But at Aztec city-state capitals (and later at Tenochtitlan), city builders erected many more of these structures than in earlier times, and they placed them in key locations within the urban epicenter to define public spaces for ceremony. Interestingly, one of the additions Late Postclassic builders made to the central plaza at Tula was a rectangular altar, built in front of Temple C.[7]

Figure 1.9 shows two small platforms or altars at the Aztec city-state capital Ixtapaluca Viejo (also known as Acozac). They are low rectangular platforms with stairs on one side; in their form these are typical of platforms at many sites. For some archaeologists in the early twentieth century, such platforms were not deemed worthy of excavation and reconstruction. They were left unexcavated next to large excavated and restored temples (figure 1.10). A number of Aztec city-state capitals have rows of platforms along one side of the main urban public plaza. The two structures at Ixtapaluca Viejo (figure 1.9) fit this pattern, which is much clearer in the plan of Teopanzolco.

Eight platforms in a rough line face the main pyramid at the Early Aztec city center of Teopanzolco (figure 1.11). They illustrate the variety of such platforms in size and form; two are circular and one is long and narrow. The southernmost platform contained an offering of ninety-two human skulls, of which about one-third showed evidence for decapitation (González Sobrino et al. 2001; Lagunas Rodríguez and Serrano Sánchez 1972). The urban center of Coatetelco in southwest Morelos also contains a row of platforms along the main plaza; in this case they are attached to the side of a large ball court (Arana Álvarez 1984; Smith 2008, figures 1.1, 3.5). There are several platforms adjacent to the main pyramids of Tenochtitlan (Olmeda Vera 2002) and Tenayuca (Noguera 1929b), and the excavated epicenter at Tlatelolco is full of these features (González Rul 1998).

In a review of architectural forms at Aztec urban centers (Smith 2008, chapter 4), I use the term *shrine* for these small platforms to distinguish them from portable altars, on the one hand, and temples on the other. I identify four types of shrine: (1) *tzompantli*, or skull rack; (2) *tzitzimime* shrine, decorated with skulls and crossed bones in relief and typically misidentified as skull racks (for discussion, see Klein 2000); (3) other rectangular shrine; and (4) circular shrine. When I began compiling data on these structures, I had hoped it might prove possible—on the basis of form, size, and location—to identify additional subtypes of the rectangular shrines beyond types 1 and 2 (I have data on over forty rectangular shrines). In fact, one goal (after reading Olivier's book) was to propose an archaeological identification of the momoztli shrine. Unfortunately, the data did not cooperate, and I have not been able to further subdivide this category or to suggest any potential momoztlis at Aztec urban sites.

FIGURE 1.9. Reconstructed small platforms or altars at Ixtapaluca Viejo (Acozac). Photograph by Michael E. Smith.

FIGURE 1.10. Unreconstructed small platform or altar in the Panteón group at Calixtlahuaca. Photograph by Michael E. Smith.

Given the wide latitude in meanings of the term *momoztli* in early sources and the wide variety in the size and form of small altars at Aztec urban sites, it seems likely that at least some of the excavated structures probably corresponded to the category of momoztli. Unfortunately, few offerings—which might tie them to

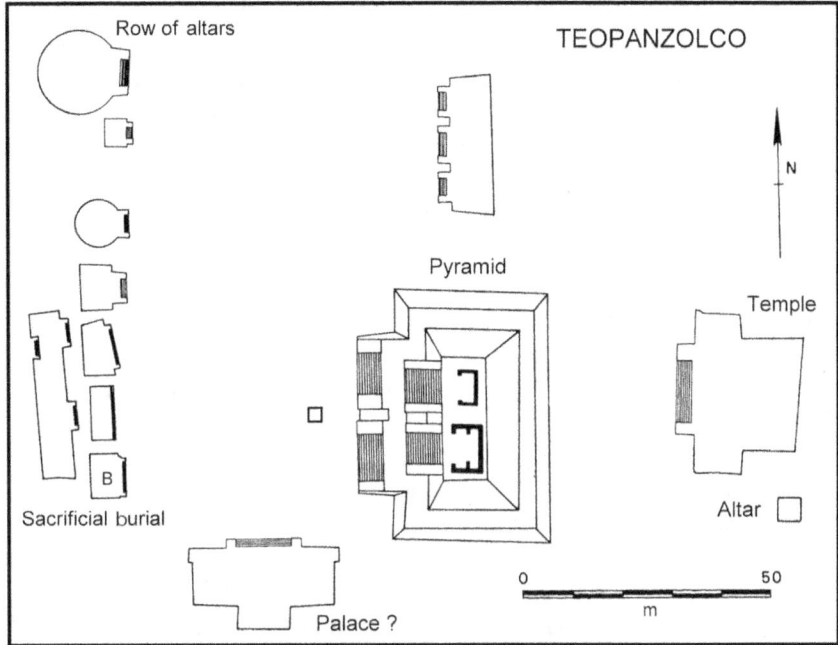

FIGURE 1.11. Plan of the epicenter of Teopanzolco, showing the row of small platforms or altars on the west side of the main plaza. Map by Michael E. Smith.

Tezcatlipoca or other identifiable cults—have been excavated at these structures. Given the low level of reporting on many of the excavations, it is impossible to tell whether the lack of offerings is the simple result of a lack of rigorous fieldwork or whether it really reflects a paucity of offerings at small platforms.

DISCUSSION

This review of material evidence for the Tezcatlipoca cult is far less conclusive than one would like. Part of the problem stems from the nature of archaeological evidence. If one starts with the chroniclers and the codices, it is easy to develop arguments for the strong association of obsidian mirrors, ceramic flutes, and momoztli shrines with the worship of Tezcatlipoca. Those sources, however, also include other uses for such objects; they are less important for mirrors but increasingly more significant for flutes and shrines. But if one starts with an isolated object without context in a museum or even a documented archaeological find with good context, it is difficult to make a rigorous argument for an object's use or significance without iconographic data or a suite of identifiable associated objects. If archaeologists were to excavate a burial or offering associated with one of the major components of the Tezcatlipoca cult, as described in the chroniclers, it would probably be relatively easy to identify the deposit correctly. But archaeologists have yet to encounter such offerings at Aztec sites.

In the absence of rich contextual and associational data of the sort provided by the excavations at the Templo Mayor since 1978 (López Luján 2005 [1994], 2006; Matos Moctezuma 1982), archaeologists and museum scholars must fall back on systematic analyses of descriptive data of the sort reviewed above. If we had larger samples of mirrors, flutes, or platforms to work with, it would almost certainly permit clearer and stronger interpretations of their roles in the cult of Tezcatlipoca (or in other contexts). I hope the above discussion helps stimulate further research in this area. We need better documentation of museum collections and archaeological findings, more systematic analyses of larger samples, and rigorous integration with parallel systematic analyses of the ethnohistoric data of the sort provided by Guilhem Olivier.

THE TEZCATLIPOCA CULT IN SPACE AND TIME

When and where did the Tezcatlipoca cult originate? This question can only be answered with archaeological data, if indeed it can be answered at all. In addition to the finds of archaeology, however, one needs rigorous methods and concepts to link the fragmentary material remains of early periods to the rich documentary and archaeological record of Tezcatlipoca at the time of the Spanish conquest. With one exception (Paddock 1985), I have not seen the application of such methods and concepts in the literature on early Tezcatlipoca. How many and which of the deity's attributes need to be present to conclude that Tezcatlipoca was known and worshipped prior to the Aztec period? Without an explicit consideration of such issues, interpretations will remain based more on the opinions of individual scholars (who may differ widely in their assumptions and standards of proof) than on empirical data. In this sense I cannot evaluate Milbrath's views (this volume) on the historical relationship between Tezcatlipoca and Kawil (see also Valencia Rivera 2006); I have no idea what criteria to use to judge the adequacy of such arguments.

In line with these observations, I will not address the "origin" of the Tezcatlipoca cult here. Olivier (2003) reviews the literature on this topic and, not surprisingly, finds it difficult to reach any firm conclusions. My approach focuses on the historical distribution of some of the key attributes of Tezcatlipoca. Most scholars would probably agree that the presence of Tezcatlipoca can be inferred from one or more of these three traits: the image of the smoking mirror, a deity with one leg cut off, or a deity with a black horizontal band of face paint. Combinations of these traits obviously provide stronger evidence than a single trait in isolation. I also review briefly a distinct suite of evidence suggesting the presence of the Tezcatlipoca cult in the Chalchihuites culture of Zacatecas in Classic and Epiclassic times.

The maps in figures 1.12 and 1.14 show sites matching these criteria for Tezcatlipoca in each of two time periods: the Epiclassic–Early Postclassic period and the Middle–Late Postclassic period. I cannot claim to have made an exhaustive study of Mesoamerican archaeological sites looking for attributes of Tezcatlipoca. I started with Olivier's (ibid.) discussion and added other material I am aware of. There does not seem to be evidence fitting my criteria from the Classic period or earlier. It is entirely possible, of course, that there was a thriving Tezcatlipoca cult in such times that did not happen to leave the kind of evidence under consideration here or perhaps one whose attributes changed through time.

Epiclassic and Early Postclassic

The clear representation of Tezcatlipoca in reliefs at the Temple of the Warriors at Chichén Itzá has been discussed by a number of authors (e.g., ibid., 65–66; Thompson 1942). The example reproduced in figure 1.13A has both the severed leg and two smoking mirrors—one replacing the lower leg or foot and the other in the headdress. The dating of the architecture and occupation at Chichén Itzá is currently undergoing revision (Kristan-Graham and Kowalski 2006), and at this point the most conservative interpretation is that these reliefs date to the Epiclassic (AD 700–900) and/or Early Postclassic (AD 900–1100) periods. Taube (1999) calls this the earliest manifestation of Tezcatlipoca in Mesoamerica.

For Tula, Olivier (2003, 65) notes that "the absence of representation of Tezcatlipoca in the prestigious Toltec city has perplexed the specialists for a long time" (e.g., Stocker 1992–93). There are two problems with this statement. First, it looks at the situation backward. Such puzzlement implies that the Aztec accounts of Quetzalcoatl and Tezcatlipoca at Tula are historically correct and that archaeologists have simply failed to locate more evidence of Tezcatlipoca at the site (since his cult must have been present and prominent). To the contrary, I argue that the archaeological record of Tula should be the starting point. We have an empirical record generated by numerous documented archaeological projects over many decades (e.g., Acosta 1964; de la Fuente, Trejo, and Gutiérrez Solana Rickards 1988; Healan 1989; Mastache, Cobean, and Healan 2002; Matos Moctezuma 1974; Sterpone 2000–1). Aztec accounts of Tula and the Toltecs, on the other hand, were ideologically motivated mythological statements to which it is difficult to attribute much historical validity (Smith 2003, 2006). Our puzzlement should instead be over why the Aztecs

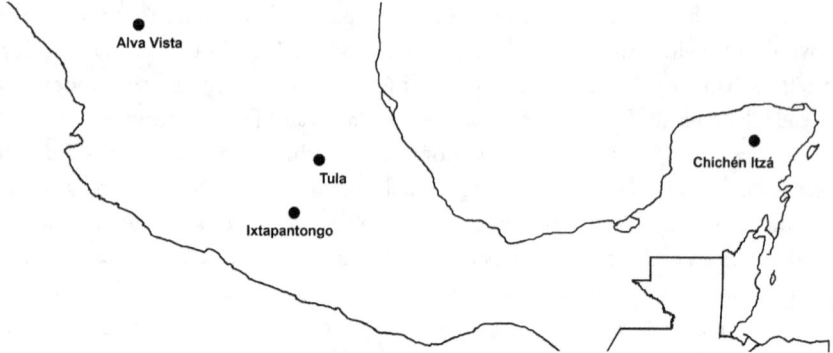

FIGURE 1.12. Distribution of Tezcatlipoca images or cult items in Mesoamerica during the Epiclassic and Early Postclassic periods. Map by author.

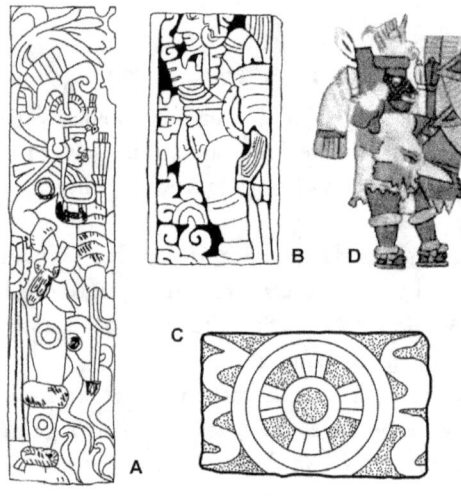

FIGURE 1.13. Representations of Tezcatlipoca and his cult during the Epiclassic and Early Postclassic periods. A: stone relief at Chichén Itzá (modified after Olivier 2003, 289); B: stone relief at Tula (modified after Stocker 1992–93, 67); C: stone relief at Tula (redrawn from Gamboa Cabezas 2007, 46); D: rock painting at Ixtapantongo (modified after Villagra Caleti 1954).

made such a big deal out of Quetzalcoatl and Tezcatlipoca among the Toltecs when the archaeological record only accords them modest presence at Tula and other Epiclassic–Early Postclassic sites.

The second difficulty with Olivier's statement is that there are in fact a good number of stone reliefs of smoking mirrors at Tula, in addition to at least one representation of Tezcatlipoca himself. The latter, a relief of the deity from Pilastra 5, lado A (figure 1.13b), has been published by Stocker (1992–93, 67), Jiménez García (1998, 126, 465), and Olivier (2003, 296). The smoking mirror reliefs at Tula seem to have gone

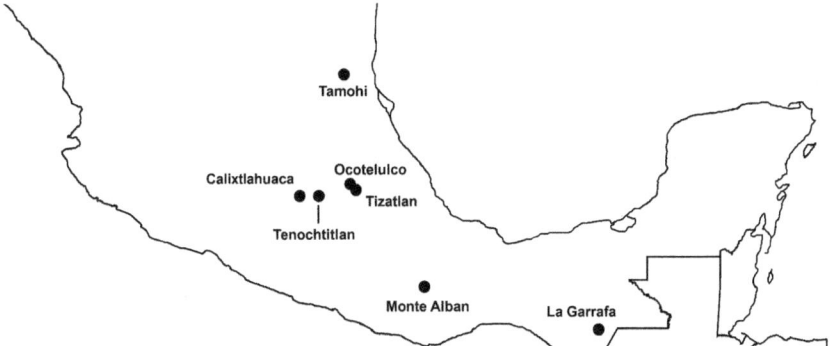

FIGURE 1.14. Distribution of Tezcatlipoca images or cult items in the Late Postclassic period. Map by author.

unidentified in the literature. Luis Gamboa Cabezas (2007, 46) recently published a photo of a newly excavated mirror relief, but he calls it a solar disk (figure 1.13c). A nearly identical relief, excavated by Joseph Acosta (1956, 97) and now in the Museo Nacional de Antropología, is identified only as a "lápida con representación de disco y volutes" by Beatriz de la Fuente and colleagues (1988, 200, and figure 144). Three other reliefs from Acosta's excavations have central circular elements very similar to these two objects but without the smoke volutes (ibid., 198–200, and figures 141–43).

While these reliefs clearly document the presence of Tezcatlipoca at Tula, archaeologists have yet to identify any temples or shrines dedicated to the deity at the site. Another possible image of Tezcatlipoca from the Toltec period is part of a complex rock painting at Ixtapantongo in the western part of the State of Mexico (figure 1.13d). This figure, a warrior who wears some kind of bird garment, has a severed leg. Agustín Villagra Caleti (1954, 3) interprets the image as Tezcatlipoca, an identification Olivier (2003, 62–63) seems to accept. Walter Krickeberg (1969, 193–95), on the other hand, labels this image Xiuhtecuhtli and identifies another figure in the painting as Tezcatlipoca. The Ixtapantongo painting can be dated to the Toltec (Early Postclassic) period on stylistic grounds (ibid., 191; Taube 1999; Villagra Caleti 1954).

A different kind of evidence suggesting the presence of the Tezcatlipoca cult during this period consists of mortuary practices of the Chalchihuites cultures of Zacatecas. Thomas Holien and Robert Pickering (1978) interpret a burial at the site of Alta Vista as that of a possible Tezcatlipoca ixiptla. Placed under the floor of a major temple at the site (the "Hall of Columns"), the burial consisted of a primary interment of a central individual, lacking the cranium, accompanied by eight secondary interments with evidence of ritual mutilation. Grave goods included a broken flute and several elaborate polychrome serving vessels. Holien and Pickering argue that this feature resembles what one might expect a burial of a Tezcatlipoca impersonator to look like (taking into account, of course, that no such burial has been encountered at Aztec sites).

Holien and Pickering make several interpretive errors, pointed out by Olivier (2003, 90–91, 200–201). For example, they misidentify the central figure in the cosmogram on page 1 of the Codex Fejérváry-Mayer (1971) as Tezcatlipoca, not Xiuhtecuhtli. Olivier (2003, 201) concludes that "the elements presented by Holien and Pickering are not enough to affirm that a ritual akin to that of Toxcatl was held in Alta Vista in the Classic period." Nevertheless, the presence of several similar burials in the region—not discussed by Olivier—does suggest to me that an identification with Tezcatlipoca or a Tezcatlipoca-like cult is a reasonable interpretation of the Alta Vista burial (Lelegemann 2000, chapter 9; Nelson 1997). In the words of Holien and Pickering (1978, 156): "Our 'Tezcatlipoca' is so labeled for convenience, not in order to claim the 'discovery' of an Aztec deity among early northern Chichimecs. In the Mesoamerican Classic generally, there is probably the cosmological context to accommodate a Tezcatlipoca-like creator god just as there are isolated archaeological indications of such a cult."

Regardless of whether one accepts the Chalchihuites burials as evidence of the Tezcatlipoca cult, the admittedly limited evidence for Tezcatlipoca in the Epiclassic and Early Postclassic periods does have a very broad distribution within Mesoamerica (figure 1.12). Previous generations of scholars might have interpreted Tezcatlipoca as a Toltec deity whose presence in other areas could be attributed to Toltec conquest or diffusion. Yet we now know that Alfred Tozzer's (1957) simplistic model of Toltec diffusion to, or influence on, Chichén Itzá is inadequate (Kristan-Graham and Kowalski 2006) and that Aztec legends of a Toltec empire were widely exaggerated, if not completely false (Smith and Montiel 2001). Nevertheless, the deity Tezcatlipoca was clearly present at Tula as well as at least one site (Ixtapantongo) with Toltec-style paintings, plus at least one area quite distant from Tula and central Mexico. It is difficult to escape the conclusion that the Tezcatlipoca cult—or at least a knowledge of the deity as an important figure—was widely distributed in Mesoamerica in Epiclassic–Early Postclassic times. If one were to speculate on the "origin" of the cult, this would most likely be found in the Classic period or earlier.

Late Postclassic

Archaeological evidence for Tezcatlipoca is more abundant during the Late Postclassic period (figure 1.14). It is often difficult to distinguish Middle Postclassic

(AD 1100–1300) and Late Postclassic (AD 1300–1521+) contexts, and some of the examples discussed in this section may in fact date to the Middle Postclassic period. Figures 1.15 and 1.16 illustrate some of the examples; these and others are discussed by Olivier (2003) and Paddock (1985). A more complete review of the literature would almost certainly turn up additional examples.[8] I divide the evidence into two groups: central Mexico and more distant areas (see figure 1.14).

One of the few cases of Tezcatlipoca from a well-documented context in Tenochtitlan is a burial urn excavated at the Templo Mayor (figure 1.15a). The presence of the deity in Tlaxcala has long been known from the Tizatlan murals (figure 1.15b; Noguera 1927). Other examples are common on polychrome ceramic vessels of the Codex style (Hernández Sánchez 2005, 159–73); an example from Ocotelulco (Contreras Martínez 1994) is shown in figure 1.15c. Gilda Hernández Sánchez (2005, 160) includes forty-five examples of polychrome vessels decorated with Tezcatlipoca-related imagery from sites ranging from Tenochtitlan to Cholula and the Puebla-Tlaxcala Valley to Veracruz. Her criteria for identifying Tezcatlipoca are different from those I use here, and it is not clear just how many of the forty-five examples have the specific attributes under discussion.

An imperial Mexica-style stone relief that may have been excavated by José García Payón at Calixtlahuaca (figure 1.15d) is a clear depiction of a smoking mirror.[9] The four examples in figure 1.15, coupled with the abundance of Tezcatlipoca in the divinatory codices and the data of Hernández Sánchez (2005), demonstrate that the Tezcatlipoca cult was present in much of central Mexico during Aztec times. For other central Mexican representations, some with known provenience and others without, see Olivier (2003, 57–73) and Gutiérrez Solana Rickards (1983).

Three Late Postclassic examples of Tezcatlipoca outside of central Mexico all lie outside the provinces of the Aztec empire; they are illustrated in figure 1.16. A mural from the Huaxtec site of Tamohi (figure 1.16a) is interpreted by Diana Zaragoza Ocaña (2003, 31–32) as Tezcatlipoca on the basis on the facial paint. John Paddock (1985) discusses a number of examples from Oaxaca, including an image carved on a bone from Tomb 7 at Monte Albán (figure 1.16b). The most distant examples, discussed by Olivier (2003, 63–64), are some Late Postclassic painted cups from La Garrafa in Chiapas; figure 1.16c shows a design from one of these cups (see Pareyon Moreno 1988, 192).

The (Middle and) Late Postclassic distribution of the Tezcatlipoca cult is concentrated in central Mexico, with several examples considerably further afield in the outer imperial provinces (Tamohi, Oaxaca) and beyond (La Garrafa). A tentative explanation for this pattern is offered below.

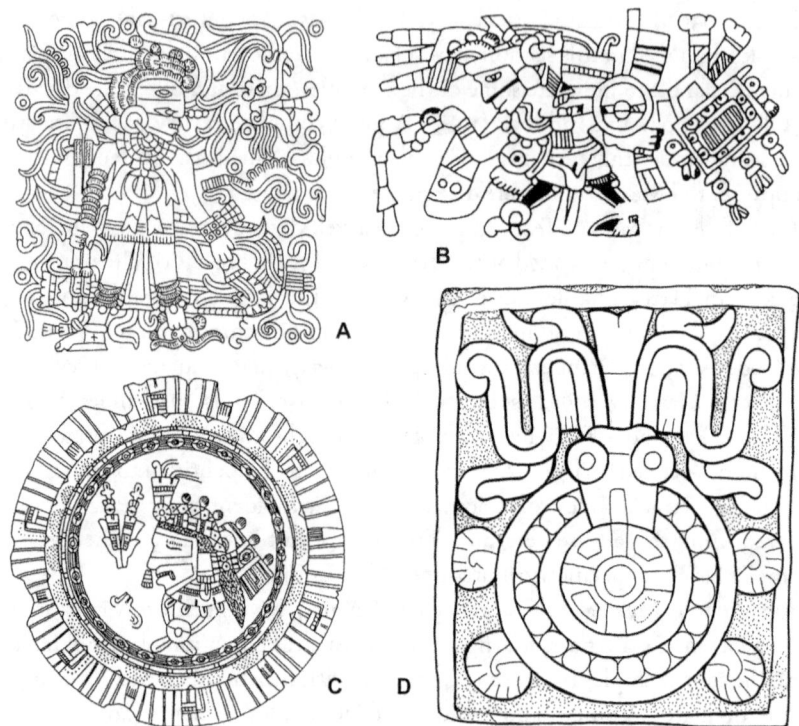

FIGURE 1.15. Representations of Tezcatlipoca and his cult in central Mexico during the Late Postclassic period. A: ceramic urn from the Templo Mayor of Tenochtitlan (modified after López Luján 2005 [1994], 178); B: mural at Tizatlan, Tlaxcala (modified after Olivier 2003, 296); C: ceramic polychrome plate from Ocotelulco, Tlaxcala (modified after Olivier 2003, 295); D: stone relief from Calixtlahuaca (catalog no. SS-91); drawing by Emily Umberger.

TEZCATLIPOCA IN THE POSTCLASSIC MESOAMERICAN WORLD SYSTEM

The Middle and Late Postclassic periods saw the most extensive development of long-distance commercial exchange and stylistic interaction in the entire Prehispanic Mesoamerican past. Goods and ideas moved freely throughout Mesoamerica, linking hundreds of independent city-states into broad interconnected networks (Smith and Berdan 2003). The commercial and fiscal institutions of the Aztec empire were part of this broad world system, but exchange and interaction were by no means limited to the imperial domain.

In comparison with earlier times, the Middle and Late Postclassic periods have many more examples of Tezcatlipoca in central Mexico and at least one additional

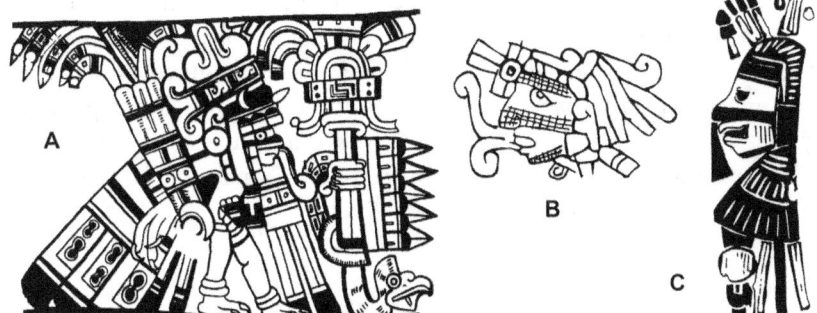

FIGURE 1.16. Representations of Tezcatlipoca outside of central Mexico during the Late Postclassic period. A: mural at Tamohi, San Luis Potosí (modified after Zaragoza Ocaña 2003, 32); B: carved bone (bone no. 65) from Tomb 7, Monte Albán (modified after Paddock 1985, 316); C: gourd cup from La Garrafa, Chiapas (modified after Olivier 2003, 295).

case of the deity in distant areas (three examples versus two; compare figures 1.12 and 1.14). I suggest that the broader distribution of Tezcatlipoca traits in the Late Postclassic period represents an expansion in the extent of this cult. In other words, it seems more likely to me that the cult was adopted in new areas in Late Postclassic times rather than being a widely distributed ancient cult for which we happen to have more material evidence from later times. This is similar to the conclusion John Paddock (1985) reached in his discussion of the nature and geographical distribution of Tezcatlipoca images in Oaxaca. Paddock argues that an indigenous cult of Tezcatlipoca did not exist in Oaxaca and that the deity "was known there only briefly during Aztec times, and in places close to the Aztec route through Oaxaca" (ibid., 309).

Paddock's interpretation was part of an older paradigm in which widespread distributions of traits were explained as resulting from "influence" from a center. In this case, he implies that the Tezcatlipoca cult was deliberately spread by invading or traveling Aztecs. Today, archaeologists are more likely to emphasize the roles of distant or provincial rulers and elites in choosing to adopt foreign traits or goods. Thus individuals in provincial or distant areas (i.e., elites or priests in Tamohi, La Garrafa, and Oaxaca in the present case) had agency in deciding whether to adopt foreign goods, traits, styles, cults, or deities (Stein 2002; Wilk 2004). These actors made their decisions based on their local context and needs, not on the wishes of distant imperial rulers. This kind of approach is particularly appropriate for Mesoamerica, where empires adopted hegemonic or indirect methods of control, as compared with the territorial or direct control exercised by empires in many other parts of the world (Sinopoli 1994; Smith and Montiel 2001).

The distribution data (figure 1.14) support the notion that the spread of Tezcatlipoca was more a result of the commercial and symbolic networks of the Postclassic Mesoamerican world system than of processes associated directly with Aztec imperialism. Two of the four central Mexican sites with Tezcatlipoca imagery (Tizatlan and Ocotelulco) are located within the unconquered enemy zone of Tlaxcala, and two of the three more distant sites (Tamohi and La Garrafa) are beyond the extent of the empire.

CONCLUSIONS

Ethnohistoric sources on Tezcatlipoca reveal a number of objects and traits that can be considered material manifestations of his cult. I have singled out three such traits—obsidian mirrors, ceramic flutes, and momoztli platforms—as nonperishable goods with particularly strong associations with the deity. These items have been excavated or collected from Aztec sites and are known to scholarship today. They all have the potential for systematic research (e.g., catalogs of museum holdings and excavated examples) that, if undertaken, would surely advance our understanding of the Aztec cult of Tezcatlipoca. My very brief analysis of the sizes of a sample of obsidian mirrors suggests the possible use of two distinct types of mirror. This exercise is meant as an example of the potentially useful information that can be generated with systematic attention to a range of objects but not with intensive focus on one or two of the finest examples.

Knowledge of the Tezcatlipoca cult and its material manifestations is hampered by the fact that, to date, no clear offering, altar, or temple dedicated to the deity has been excavated at a Late Postclassic site (apart from the segment of stairs at the Tezcatlipoca temple south of the Templo Mayor; see note 2). More precisely, archaeologists have not yet identified such excavated features; it is entirely possible that early excavators uncovered a Tezcatlipoca temple or momoztli platform but failed to identify it because of the fragmentary nature of the finds or incomplete excavation.[10] This lacuna makes it difficult to evaluate enigmatic features such as the Alta Vista burial because there is no well-documented central Mexican example for comparison.

The distribution of key representations and traits of Tezcatlipoca in space and time suggests some patterns for the development and spread of the cult, although the number of cases remains somewhat small to reach confident conclusions. Although it is certainly possible that the cult of Tezcatlipoca had deep origins in Mesoamerica, the clear markers of the Aztec period deity and cult do not appear until the Epiclassic–Early Postclassic period, where they are quite widely distributed in space (figure 1.12).

In the Middle and Late Postclassic periods, the number of representations of Tezcatlipoca and smoking mirrors in central Mexico increased dramatically, and their spatial extent outside of central Mexico also expanded. Like so many aspects of Aztec political, religious, and elite culture, the Tezcatlipoca cult was adopted from Toltec models. The Aztecs probably expanded and elaborated the cult and its mythology to a much greater extent than had their Toltec ancestors, although this is difficult to prove with current data. Representations in the codices, murals, and elaborate polychrome ceramics—in both the Valley of Mexico and the Puebla-Tlaxcala area—suggest a widespread cult of high prestige. It is likely that distant elites and priests adopted elements of this cult because of that prestige; there is no evidence that imperial armies or administrators actively promoted the cult in conquered or distant areas.

Acknowledgments. I thank Elizabeth Baquedano for inviting me to write this chapter. Some of the data in table 1.1 were initially assembled in a term paper by Kate Sullivan for a class at the University of Albany, SUNY. Adje Both provided helpful information on ceramic flutes and the context of Aztec music more generally. He sent me several of his papers and kindly allowed me to reproduce three of his drawings of flutes. I want to thank a number of museum personnel for responding to my inquiries about obsidian mirrors; they are listed in note 4. In many ways this chapter is merely an update, extension, and reorganization of parts of Guilhem Olivier's book, *Mockeries and Metamorphoses of an Aztec God: Tezcatlipoca, "Lord of the Smoking Mirror,"* and I acknowledge the inspiration of that work and its author. I thank Elizabeth Baquedano, Frances Berdan, Adje Both, Guilhem Olivier, and Emily Umberger for their helpful comments on an earlier draft of this chapter.

NOTES

1. There are other monographic treatments of Aztec deities, of course, but they tend to focus either on a limited range of source material (e.g., Boone 1989; Vié-Wohrer 1999) or on a particular aspect of the deity (e.g., Carrasco 1982; Nicholson 2001). No other work takes such a comprehensive approach to an individual deity.

2. Excavations of the Programa de Arqueología Urbana, an outgrowth of the Templo Mayor project, have located a portion of the stairway of the Tezcatlipoca temple under the Antiguo Palacio del Arzobispado south of the Templo Mayor (Matos Moctezuma 1992, 1997; Olmo Frese 2003); unfortunately, these excavations revealed no offerings or other clear Tezcatlipoca-related elements. The so-called Cuauhxicalli de Motecuhzoma Ilhuicamina, uncovered not far from the Tezcatlipoca temple (Graulich 1992; Pérez-Castro et al. 1989),

does have Tezcatlipoca imagery, but this relates more to the political message of the stone than to the Tezcatlipoca cult per se (Umberger, this volume).

3. For historiographic discussion of how the examples in Paris and Madrid may have made their way from Mexico to Europe, see Meslay (2001) or Feest (1985, 1990).

4. I thank these museum personnel for information and help with my brief survey: Felipe Solís of the Museo Nacional de Antropología for nos. 6, 12, and 13; Martín Antonio M. and Patricia Aguirre M. of the Instituto Mexiquense de Cultura for no. 1; Colin McEwan and Steward Watson of the British Museum for nos. 3–5; Ana Verde of the Museo de América for no. 7; Elise Alexander and Christina Elson for no. 2; Shelby Spaulding of the Nasher Museum of Art at Duke University for no. 8; Begonia Sánchez and Aurelio Nieto Codina of the Museo Nacional de Ciencias Naturales for no. 11; and Alexander Benitez and Janet Pasiuk for no. 14.

5. The analysis carried out by Calligaro et al. (2005), while perhaps technically sophisticated, is quite crude when compared with standard archaeometric source analyses of obsidian that employ many source samples and large databases (e.g., Glascock 2002). Now that portable X-ray fluorescence machines are becoming more common, it would not be difficult to analyze obsidian mirrors with greater rigor (i.e., to use a larger number of reference samples from known sources to improve the ability to assign geological sources to the objects).

6. Communication with Adje Both and Susan Rawcliffe about Aztec wind instruments indicates that it is more difficult than I had thought to distinguish flutes from whistles when dealing with fragmentary remains. Thus my classification of these types (Smith n.d.a, n.d.c) will require revision. I thank Adje Both for agreeing to help with this endeavor in the future.

7. My offhand explanation of this act has generally been that the Aztec period builder of the platform was stamping Tula with the mark of a proper Aztec city (since Tula had many fewer such altars than specified by the norms of Aztec urban planning). In terms of Tezcatlipoca, one could also speculate that this was meant to be a momoztli dedicated to Tezcatlipoca, placed in the Tula plaza as part of a deliberate effort by the Aztecs to materialize the Tezcatlipoca cult posited in politically charged legends of the Toltecs. Or perhaps the Aztec period builder thought Tula, as the mythical home of Tezcatlipoca, needed a physical symbol of the deity. In any case, the altar in front of Temple C provides one more example of Tula's great ideological importance for the Aztecs.

8. Another underutilized source of information on the distribution of the Tezcatlipoca cult in the Late Postclassic period is the wealth of local documentation from throughout Mesoamerica. The *Relaciones Geográficas* (Acuña 1984–88) often mentions the major deities in the towns covered, and these data have been analyzed in a number of regional studies. Druzo Maldonado Jiménez (2000, 108–19; 2004), for example, discusses the possible presence of Tezcatlipoca worship in Morelos using data from the *Relaciones Geográficas*. A systematic look at this body of data would provide a very useful complement to the archaeological data discussed in this chapter.

9. This relief is from the collection originally stored in the Museo Regional de Toluca. That collection consisted primarily of materials excavated at Calixtlahuaca by García Payón but with other pieces added over the years without clear documentation. This relief is likely from Calixtlahuaca, but that cannot be proven with current information (Smith, Wharton, and McCarron 2003; Umberger 2007a).

10. Native historical sources mention a temple dedicated by Tezcatlipoca at or close to Tlalpitzahuac, a town near Chalco (see discussion in Umberger 1996a), but this has not been excavated or studied. A nearby Epiclassic/Early Postclassic site at Tlalpitzahuac—without Tezcatlipoca imagery—has been excavated (Granados Vázquez et al. 1993; Tovalín Ahumada 1998).

2

Iconographic Characteristics of Tezcatlipoca in the Representations of Central Mexico

The Ezpitzal Case

JUAN JOSÉ BATALLA ROSADO

The representation of Tezcatlipoca has a set of very similar iconographic features in most Mesoamerican cultures. They consist primarily of the "smoking mirror," the absence of one leg, and the characteristic breast-plate, among others. In addition, through iconographic sources (especially Mesoamerican codices), one observes that in central Mexico, during the Postclassic period as well as in Early Colonial times, there is an additional element not found in any other area or indigenous culture. I am referring to what Sahagún's sources call the *ezpitzal*. This particular iconographic feature is formed by a stream of blood on the deity's forehead, in which floats a heart. I begin by explaining the etymology of the term *ezpitzal*; I then demonstrate its presence in several codices, including Borbonicus, Tudela, and Telleriano-Remensis. I also illustrate how in other cultural areas we see that the ezpitzal does not appear in representations of Tezcatlipoca (e.g., in the so-called Borgia Group). Also, it is possible that the Codex Porfirio Díaz (Cuicateca area) could represent the ezpitzal in Tezcatlipoca's depiction in the religious-calendric section.

The term *ezpitzal* appears written in folio 261r of the Codex Matritense (Sahagún 1993 [1559–61]), which is preserved in the Library of the Royal Palace in Madrid and attributed to Fray Bernardino de Sahagún and his informants. This page is dedicated to the depiction of the main deities and their characteristic attire (figure 2.1). It is here where we encounter the first page of information, which goes from folio 261r, mentioned above, to 267r: thirteen pages in which, in all but the last page,

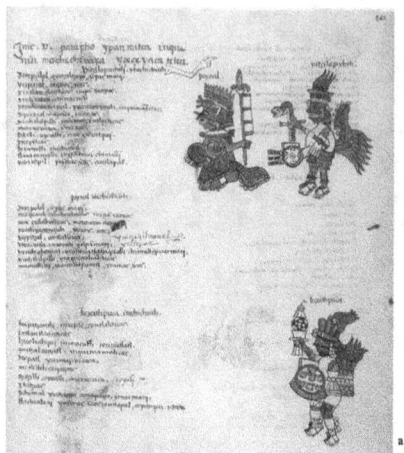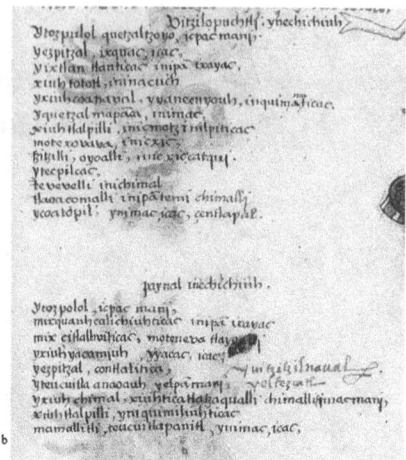

FIGURE 2.1. Folio 261r of the *Primeros Memoriales* by Sahagún and detail of the explanatory text (Sahagún 1993 [1559–61]).

three deities appear depicted vertically in relation to the others with a description written to the left. The images of this section were later copied at the beginning of the Florentine Codex, although in this case its function was to indicate the chapter dedicated to all of the deities and its description.

In this first page of this section of the Codex Matritense, one observes several inconsistencies (see figure 2.1). First, there are two associated images, Painal and Huitzilopochtli, which breaks the verticality of the other three images and the corresponding text (also vertical). Second, next to the image of the third god, Tezcatlipoca, we clearly see the sketch of the head and body of the other deity that, when compared with the next page, can only be Quetzalcoatl (but it is difficult to discern the intention of writing any text). In my opinion, on folio 261r the scribes are carrying out tests to develop in consecutive pages the main deities of the Aztec pantheon. I believe the initial idea was to present at least four deities per page. The problem arises when it comes to the corresponding explanatory text. This is why I think they ultimately corrected the presentation system, although Painal and Huitzilopochtli remain painted in the same line and thus the explanation of the first deity is second, below Huitzilopochtli. Third, it is possible to see that another scribe added something to the original text. Focusing on the text referring to Painal, *yuitzitzilnaual* was added in the fifth line of the text and *yeltezcatl* in the sixth line (see figure 2.1, detail). If we compare the way these letters are written in comparison to the others, we see clear differences when tracing the "y" and "l," although it could be said that these additions have cursive tracing and were perhaps done more quickly.

What *is* clear is that the ink is a different color, which is why I remain convinced that there were two different writers. Finally, there is another clear inconsistency on this page, not involving the document's physical attributes but rather its contents. I refer to the word *ezpitzal* as part of the attire of both Huitzilopochtli and Painal. As I will prove, the ezpitzal is an element pertaining to Tezcatlipoca and not to Huitzilopochtli and his acolyte Painal. Furthermore, the image of Huitzilopochtli does not show this element, despite the text mentioning it (see figure 2.1).

THE TERM *EZPITZAL*

Determining the etymology of the word *ezpitzal*, which appears in the *Primeros Memoriales*, is not an easy task. Expanding on the opinion expressed by Henry Nicholson (1988, 233–34), Thelma D. Sullivan (1997, 94n2) goes deeper into the meaning of the term, indicating that

> it "is apparently derived from eztli, blood, and pitza, to blow, to play a flute or similar instrument, and to cast gold or silver, in which blowing as a process was used. There is a verb, tototlapitza, which means to fashion a decoy. The same term is included in the itemization of the costume and insignia of the next deity, Painal, where what appears to be a marginal annotation identifies it as ihuitzitzinahual, 'his hummingbird disguise.'" This led Eduard Seler (1902–23, 2: 424) to conclude that *ezpitzalli* probably refers to this element in Huitzilopochtli's costume, often depicted as a helmet mask. However, it is also possible that it refers to the vestigial bird motif worn on the god's forehead.

Ángel María Garibay (Sahagún 1982 [1977], 885) and Miguel León-Portilla (1958, 113, 115) translate the term as a "flow of blood," which, according to the text, should be worn on the forehead by both Huitzilopochtli and Painal. As noted, however, it is observed only on the latter.

My opinion on this matter is not definitive. What I believe we *can* be sure of is that the term *ihuitzitzinahual*, depicted with different ink and writing (see figure 2.1, detail), does not necessarily refer to ezpitzal. The term was depicted in the same line but does not follow the line of text. For this reason, this addition informs us of another element that refers to Painal but has no relation to the ezpitzal. However, to translate it as a "flow of blood" fits the iconography on Painal's forehead: a river or jet of blood with several streams, each decorated at the end with precious stones—*chalchihuatl*, or "precious water" (see Batalla Rosado 1994a)—in which a heart is floating. In the examples below, we can observe this more clearly.

The term *ezpitzal* seems to derive from *eztli* (blood) and the verb *pitza*. The meaning of pitza as a reflexive verb is "to rise oneself with anger or to fire oneself with anger" (Molina 1977 [1571], 82v), "to get oneself red, to mount oneself with anger" (Siméon 1988 [1885], 387), or "to huff and puff with anger" (Karttunen 1992 [1983], 197). In this way, if we turn our attention to the depiction, I think ezpitzal defines an attribute related to the rage or madness of the deity. If we consider the iconography composed of a heart submerged in a river of blood, we find terms such as *yollopoçoni*, *yollococolcuic*, and *yollococoltia* (Molina 1977 [1571], 40v; Siméon 1988 [1885], 197–99), which refer to getting angry, getting mad, cruelty, irascibility, violence, confrontation, and spreading discord. The terms *cocolcuic* and *cocoltia*, together with *yollo*, are translated as similar to "rage" and "discord," and *poçoni* indicates "boil," "bubble," and "agitate," referring to a fluid (ibid., 390), which itself can also refer to a "river of blood" and rage through its "boiling" aspect. All of these characteristics can be applied to Tezcatlipoca as creator of discord and conflict wherever he goes (see Olivier 2004b).

The one aspect I can affirm with certainty about ezpitzal is that it makes reference to the "river of blood" with a heart floating in it, painted over a deity's forehead—in this specific case, Painal (Sahagún 1993 [1559–61], folio 261r).

Once I have developed the term's possible significance, I will show that the element mentioned above in fact refers to the god Tezcatlipoca. For this reason, my opinion shifts toward a new iconographic "mistake" in Fray Bernardino de Sahagún's *Primeros Memoriales* (see Batalla Rosado 2008, 52–53), which, as we will see, was moved when introduced to the Florentine Codex.

THE EZPITZAL AS A DISTINCTIVE ELEMENT OF TEZCATLIPOCA

The ezpitzal is an iconographic feature that, despite the large number of examples of deity representations, is depicted on very few occasions. In fact, I could find it depicted only in the codices of central Mexico and possibly, but not certainly, in a Cuicateco document. To be precise, it is present in the Codices Borbonicus, Tudela, Telleriano-Remensis, Vatican A or Ríos, *Primeros Memoriales*, and Florentine, and we could probably add the Porfirio Díaz. From my research on these codices I can conclude that the Codex Borbonicus is the only sample of a calendric-religious codex of pre-Columbian origin preserved in central Mexico (see Batalla Rosado 1992, 1993a, 1993b, 1994a, 1994b, 1994c).

Before I show the various images of the ezpitzal, I wish to point out the paradigm of Tezcatlipoca's iconography—his representations in the murals of Tizatlan and in the paintings of the Codex Borgia (figure 2.2). Here we can clearly observe that the ezpitzal is not depicted on the deity's forehead, a feature that can be applied to the entire group of the Borgia manuscripts (see Spranz 1964). This absence is common in most of the representations of this god, even in his representations

FIGURE 2.2. Representations of Tezcatlipoca. A: murals of Tizatlan (Noguera 1929a, figure 1); B: Codex Borgia (1976, 21).

in sculpture (see Olivier 2004b, 90–156, 493–520). Nevertheless, the Codex Borbonicus of central Mexico *does* show the ezpitzal over Tezcatlipoca's forehead.

Beginning the analysis with the Codex Borbonicus, we observe that the ezpitzal appears painted a total of twenty-four times: nineteen in the *tonalamatl* and five in the *xiuhpohualli*. I can confirm that each instance is an attribute of Tezcatlipoca. The tonalamatl of the Codex Borbonicus contains the representation of Tezcatlipoca as the tenth Lord of Day. With eighteen of the *trecenas* (thirteen-day periods) preserved, having lost the first two, his representation is thus repeated eighteen times. They all share one common iconographic trait: the smoking mirror on the temple, with the "river of blood" with a heart floating on it on the forehead. Bearing in mind that the calendric signs in this section were painted by at least two different *tlacuiloque* (painter)—one for the trecenas 3–10 and the other for 11–20 (see Batalla Rosado 1993a)—it is interesting that in both cases Tezcatlipoca is depicted with his ezpitzal (figure 2.3) (though it is colored only in trecenas 3, 4, 5, 6, and 13), showing this feature in addition to the smoking mirror in the rest of the trecenas.

The other example in which the ezpitzal appears in conjunction with Tezcatlipoca is the main frame in the trecena 3, where Tepeyollotl-Tezcatlipoca has a huge jet of blood over his head that expands in six streams, in which a heart floats (figure 2.4). By comparing the iconography of this ezpitzal with the one that appears in figures 2.1 and 2.3 and the figures we will see henceforth, we see that this depiction is much more impressive and surprising because of its size and precision. Although the main frames of the trecenas of the Codex Borbonicus have other depictions of Tezcatlipoca (or other deities with his characteristic features), none depicts the ezpitzal, not even Tezcatlipoca on page 22.

FIGURE 2.3. Tezcatlipoca as Lord of Day (Codex Borbonicus 1974, 4, 13).

In the xiuhpohualli, the image of Tezcatlipoca appears five times in different festivities. In all of them, made by the same tlacuiloque (Batalla Rosado 1994b), the ezpitzal is present in addition to the characteristic iconographic features of the deity. Tezcatlipoca participates in the festivities shown in pages 26, 31, 33, 34, and 36. Using the month of Ochpaniztli as an example, we can clearly see the ezpitzal over the god's forehead (figure 2.5).

In contrast to Tezcatlipoca's ezpitzal, the Codex Borbonicus depicts a female with a red headband fitted on her forehead with two hearts painted on it. She is painted on pages 23, 26, 27, 28, 36, and 37 (figure 2.6); on some occasions she is accompanied by Tezcatlipoca himself. Because of this, I can confirm that the headband is not the ezpitzal and that the tlacuiloque who painted the xiuhpohualli in the Codex Borbonicus distinguished clearly between the two iconographic features. I can confirm that the depictions of Tezcatlipoca in the Codex Borbonicus have, as one of the characteristic features of the deity, include either the ezpitzal or the river of blood with its streams ending in precious stones and a heart floating on it.

If we consider other documents from central Mexico, we can confirm that in this distinctly colonial codex, Tezcatlipoca still has the ezpitzal as one of the elements of his iconography. In the Codex Tudela, or Codex of the Museum of America, a calendric-religious document from central Mexico (either its paintings or those of the Libro Indígena [Native Book] were the origin of the Magliabechiano Group [Batalla Rosado 2002]), we find two Tezcatlipoca depictions, which stand out because of the ezpitzal. Both images are made by the same tlacuilo and are compiled as a single description of the months of Toxcatl and Tlaxochimaco, or Miccailhuitl in the xiuhpohualli. In the first instance, in folio 15r, we see Tezcatlipoca with his smoking mirror, characteristic breast-plate, and the depiction of the ezpitzal

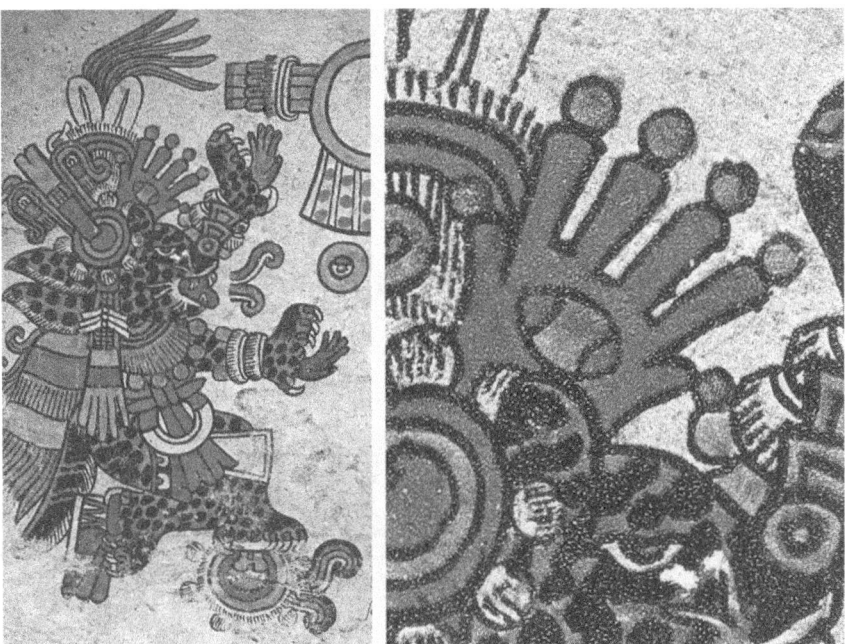

FIGURE 2.4. Representation of Tepeyollotl-Tezcatlipoca in the Codex Borbonicus (1974, 3).

FIGURE 2.5. Representation of Tezcatlipoca in the month of Ochpaniztli (Codex Borbonicus 1974, 31).

FIGURE 2.6. Cihuacoatl depicted on the xiuhpohualli of the Codex Borbonicus (1974, 23).

(figure 2.7) standing out over his forehead. Three streams of blood are clearly visible, although only two end in precious stones and have a heart submerged in them.

The other representation of Tezcatlipoca with the ezpitzal in the Codex Tudela appears on folio 19r, where he is depicted presiding over another monthly festivity, Tlaxochimaco-Miccailhuitl (figure 2.8). In this case, the ezpitzal, despite having been made by the same tlacuilo, has some differences. The blood streams expand not only toward the front but also upward. Furthermore, instead of three jets ending in precious stones, there are five. In fact, the iconography of this ezpitzal is more similar to the one shown by Tepeyollotl in the Codex Borbonicus (see figure 2.4). An interesting aspect of the depiction of Tezcatlipoca's ezpitzal in the Codex Tudela is that, in my opinion, it shows that the tlacuilo who created it (around 1540) still maintained most of the purity of his pre-Columbian style. A consideration of the tlacuilo's knowledge of pre-Columbian style is the only way to understand the quality of his depictions.

As I have shown (ibid.), the paintings of the Codex Tudela gave way to different copies, which compose the so-called Magliabechiano Group. In these works, the tlacuiloque did *not* already know how to interpret many of the iconographic features compiled in the Codex Tudela. Thus the depiction of the ezpitzal becomes an example of the degeneration of the copies as a result of misinterpretation of the original (see ibid., 187–89, 199–201), and so the copies are transformed into

FIGURE 2.7. Tezcatlipoca as patron of the month Toxcatl (Codex Tudela 2002, folio 15r).

FIGURE 2.8. Tezcatlipoca as patron of the month Tlaxochimaco-Miccailhuitl (Codex Tudela 2002, folio 19r).

something quite different (figure 2.9). As can be appreciated, in the images of the copies made using the Codex Tudela as an example, the Codices Magliabechiano and Ixtlilxochitl (both versions of a document currently lost), the Codex Ritos y Costumbres (also a copy of another document unknown to us), and the *Libro de Figuras*, from which images were copied to the Codex Tudela, all show the transformation of the ezpitzal of Tezcatlipoca in a headband or garland of flowers that ended with flowers instead of precious stones. Also, the heart submerged in the blood is not present in any of these images. They are all features that seem to be descended from a common iconographic source. These characteristics are shown in many other iconographic features descended from the source copy that gave rise to the Codex Tudela, the *Libro de Figuras*, and the strange features of the Magliabechiano

50 ICONOGRAPHIC CHARACTERISTICS OF TEZCATLIPOCA

FIGURE 2.9. A: Native book of the month Toxcatl in the Magliabechiano Group (Batalla Rosado 2002b, 188, figure 21); B: Native book of the month Tlaxochimaco in the Magliabechiano Group (ibid., 200, figure 25).

and Ixtlilxochitl Codices (see ibid. for the genealogy of the documents, the order in which the components of the Magliabechiano Group were created, and how they were corrupted by the copyist's misinterpretations).

Resuming the analysis of the ezpitzal in the colonial codex, we find it depicted again in the documents from central Mexico. This is the case with the Codices Telleriano-Remensis and Vaticanus A (or Ríos), both copies of the same unknown original (or possibly, in the case of the latter, a translation of the former). Both documents have several missing folios, and others are loose or have been misplaced. Because of this, the references I will make to them are taken from the 1995 edition for the first reference and from the 1979 edition for the second. Despite the impossibility of establishing the degree of relationship between them, I will always use the Telleriano-Remensis first and then the Vaticanus A because I believe the images in the Telleriano show a lesser degree of iconographic corruption.

Beginning with the xiuhpohualli, we find a depiction of Tezcatlipoca in the month of Pachtontli. In both cases we can see the characteristic features of the deity: the smoking mirror, the absence of one foot, the *anahuatl*, or circular breast-plate, and

ICONOGRAPHIC CHARACTERISTICS OF TEZCATLIPOCA 51

FIGURE 2.10. Depictions of Tezcatlipoca in the month of Pachtontli. A: Codex Telleriano-Remensis (1995, folio 3v); B: Codex Vaticanus A (1979, 46v).

so on. Both images also show the ezpitzal (figure 2.10). Despite the missing details, in this case it is possible to confirm that both the Telleriano and the Vaticanus A lack a stylistic quality that is present in the Codices Borbonicus and Tudela. In Telleriano and Vaticanus A, the big jet or "river of blood" that runs along the head from the temple to the forehead has disappeared. The only features in these codices that remind us of the ezpitzal are the painted hearts—four in both examples—and the red ending, which is divided into three or four lines. It is clear that this image is the ezpitzal, considering the depictions from the Codices Borbonicus and Tudela. However, an individual analysis of the figures indicates that any meaning is lost, and it would be difficult to identify it with the lack of detail, as already mentioned.

Another occurrence of Tezcatlipoca is found painted in the codices accompanying Xochiquetzal in the trecena 1 Eagle. Although in this case he appears disguised as a coyote (Olivier 2004b, 494, figure 2), again we find that he has the ezpitzal (figure 2.11), thus bearing a striking similarity to his other depictions. In this example the hearts are bigger and the streams of blood, which are not very clear,

FIGURE 2.11. Tezcatlipoca as coyote. A: Codex Telleriano-Remensis (1995, folio 23r); B: Codex Vaticanus A (1979, folio 36r).

end in precious stones. Despite the corruption present in its depiction, it is clear that it is the ezpitzal.

As a result of the analysis of these two documents, I can suggest that they both reach a remarkable state of iconographic corruption in looking at the way they represent the ezpitzal. Comparing its style with the one shown in the Codices Borbonicus and Tudela, we can confirm outstanding differences. There are other representations of Tezcatlipoca in the Codices Telleriano-Remensis and Vaticanus A, but the ezpitzal does not appear in any of them. As an example, although depicted in the image of the month of Toxcatl, preserved only in folio 44v of the Vaticanus A, an adornment containing red circles can be seen over Tezcatlipoca's forehead (figure 2.12), which I believe is not the ezpitzal unless it has been transformed dramatically from its original form.

Chronologically, the last depiction of the ezpitzal in the codices of central Mexico is found the *Primeros Memoriales* and Florentine Codex of Fray Bernardino

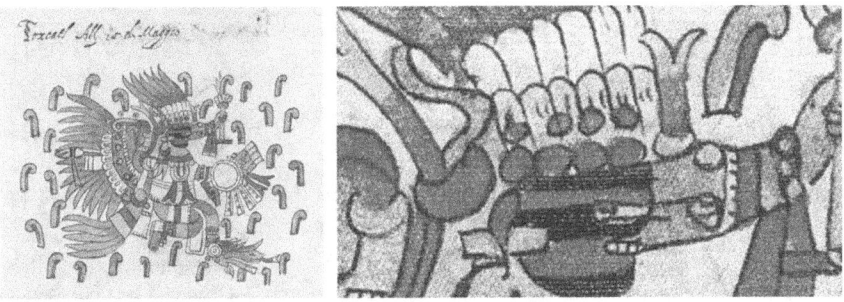

FIGURE 2.12. Tezcatlipoca as patron of the month of Toxcatl in the Codex Vaticano A (1979, folio 44v).

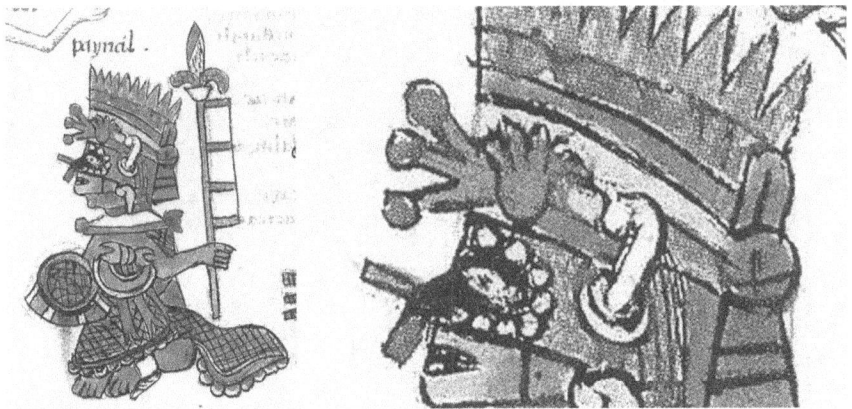

FIGURE 2.13. Representation of Painal in the *Primeros Memoriales* (1993, folio 261r).

de Sahagún. Considering the first of these, we have seen that it only shows the ezpitzal over Painal's forehead (figure 2.13). In this case, the corruption is also evident because the blood is a clear red color and the heart is only identified as such because we know the ezpitzal contains an iconographic one. It would be difficult to confirm that the object painted here is a heart without this prior knowledge. The images of Huitzilopochtli and Tezcatlipoca do not depict the ezpitzal (see figure 2.1), even though in the first of these, the explanatory text indicates its presence.

As a possible mistake in the iconography of the *Primeros Memoriales*, I must point out that Painal usually bears other characteristic elements of Tezcatlipoca, which this figure does not have. I refer to the smoking mirror, the breast-plate (*anahuatl*), the arrow as a nose ornament, the ezpitzal, and so on. Because of this, I must again insist that this source be used cautiously for research concerning its

54 ICONOGRAPHIC CHARACTERISTICS OF TEZCATLIPOCA

FIGURE 2.14. A: Painal in the Florentine Codex (1979 I, folio 10r); B: Huitzilopochtli in book III of the Florentine Codex (1979 I, folio 6r).

iconography, which contains serious mistakes. This is the case involving one such mistake, which I have pointed out elsewhere (Batalla Rosado 2008, 53), concerning the miswriting of years and days. In this case, the cartouche or vignette—generally blue or red—to avoid any confusion with the days (see Batalla Rosado 1995), frames the days instead of the years, so the one who used this information did not know how to write. When the *Primeros Memoriales* was written, it was the second half of the sixteenth century, and the tlacuiloque in charge of its paintings seem to have lost part of the pre-Columbian tradition. Nevertheless, the style is still strongly influenced by that tradition.

In the Florentine Codex we find the ezpitzal associated with Painal and Huitzilopochtli (figure 2.14). First, in the copy of the itemization of deities in the *Primeros Memoriales*, compiled before book I, the ezpitzal appears with Painal. Second, in

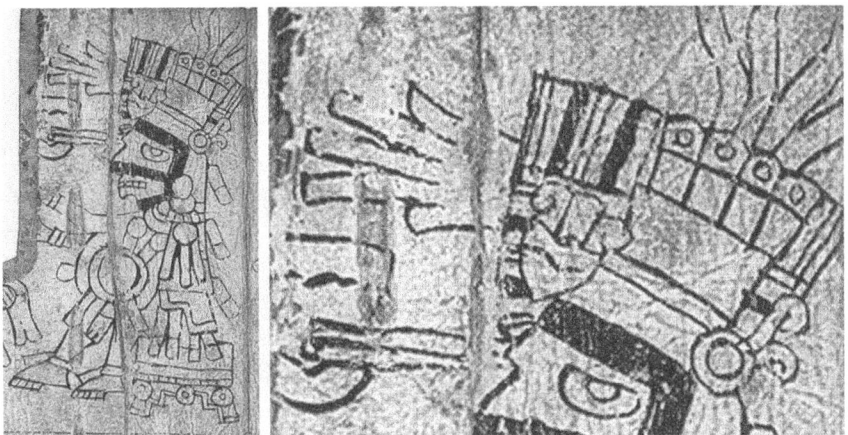

FIGURE 2.15. Image of Tezcatlipoca-Itztlacoliuhqui in the Codex Porfirio Díaz (Doesburg 2001, 16).

book III of the principles of deities, there is a figure of Huitzilopochtli that also carries it. In both cases, the corruption of the ezpitzal is evident, and the ezpitzal is only recognized because it is the only element that could be present. The heart has disappeared, and the blood is no longer red.

Finally, I point out as something quite exceptional the possible presence of the ezpitzal in the Codex Porfirio Díaz (Olivier, personal communication, November 26, 2005), a document from the area of Cuicateca. In its calendric-religious section, this codex contains an image of Tezcatlipoca-Itztlacoliuhqui (Olivier 2004b, 498, figure 6b), which shows a heart on his forehead (figure 2.15).

In this case, the organ is attached to the forehead, not "floating" in a river or jet of blood. Despite the absence of color, I can confirm that it is a heart, though not specifically the ezpitzal, as I have defined it through the codices of central Mexico. Nevertheless, the left side of the heart comes out of Tezcatlipoca's head, an element composed of two short sections (upper and lower) and three longer ones that could be blood, being very similar to the jet of "precious liquid" flowing from the victims depicted on the next page (see Doesburg 2001, 17). The absence of color in this part of the document does not allow me to confirm that it is the ezpitzal, although I believe it is; however, once more the heart is disfigured because it is not floating in the "precious liquid."

These images are those I have identified of the ezpitzal, all of them in the codices from central Mexico except one from the Codex Porfirio Díaz. Nevertheless, before I present the findings of this research, I must refer to another iconographic feature that could be related to the ezpitzal. This I identified in the Magliabechiano

Group (specifically in the Codices Tudela and Magliabechiano) because the Codex Ixtlilxochitl and its copy, the Codex Veitia, do not include this section. I refer to the itemization of the eleven gods of Pulque, painted in both documents.

These gods are defined by a series of iconographic features, identified by other scholars (see Batalla Rosado 2002b, 233–48). A remarkable feature here is the facial paint called *mixchictlapanticac*, which consists of painting the face red and the rest of the figure black or dark; painting a stain of a green color with two yellow brushstrokes on the left side of the face; a white crescent nose ornament, or *yacameztli*; the square shield, or *ometochchimalli*; the *itztopolli* or *tecpatopolli* (ax) carried in their hands; and finally the necklace of *malinalli* or *yauhtli*, known as *tlachayaualcozcatl*.

In contrast, six of the images in the Codex Tudela (folios 31r, 32r, 33r, 34r, 36r, and 38r) have as an iconographic and characteristic feature a little double-coned yellow hat that "floats" over something similar to the depiction of the river of blood, although its color is green and the "streams" end in yellowish circles. Although the change is evident in the Codex Magliabechiano, the element is found painted in its folios 49r, 50r, 51r, 52r, 53r, 54r, 55r, 56r, 57r, 59r, and 64r on eleven deities, although the last one (Techalotl, folio 64r) is a god that belongs to the section dedicated to the gods of death.

If we analyze, for example, the iconographic feature in the image of Totoltecatl (figure 2.16), we can confirm that it has some likeness to the ezpitzal. In the grand scheme of things, we should keep in mind that the colors red, blue, and green can be interpreted similarly to the *chalchihuatl*, or precious liquid: blood (see Batalla Rosado 1994a). In fact, in the Codex Borbonicus (1974, trecena 20) we find a cuauhxicalli—plenty of hearts submersed in a big jet of blood. This one is blue, which demonstrates that it is either a mistake by the tlacuilo or that both colors are valid to represent the chalchihuatl.

Nevertheless, in this case I think it is a clear reference to the *malinalli*, the presence of grass in the breasts of the deities. Its depiction over the deities' foreheads could be linked to the ezpitzal of Tezcatlipoca, switching the red color of blood with the green of the malinalli and the heart with the cone-shaped hat of Xipe Totec, the Red Tezcatlipoca.

Therefore, what I believe the tlacuilo did in the Codex Tudela was produce a similar element to the ezpitzatl on the six pulque deities using the green color (the one in folio 31r is not finished properly), given that green is a substitute for red and blue as indicative of something precious, from *xiuitl*—"turquoise." In its interior, instead of the heart that appears in the depictions of Tezcatlipoca, there is the cone-shaped hat of Xipe Totec, which can be represented as either a single cone (see Vié-Wohrer 1999) or as two cones (see trecena 14 in the Codex Borbonicus). We must not forget that Xipe Totec is fairly close to Tezcatlipoca (see Olivier 2004b). As I pointed out

FIGURE 2.16. Representations of Totoltecatl. A: Codex Tudela (2002, folio 34r); B: Codex Magliabechiano (1970, folio 52r).

in the case of the ezpitzatl of Tezcatlipoca, in the manner of the Libro de Figuras, the Codex Ritos y Costumbres, and Codex Magliabechiano, the element present in the gods of pulque becomes a feature impossible to decipher—including the hat of Xipe Totec, which cannot be interpreted either (see figure 2.16b).

CONCLUSIONS

Through the analysis in this chapter, I have been able to determine that in the iconography of the calendric-religious codices of central Mexico, the representation of Tezcatlipoca has a defining feature: the ezpitzal. Although the etymology of this term is not clear, I think that it refers to the wrath and discord this deity invoked in humans (Olivier 2004b, 65–66). However, the translation a "flow of blood" could also be valid.

In addition, I was able to confirm that the ezpitzal is already represented in pre-Columbian documents (e.g., Codex Borbonicus) and in Early Colonial manuscripts (e.g., Codex Tudela) and that its style is mostly preserved in the colonial manuscripts. As the Colonial period progressed, we get the impression that the new tlacuiloque and codex copyists did not know how to interpret this element. I believe that in their culture, they could not conceive of the notion of a "jet of blood" running along the head, from the temple to the forehead; therefore the change is vast, and among certain members of the Magliabechiano Group the corruption is complete and the blood and the heart disappear altogether. In other documents, such as the Telleriano-Remensis, Vaticanus A, *Primeros Memoriales*, and Florentine Codices, there is still an obvious intention to represent the ezpitzal, but its depiction varies in other documents that precede them (Codices Borbonicus and Tudela). Even in Sahagún's codex, the ezpitzal becomes a feature that defines Huitzilopochtli and his acolyte Painal. In this case, I think it is a result of the many "mistakes" already included in these works. Although Sahagún's writings were never questioned, more people, including myself, make a point of treating them like any other source and study them in-depth. Finally, it is possible that a codex painted in the Cuicateca cultural area, the Porfirio Díaz, also depicts Tezcatlipoca with his ezpitzal, even if it is disfigured. If the ezpitzal is mentioned in the religious-calendric section of the Porfirio Díaz, it would also be close to the documents from central Mexico and not only to the so-called Borgia Group.

I end by pointing out the possibility that the section dedicated to the gods of pulque in the Magliabechiano Group (Codices Tudela and Magliabechiano) show an element similar to the ezpitzal, or at least one we could relate it to, which forges a relationship between these deities and Xipe Totec and thus Tezcatlipoca as well. Nevertheless, in this case everything seems to point to malinalli painting as a substitute for the river of blood.

3

Enemy Brothers or Divine Twins?

A Comparative Approach between Tezcatlipoca and Quetzalcoatl, Two Major Deities from Ancient Mexico

GUILHEM OLIVIER
Translated by Michel Besson

to Henry B. Nicholson

According to Jean-Pierre Vernant (1974, 110), the great specialist on the pantheon of ancient Greece, "investigations done by historians of the religions, such as Georges Dumézil, have shown that one can understand a religious system as being a linguistic system only by studying the relationship between gods."[1] This introduction may come as a surprise, especially from one who spent several years working on the monography of a single deity, Tezcatlipoca, chosen from the particularly rich Mesoamerican pantheon. That said, let me quote from the conclusion of the book I wrote about him: "As I kept tracking Tezcatlipoca, I felt ever more strongly that an important and complementary part of the journey remained to be undertaken. In the shadow of my hero, at his side or facing him, Quetzalcoatl unfailingly appeared as a faithful or at times inverted reflection. Little by little I grew more confident in affirming that the stark opposition often remarked upon in modern studies did not fit perfectly with the indigenous vision of their places in the pantheon" (Olivier 2003, 274).

Space limitations do not allow me to detail here all of the common points as well as oppositions that characterize these two giants of Mesoamerican mythology. I have thus deemed it more advisable to concentrate on a series of cues—each of them constituting a potential field of investigation—that reveal a number of traits and functions Quetzalcoatl and Tezcatlipoca have in common. These factors betray a certain kinship between the two gods, a sort of "twin-ness" that we can find among the heroes of many indigenous mythologies on the American continent.

DOI: 10.5876/9781607322887.c003

I will start with the numerous divine names the native people attributed to both Tezcatlipoca and Quetzalcoatl. On the one hand, both deities could be invoked under several names allocated to the supreme deity. For example, Tezcatlipoca was also called Moquequeloa ("He who mocks himself"), another name of the supreme god that fit his propensity to ridicule humankind (Sahagún 1950–82, book I: 5; book VI: 18, 42, 51). In fact, the "jokes" played by the Lord of the Smoking Mirror were akin to real trials, at the end of which men could catch a glimpse of what their fate might be (Olivier 2003, 15–20). Quetzalcoatl was also linked to fate. He, too, was called Moquequeloa in an invocation preserved by Hernando Ruiz de Alarcón (1984, 75, 77), and many texts give him the paternity of the origin of the calendar (Sahagún 2000, 716).

Quetzalcoatl, as well as Tezcatlipoca, bore names that included the word *Ehecatl*— "Wind," "1 Wind," and "9 Wind" were Quetzalcoatl's calendar names (Sahagún 1950–82, book IV: 101; Codex Telleriano-Remensis 1995, folio 8v; Nicholson 1979, 40); under his guise of Ehecatl, he was often represented in statues and pictographic manuscripts alike with a mouth mask in the shape of a bird's beak (Nicholson and Quiñones Keber 1983, 78–79) (figure 3.1). Furthermore, according to the interpreter of the Codex Tudela (1980, folio 42r; see also Codex Magliabechiano 1996, folio 60v), "this [Quetzalcoatl] was considered by the Indians as god of the airs, and the Indians used to paint him with the lower half of his face, from the nose down, made of wood, like a trumpet, which he used to blow out air."[2]

Associated with sacrifice and self-sacrifice, wind had a creative role, illustrated by Quetzalcoatl's birth, as he was conceived by the breath of the supreme deity (Codex Telleriano-Remensis 1995, folio 8v; Olivier 2003, 20–22). At the moment when the sun and the moon were created in Teotihuacan, Quetzalcoatl-Ehecatl started the movement of the sun by blowing on him (Sahagún 1950–82, book VII: 8).

As Yohualli Ehecatl, or "Night Wind," the Lord of the Smoking Mirror was closely associated with the idea of destruction (Alva Ixtlilxóchitl 1985, 1: 264; Historia de los mexicanos por sus pinturas 1941 [1543], 213–14), including the cyclical destruction of the cosmic eras and also of the earthly kingdoms and fortunes that he allotted to men but took away from those who lacked respect (Olivier 2003, 20–25). An inspirer of evil activities among sorcerers, Tezcatlipoca was also the origin of a number of illnesses, carried around by those "airs of the night" today's Indians still fear (ibid., 23–24). In the Codex Borgia (1963, 35, 36), the Lord of the Smoking Mirror, as Night Wind, is also represented with the same mouth mask as Quetzalcoatl (figure 3.2). Although usually applied to Tezcatlipoca, the title Yohualli Ehecatl is presented in the Historia de los mexicanos por sus pinturas (1941 [1543], 209) as one of the names of the "Plumed Serpent." The interpretation, however, by which the former is associated with the nightly and evil characteristic of

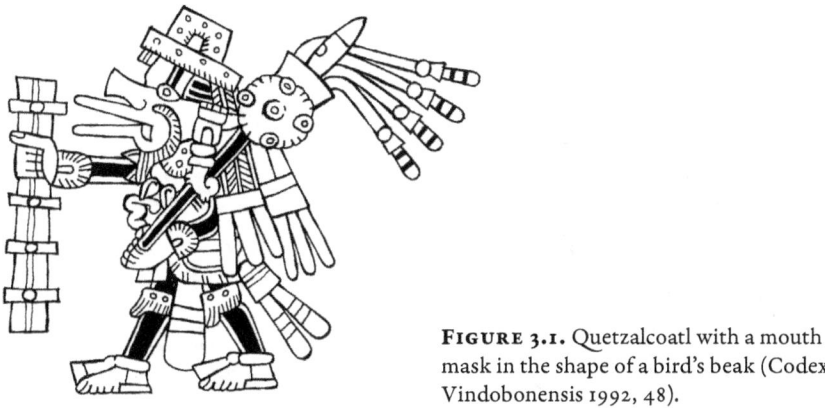

FIGURE 3.1. Quetzalcoatl with a mouth mask in the shape of a bird's beak (Codex Vindobonensis 1992, 48).

the wind and the latter with the creative wind that blows during the day, should be taken with caution (Graulich 1988, 144). The *temalpalitotique*, sorcerers who did their evil deeds only at night, venerated Quetzalcoatl under the name Ce Ehecatl (Sahagún 1950–82, book IV: 101–6). Furthermore, in the Codex Vaticano A (1996, 71), we find mention of the fear that Quetzalcoatl would destroy the world by sending hurricanes into it.

The warrior aspect of Tezcatlipoca was made evident under his title Yaotl, "Enemy," a title also applied to the war-like gods Huitzilopochtli and Xipe Totec (Anales de Cuauhtitlan 1992a, 14–15, 1992b, 39–40; Durán 1967, 1: 153; Olivier 2003, 28–32). To our knowledge, Quetzalcoatl is only called Yaotl once, in an invocation collected by Ruiz de Alarcón (1984, 75): "It is I in person. I am Quetzalcoatl. I am Matl. I indeed am Yaotl."[3] But the god's war-like nature is attested in myths relating to both his youth and when he vanquishes and sacrifices his brothers or his uncles, depending on the version of the myth one reads (Leyenda de los Soles 1992a, 94–95, 1992b, 154). Diego Durán (1967, 1: 40) affirms that warriors invoked the Plumed Serpent to capture prisoners on the battlefield. Fray Juan de Torquemada (1969/1975–83 [1613–15], 1: 224), speaking about the city of Cholula, whose main deity was Quetzalcoatl, said: "And for this war, the Chololtecs took their god Quetzalcoatl with them, since the demon always talked to them through the voice of this idol, they wanted to have him close by to know at all times what was the best thing they had to do."[4] Finally, in the Maya lands, the war-like qualities of the Plumed Serpent are well documented in iconographic and written sources (Seler 1998 [1908]).

Among Quetzalcoatl's and Tezcatlipoca's calendar names, sources mention "1 Reed" and "2 Reed," respectively (Caso 1961, 90; Codex Telleriano-Remensis 1995, folio 14v; Sahagún 1950–82, book I: 33–34; book IV, 29, 56). Among the various

FIGURE 3.2. Tezcatlipoca as Yohualli Ehecatl, "Night Wind," with Quetzalcoatl mouth mask (Codex Borgia 1963, 35).

symbolic associations linked to the reed, I will mention only the importance of reed mats as symbols of power among the Mexica as well as the Mixtecs or Mayas (Boone 2000, 46, 56, 134; Thompson 1950, 48, 107). The craftsmen who made those mats adored the god Nappatecuhtli, a deity who was very close to Quetzalcoatl, according to Alfredo López Austin (1990, 333), but who could also well have been an avatar of Tezcatlipoca, since a deity called Nappatecuhtli Tezcatlipoca is mentioned in Chalco (Historia de los mexicanos por sus pinturas 1941 [1543], 219). In codices as well as on bas-reliefs, the sign "1 Reed" is often associated with Quetzalcoatl (Caso 1961, 90) (figure 3.3). According to several sources, the day Ce Acatl could be the calendar name, the birth name of Quetzalcoatl, or the name of the day of his death (Codex Telleriano-Remensis 1995, folio 10r; Historia de los mexicanos por sus pinturas 1941 [1543], 217; Sahagún 1950–82, book IV: 29). The sign Ome Acatl—which is also the name of the god Omacatl—was the calendar name of Tezcatlipoca (Sahagún 1950–82, book I: 33–34; IV: 56) (figure 3.4). "2 Reed" is a lunar sign associated with fertility (Olivier 2003, 40–42). These favorable characteristics could explain the choice of a year 2 Reed to celebrate the feast of the New Fire, a ceremony whose mythical prototype represents Tezcatlipoca lighting a fire after the flood, specifically during a year Ome Acatl (Historia de los mexicanos por sus pinturas 1941 [1543], 214–15). Quetzalcoatl is also linked with the moon, especially in Tollan, where he performed penitential acts similar to those practiced by Tecuciztecatl-Moon in Teotihuacan (Anales de Cuauhtitlan 1992a, 8, 1992b, 30; Graulich 1997, 190; Sahagún 1950–82, book VII: 4). Furthermore, Durán (1967, 1: 64) describes how a Quetzalcoatl impersonator was treated in Cholula: "At midnight, after having honored him greatly with incense and music, they took him and

FIGURE 3.3. Quetzalcoatl with his calendar name Ce Acatl, "1 Reed" (Codex Telleriano-Remensis 1995, folio 22r).

FIGURE 3.4. Tezcatlipoca with his calendar name Ome Acatl, "2 Reed" (Codex Zouche-Nuttall 1992, 14).

sacrificed him in the manner already mentioned, upon that very same hour of the night, and offered his heart to the moon."⁵

Having examined the names of Tezcatlipoca and Quetzalcoatl, I will briefly mention a number of characteristics of their sacred bundles, symbolic objects wrapped in pieces of cloth, which the Nahuatl-speaking Indians used to call *tlaquimilolli*

(Olivier 1995, 2006). The discovery of the role of Huitzilopochtli's and Tezcatlipoca's tlaquimilolli during the ceremonies of enthronement allows us interpret that rite as the symbolic death of the future king, a death that reenacted the apparition through the tlaquimilolli of both of his tutelary deities (Florentine Codex 1979, 2, book VIII: folio 46r; Olivier 2003, 78–81) (figure 3.5). It is even possible that similar rites could have been completed using Quetzalcoatl's relics, even if sources remain very discreet about enthronement ceremonies in cities such as Cholula. Whatever the case may have been, we know how important those bundles were among the Quiché of Guatemala, who called them Pisom C'ac'al (glorious bundles) and who gave Nacxitl Quetzalcoatl a foremost role in the transmission of power (El Título de Totonicapán 1983, 175, 177, 187, 189; Popol Vuh 1985, 198–204). Similarly, in Mixtec codices, the presence of the sacred bundles of 9 Wind–Quetzalcoatl seems closely associated with the establishment of the main Mixtec dynasties (Jansen 1982, 318–32; Pohl 1994, 23–31).

Animals were considered potential epiphanies through which Mesoamerican deities could make themselves present. The number of animals whose guise Tezcatlipoca and Quetzalcoatl could adopt is truly remarkable. Many Mesoamerican animals have ambiguous attitudes as far as divine "possessions" are concerned. For example, the monkey, usually identified with Quetzalcoatl—especially in statues (Nicholson and Quiñones Keber 1983, 126–27)—may also indicate the presence of Tezcatlipoca, whose facial marking he wears in the Codex Borgia (1963, 49), attested to in a passage from André Thévet (1905, 33) that speaks of a simian metamorphosis of the Lord of the Smoking Mirror (figure 3.6). The opossum, *tlacuache*, superbly analyzed as Quetzalcoatl's double by Alfredo López Austin (1990), nevertheless also presents ornaments that are characteristic of Tezcatlipoca in the Codex Fejérváry-Mayer (1901–2, 38–43; Seler in ibid., 194–95). As for the jaguar, it was the favorite animal double of Tezcatlipoca, who in this guise was assimilated to Tepeyollotl, "Heart of the Mountain"; the jaguar also entertains a very close relationship with Quetzalcoatl (Olivier 1998, 119–21) (figure 3.7). In the form of a jaguar, Tezcatlipoca was the agent of the destruction of all creatures at the end of the first age (Historia de los mexicanos por sus pinturas 1941 [1543], 213). Similarly, at the end of the Toltec era, "he [Tezcatlipoca] drove out Quetzalcoatl, who had been lord of Tula for several years, because, while he was playing the ball game with him, he changed into a tiger, and the spectators got such a fright that they ran away and, in their precipitation and rendered blind by fear, they fell into the ravine of the river that flows by there and they drowned"[6] (Mendieta 1980 [1870], 82).

Tezcatlipoca's presence was foreseen during the cataclysm that is supposed to destroy the last sun (Sahagún 1950–82, book III: 12). As master of the night spaces, both above and underground (of which the cave is the most accomplished

FIGURE 3.5. Presence of a sacred bundle, *tlaquimilolli*, during the rites of enthronement (Florentine Codex 1979, 2, book VIII: folio 46r).

FIGURE 3.6. Monkey with the facial marking of Tezcatlipoca (Codex Borgia 1963, 49).

FIGURE 3.7. Tepeyollotl, "Heart of the Mountain," the jaguar aspect of Tezcatlipoca (Codex Borbonicus 1991, 3).

manifestation), the jaguar belongs to the world of humidity ruled by Tlaloc. The latter shares with Tepeyollotl the quality of being "God of the earth" but also the role of rain provider, a role sometimes attributed to Tezcatlipoca (Olivier 2003, 98–100). Similarly, Quetzalcoatl Ehecatl was the god who opened the way to the gods of rain with his breath (Sahagún 1950–82, book I: 9). Represented performing rituals of self-sacrifice and described as the animal in front of which the Indians confessed their sins, the jaguar is merged with Tezcatlipoca but also with Tlazolteotl, the patron of the day Ce Ocelotl (1 Jaguar) (Codex Borgia 1963, 12; Codex Vaticanus B 1901–2, 30; Las Casas 1967, 2: 224). In this respect, he is also very close to Quetzalcoatl, who numerous documents show as the initiator of self-sacrifice practices. A manifestation of the forces of origin, of the earth and the moon, Tepeyollotl-jaguar appears in manuscripts together with the masters of human genesis, Tlazolteotl or Quetzalcoatl, who wear many jaguar-skin ornaments (Codex Borbonicus 1991, 3; Codex Borgia 1963, 63) (figure 3.8). Alva Ixtlilxóchitl (1985, 2: 387) affirms that Quetzalcoatl's sacred bundle was formed from his ashes, wrapped in the skin of a jaguar. Furthermore, his Quiché equivalent, Gucumatz, could also transform into a jaguar (Popol Vuh 1985, 212).

In addition to their names, representations, and animal doubles, the gods could appear through "images"—mortals who represented them—especially during the feasts of the *veintenas* (a "month" of twenty days). The problem is that most of our sources describe ceremonies carried on in Mexico City, and data about other cities (notably Cholula, where Quetzalcoatl was venerated) are sorely lacking. Though Tezcatlipoca enjoyed in Tenochtitlan a main feast, that of Toxcatl, the Plumed Serpent was not celebrated in the Mexica capital during any specific veintena. In fact, Michel Graulich (1999, 191–93) shows that the Mexica had replaced Quetzalcoatl with Huitzilopochtli as patron of the celebration of Panquetzaliztli, which celebrated the birth of their tutelary god.

Whatever the case may be, it seemed interesting to compare the respective impersonators (*ixipla*) of Tezcatlipoca and Quetzalcoatl in both Mexico City and Cholula. The image of Tezcatlipoca was usually chosen from among war prisoners of noble origin (Sahagún 1950–82, book II: 66–68). Durán (1967, 1: 44, 59), however, states that he was chosen from among the slaves. Similarly, the Dominican describes the representative of Quetzalcoatl in Cholula as a slave bought by the merchants (ibid., 63–64). According to Durán (1971, 131), the representative of Quetzalcoatl should be "flawless of hands and feet, without stain or blemish, nor one-eyed, nor with a cloud in his eye, nor lame, nor lacking one hand, nor crippled, nor with bleary eyes, nor drooling, nor lacking teeth. He was to have no blemish—none whatsoever—the sutures of his skull closed, nor signs of a cleft chin, nor pustules, nor scrofula—he was to be free of all imperfections."[7]

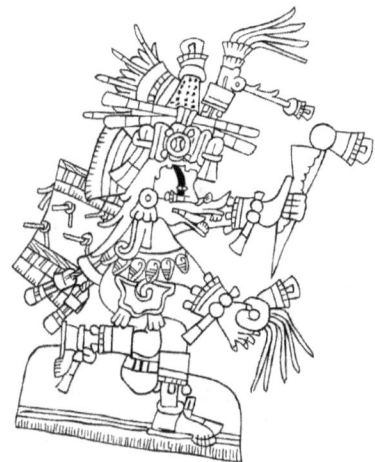

FIGURE 3.8. Quetzalcoatl with a conical jaguar-skin hat (Codex Telleriano-Remensis 1995, folio 8v).

FIGURE 3.9. Representative of Tezcatlipoca during the Toxcatl feast (Florentine Codex 1979, 1, book II: folio 30v).

This list of negative attributes, all of which must be absent in the chosen person, is very close to the description given by Sahagún's informers, who wrote in Nahuatl a long list of physical defects the young man who represents Tezcatlipoca should not display (Sahagún 1950–82, book II: 66–68) (figure 3.9). These testimonies, in addition to the unique views they offer on the pre-Columbian idea of masculine beauty, agree on the necessity of physical perfection in the impersonators of Quetzalcoatl and Tezcatlipoca, a quality they must therefore have had in common with both deities.

Another common trait that representatives of both Tezcatlipoca and Quetzalcoatl shared was the knowledge of the ultimate phase in their respective divine roles. According to Juan Bautista de Pomar (1986, 67), concerning the representative of the Lord of the Smoking Mirror, "though he was certain of his own upcoming death, it was never heard that among all those that were chosen for that, any had ever flown even though he could, but it seemed to him so inconceivable for men who represented such a majesty as the one of that idol."[8] Also, the one who impersonated Quetzalcoatl in Cholula was told by two priests: "Oh Lord, let your worship know that nine days from now your task of singing and dancing will end. Know that you are to die! And he was expected to answer, So be it"[9] (Durán 1967, 1: 63; 1971, 132).

It seems that Tezcatlipoca's and Quetzalcoatl's representatives were chosen from among persons willing to fill the role that was to be theirs. They were prone to adhere to the mystical and warrior-like ideology that assured them that, if they died on the sacrificial stone, they would live a glorious afterlife in the house of the sun (Sahagún 1950–82, book III: 49).

I have insisted on the role and symbolism of the flute of Tezcatlipoca's representative in Toxcatl (Olivier 2003, 223–26). Indeed, several metaphors betray the narrow links that existed among Tezcatlipoca, the flute, and the ruler. The instrument allowed the deity to communicate his will to the king, and the latter himself was assimilated to the flute of the Lord of the Smoking Mirror. When he broke his flutes on the steps of the temple, Tezcatlipoca's representative was expressing the temporary break in relations between men and the gods, which coincided with the symbolic death of the king (figure 3.10). He also reenacted, in reverse, the myth of the solar origin of music. With the apparition of new representatives of the gods, the king was reborn, and the sound of the flutes again manifested the contact with Tezcatlipoca.

An interesting parallel to this association of a deity with a musical instrument is found in the case of Quetzalcoatl. In effect, Durán (1967, 1: 63–65) tells how a priest who resided permanently in Quetzalcoatl's temple in Cholula was responsible for playing that god's drum. The comparison with Tezcatlipoca's impersonator, who played the flute in the streets of Mexico City, has been noted by Durán (ibid., 63, 1971, 132): Quetzalcoatl's impersonator, he affirms, "sang and danced in order to be recognized as the impersonator of the god. These things [were] substituted [for] the flute which the other [Tezcatlipoca] played for the same reason—that of being recognized."[10]

I should now analyze more deeply the symbolism of the drum, undoubtedly a *huehuetl*, used by Quetzalcoatl. The flute could be associated with some sort of solar symbolism, while the drum more probably refers to the surface of the earth or the

FIGURE 3.10. Sacrifice of Tezcatlipoca's representive in Toxcatl (Florentine Codex 1979, 1, book II: folio 30v).

underworld. Whatever the case, Tezcatlipoca, the tutelary deity of the *tlatoani*, as Quetzalcoatl was, had a close relationship with power. Indeed, it was said that the main political personages had to come to Cholula to have their power confirmed before Quetzalcoatl: "The said kings and chiefs, upon inheriting the kingdom or the chiefdom, used to come to this city [Cholula] to pledge allegiance to the idol that was there, Quetzalcoatl, to whom they offered sumptuous feathers, cloaks, gold and precious stones, and other valuable things"[11] (Rojas 1985, 130–31).

As for the musical instruments, they were among the power insignia that Nacxit, the Quiché equivalent of Quetzalcoatl, gave to future lords (El Título de Totonicapán 1983, 183; Popol Vuh 1985, 142).

Mythic data relating to Quetzalcoatl and Tezcatlipoca obviously constitute a rich lode of information for our investigation. Here we find important data related to what could be called the incomplete twin kinship between the two deities (Olivier 2010). Recall that Mayan myths included in the Popol Vuh (1985) present at least two sets of twins: first, Hun Hunahpu and Vucub Hunahpu, and second, the twin sons of the former, Hunahpu and Ixbalamque, who are transformed into the sun and the moon. To Hun Hunahpu is also attributed the anterior paternity of two other sons, Hunbatz and Hunchouen, later defeated by their younger twin brothers. The Mixtec myths also illustrated in the codices depict a divine and supreme couple who share the same calendar name, 1 Deer, meaning both deities were born on the same day (Codex Vindobonensis 1992, 51; García 1981 [1607], 327–29; Selden Roll 1955) (figure 3.11).[12] These primordial twins also have twin sons,

FIGURE 3.11. The Mixtec supreme couple shares the same calendar name, 1 Deer (Codex Vindobonensis 1992, 51).

both of whom have the name 9 Wind, one of Quetzalcoatl's names in the Mixtec area (Nicholson 1978).

The data from central Mexico also show a supreme deity (here again a double one), Ometecuhtli (Lord 2) and Omecihuatl (Woman 2), who gave birth to four sons: Red Tezcatlipoca, Black Tezcatlipoca, Quetzalcoatl, and Huitzilopochtli (Historia de los mexicanos por sus pinturas 1941 [1543], 209–10). The fact that the first two share the same name raises the possibility that they were twins,[13] while the last two are very close in many respects. For example, Quetzalcoatl appears wearing a hummingbird headdress in the Codex Borgia (1963, 44) (the hummingbird is the animal double of Huitzilopochtli); and the story of the group that carries the sacred bundle of the Plumed Serpent in the Selden Roll (1955) seems to reproduce many events from the Mexica migration led by the "Left Handed Hummingbird" (figure 3.12). It is undoubtedly significant that some sources attribute the same mother to both Quetzalcoatl and Huitzilopochtli: Coatlicue (Muñoz Camargo 1998, 84; Sahagún 1950–82, book III: 1–5).

The omnipresence of twin figures in the Mesoamerican myths of origin is remarkable. In the first phase, we see the transition from double creator deities to divine beings who also have twin-like features. These gods are then put in charge of various creations, during which a number of original units, both twin-like and androgynous, are broken into single units. The example of Tlalteotl, "Earth Goddess," cut in half by the "twins" Quetzalcoatl and Tezcatlipoca to form heaven and earth, is a clear example of this process, to which I will return. Similarly, in many contemporaneous indigenous myths, the twins who are the origin of the sun and the moon—sometimes proceeding from a single egg—grow progressively farther apart before their final astral metamorphosis (Báez-Jorge 1992; López Austin 1994).[14]

FIGURE 3.12. Quetzalcoatl wearing a hummingbird headdress (Codex Borgia 1963, 44).

I propose, starting with the myth of the origins included in the Historia de los mexicanos por sus pinturas, a possible equivalence between this theogonical model and the composition of the Mexica central government. Indeed, it has been shown that the king (*tlatoani*) was accompanied by a personage the Spaniards described as a vice-king, who was called *cihuacoatl* ("Female Serpent") (Acosta Saignes 1946, 171–86; Klein 1988) or again "Female Twin," if we translate *coatl* as "twin" (Molina 1970, folio 23r). We would then find heading the Mexica state a twin-like figure, equivalent to the one who ruled the Nahua pantheon through Ometecuhtli and Omecihuatl.[15] Possibly, an echo of this mythic model could be found in the story of the birth of an Aztec king and his cihuacoatl. In effect, Chimalpahin Cuauhtlehuanitzin (2003, 70–73) states that Motecuhzoma Ilhuicamina and his future vice-king, the famous Tlacaellel (prototype of the Aztec cihuacoatl), were born on the same day to different mothers but the same father, the king Huitzilihuitl. In other words, they were almost twins.[16] As for the famous council of four members that helped the king in his work (Piho 1972), one hypothesis could be to compare it to the four sons of the supreme deity. Whatever the case may have been, and while I acknowledge that a more profound study of those possible correlations is needed, the concept of a "twin-like royal figure" has been attested to in other civilizations, especially in Africa, which elaborated systems of sacred royalties very close to the Mesoamerican royalties (Heusch 1986, 236–38, 264; Olivier 2007).[17]

Returning to our "twins" in the Nahua myths, I will examine the differential evolution of their respective activities. As Claude Lévi-Strauss (1991) has amply demonstrated, the twins in the myths of Amerindians tend to grow further apart as the myths multiply. In the same manner, Tezcatlipoca and Quetzalcoatl cooperated during the first part of their mythical existence, only to later fight against each other during the great cosmological cycles. First we find them closely associated with the creation of the earth and heaven from the rending of the primordial deity, Tlalteotl.

According to one version of the myth, Quetzalcoatl and Tezcatlipoca were transformed into two serpents to penetrate, and undoubtedly to fecundate, Tlalteotl (Thévet 1905, 29). But we have seen that in Nahuatl, coatl, or serpent, may also mean "twin" (Molina 1970, folio 23r). Commentators have often stressed the bipolar character of Quetzalcoatl, sometimes translated as "Precious Twin." They insist that, accompanied by his double (*nahualli*), he went down to the underworld to gather the bones of past generations to create humankind anew from them (Leyenda de los Soles 1992a, 88–89, 1992b, 145–46). Other versions attribute this creation to Xolotl, who is thus rendered identical to Quetzalcoatl (Mendieta 1980 [1970], 78) (figure 3.13). In the tale of the creation of the sun and the moon in Teotihuacan, Xolotl's role in the origin of "double" plants and animals is very significant:

> He [Xolotl] said to the gods: "Let me not die, O gods." Wherefore he wept much; his eyes and his eyelids swelled. And when death approached near unto him, he fled from its presence; he ran; he quickly entered a field of green maize and took the form of, and quickly turned into, two young maize stalks [growing] from a single root, which the workers in the field have named xolotl. But there, in the field of green maize, he was seen. Then, once again he fled from him; once more he quickly entered a maguey field. There also he quickly changed himself into a maguey plant [consisting of] two [parts] called mexolotl. Once more he was seen, and once more he quickly entered into the water and went to take the shape of [an amphibious animal called] axolotl. There they could go to seize him, that they might slay him.
>
> Quimilhui in teteu. Macamo nimiqui teteuie. Ic cenca chocaia, vel ispopoçaoac. Auh in ie itech onaci miquiztli, çan teispāpa eoac, cholo, toctitlan calactiuetz: ipan onmixeuh, ic mocueptiuetz, in toctli ome manj, maxaltic: in quitocaiotica millaca, xolotl. Auh vncan ittoc in tocitlan: ie no ceppa teispampa eoac, ie no cuele metitlan calactiuetz: no ic ōmocueptiuetz in metl, ome manj, in itoca mexolotl. Ie no ceppa ittoc, ie no cuele atlan calactiuetz, axolotl mocuepato: ie vel vmpa canato, inic conmictique. (Sahagún 1950–82, book VIII: 8).

Finally, according to another mythological version of the creation of humankind transmitted by Thévet (1905, 26–27), Quetzalcoatl's name was Ehecatl. There is a symmetrical myth in which Tezcatlipoca's double, also called Ehecatl, travels to the abode of the sun instead of going to the underworld to bring the multicolored musicians back to earth (ibid., 32–33). This is the myth of the origin of music and of the prayers that permitted humankind to venerate the gods and communicate with them (Olivier 2003, 218–19).

Davíd Carrasco (1992 [1982], 100–101) rightly remarked on the incomplete character of the creations attributed to Quetzalcoatl, such as the discovery of

FIGURE 3.13. Xolotl, Quetzalcoatl's twin (Codex Borgia 1963, 10).

corn and the appearance of agave. It seems that Tezcatlipoca's interventions anticipate or complete these "incomplete creations." Indeed, in the case of corn, Tezcatlipoca appears both as the father of the precious cereal, which he conceives together with Xochiquetzal in Tamoanchan, and as the fruit of that conception; thus the Lord of the Smoking Mirror merged with Itztlacoliuhqui-Corn (Olivier 2000, 2003, 117–23) (figure 3.14). Quetzalcoatl then intervenes as the deity who discovers corn, a plant already created by his enemy brother (Leyenda de los Soles 1992a, 89–90, 1992b, 146–47). As for the agave, the Plumed Serpent contributes to its birth by sowing the bones of Mayahuel, from which the plant would be born (Thévet 1905, 27–28). Regarding Tezcatlipoca, by sacrificing Ometochtli, the god of pulque who is then reborn, he allows mankind to consume that drink, which until then was lethal (Chávez 1986, 62). Their mythical actions thus overlap but also become complementary. We have seen that they acted together to create heaven and earth from the deity Tlalteotl. I strongly suspect that they also collaborated in the creation of time, even if the Historia de los mexicanos por sus pinturas (1941 [1543], 210) mentions Huitzilopochtli at Quetzalcoatl's side. In that case, the Mexica placed their tutelary deity in lieu of the Lord of the Smoking Mirror, with whom he often merges. To support this hypothesis, one plate from the Codex Borbonicus (1991, 22) precisely presents Quetzalcoatl and Tezcatlipoca as the patron deities of the fifty-two-year cycle, accompanying Cipactonal and Oxomohco, the personages associated with the creation of the divinatory calendar (ibid., 21) (figure 3.15).

That said, despite their collaborative efforts and complementary creations, Tezcatlipoca and Quetzalcoatl fight ferociously. Graulich (1997, 82–86) has demonstrated

FIGURE 3.14. Itztlacoliuhqui-Corn, an aspect of Tezcatlipoca (Codex Telleriano-Remensis 1995, folio 16v).

FIGURE 3.15. Quetzalcoatl and Tezcatlipoca as patron deities of the fifty-two-year cycle (Codex Borbonicus 1991, 22).

how they alternated as the sun throughout the various cosmic eras. The identification of the divine twins with the sun and the moon has also been underlined by Alfred Métraux (1946) in South America, and in addition we find it in many ancient and modern myths of Mesoamerica. In the case of Quetzalcoatl and Tezcatlipoca, the astronomical implication is more complex inasmuch as each of them can alternately appear as the sun, the moon, or Venus, according to the cosmic cycles (Olivier 2003, 271–72). Thus Tlahuizcalpantecuhtli-Venus, generally identified as Quetzalcoatl (Anales de Cuauhtitlan 1992a, 12, 1992b, 36), can also appear with its foot replaced by Tezcatlipoca's mirror in the Codex Laud (1966, 1) (figure 3.16).[18] Only by evaluating the cosmogonical context can one understand these apparently contradictory metamorphoses.

FIGURE 3.16. Tlahuizcalpantecuhtli-Venus with its foot replaced by Tezcatlipoca's mirror (Codex Laud 1966, 1).

For instance, during the terrible confrontation between Quetzalcoatl and Tezcatlipoca in Tollan, we find, with their roles reversed, many elements relating to their previous fights as suns. Several scholars have identified Nanahuatl as Quetzalcoatl, and Graulich (1997, 180–87) proposed identifying the era created in Teotihuacan as the Sun of Quetzalcoatl rather than the Sun of the Toltecs.

Several transgressions caused the demise of both Quetzalcoatl and Toltec city. First, the drunkenness of the master of Tollan recreates (through inversion of their roles) the transgression that provoked the expulsion of Tezcatlipoca-Itztlacoliuhqui from Tamoanchan (Olivier 2003, 142–46). Similarly, on the eve of the Spanish conquest—and assimilated by the natives to the return of Quetzalcoatl, as Henry B. Nicholson (2001a) shows—Tezcatlipoca naturally appears as a "drunken prophet" under the features of a chalca (Sahagún 1950–82, book XII: 33–35) (figure 3.17). These moral flaws—drunkenness, to which is added a sexual transgression—were at the source of extraordinary changes that can assume a cosmic dimension, such as the end of an era or the expulsion from Tamoanchan (Carrasco 1992 [1982], 174–78; Graulich 1997, 187–206; Olivier 2003, 142–51). The comparison with the latter myth is amply justified by the presence of Xochiquetzal in the Toltec tales (figure 3.18). Seduced by Tezcatlipoca in Tamoanchan (in one version, the Lord of the Smoking Mirror ravishes her at the side of her first husband, Tlaloc), Xochiquetzal the "prostitute" is

FIGURE 3.17. Tezcatlipoca as a "drunken prophet" under the features of a chalca (Florentine Codex 1979, 3, book XII: folio 18v).

introduced in the cell of the virtuous Topiltzin by Tezcatlipoca and thus appears as the Master of Tollan's instrument of sin (Durán 1967, 1: 14; Muñoz Camargo 1998, 165–66). Furthermore, Xochiquetzal also fills the same augural function as the Lord of the Smoking Mirror on the eve of the conquest: Cervantés de Salazar (1985, 343) affirms that Motecuhzoma, after Cortés destroyed the "idols" in the Templo Mayor of Mexico-Tenochtitlan, "hid very well the pain he felt in his heart in front of those events. He then ordered the destruction of a house of ill repute where public women worked in Tlatelolco ... These were around 400 women, and he was saying that the public sins committed by them had caused the gods to allow his city and kingdom to be invaded by Christians who should be more powerful than him."[19]

Thus the Mexica tlatoani, following the model of cosmogonic eras ended by major transgressions, attributes the coming of the Spaniards to the sins of the prostitutes whose tutelary deity was Xochiquetzal (Olivier 2004a, 324–26).

Through the rather amusing history of the *tohueyo*, one of Tezcatlipoca's avatars, Sahagún's informants offer a precious variation on the theme of Quetzalcoatl's

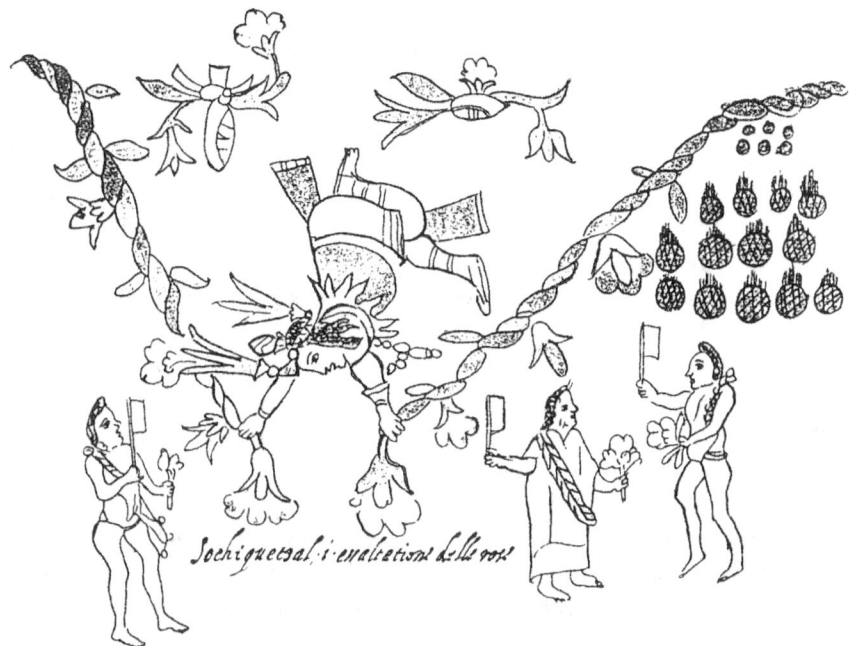

FIGURE 3.18. Descent of Xochiquetzal at Tollan (Codex Vaticano A 1996, folio 7r).

sexual transgression (Sahagún 1950–82, book III: 19–22). Here, the sin lies in the misalliance into which Huemac is forced through Tezcatlipoca's deeds. Unable to react in the proper way, Huemac appears, just as Quetzalcoatl did, as a star from the past, on the verge of being replaced by some newcomers. But like the twins Hunahpu and Ixbalamque in the Popol Vuh, the Mexica understand the true meaning of the questions that confront them and of the situations in which they find themselves (Olivier 2003, 149–53). The adorers of Huitzilopochtli are clearly designated as the successors of Quetzalcoatl's disciples, while the victory of the tohueyo-Tezcatlipoca over the Coatepec foresees the gest of Huitzilopochtli and the beginning of the Mexica era (Graulich 1988, 207–39; Olivier 2003, 149–64). We find this idea of a competition for succession occurring between twin deities or heroes vying for power—such as the twins before their metamorphosis into the sun and the moon in modern-day indigenous myths—in many Indo-European myths and sagas as well, which Georges Dumézil (1994, 19–165) has superbly analyzed.

Quetzalcoatl's and Tezcatlipoca's respective attitudes regarding human sacrifice have also been used to place these deities in strong opposition: the "peace-loving" Quetzalcoatl facing the "bloodthirsty" Tezcatlipoca. But this caricature does not hold up well under a careful scrutiny of the sources. Indeed, as Graulich (1988, 214–16) showed, the introduction of human sacrifices in Tollan responds to the need to recreate and feed the earth and the sun at the time of the rising of Huitzilopochtli's era. This theme becomes especially sensitive as soon as the Spaniards arrive and begin their domination, as the origin of ritual executions has often been attributed to the "bloody" Tezcatlipoca. However, Quetzalcoatl sacrificed either his own brothers or his uncles on the Mixcoatepetl, after having tortured them (Leyenda de los Soles 1992a, 95, 1992b, 154). Similarly, André Thévet (1905, 35) relates that Quetzalcoatl "went to Tula, where they did not as yet know what it meant to make a sacrifice, and thus, as he brought the use of sacrifice, he was held as a god."[20]

Actually, several priests who bore his name were in charge of immolating the victims in Tenochtitlan, Texcoco, and other cities (Alvarado Tezozómoc 1980 [ca. 1598], 516; Durán 1967, 1: 31–32; Pomar 1986, 62; Sahagún 1950–82, book III: 6) (figure 3.19). At the time of the fall of Tollan, the image of a young solar Quetzalcoatl, a warrior and maker of sacrifices, is thus replaced by the portrait of an old priest, peaceful and associated with the moon. It is obvious that the introduction of sacrifices in Tollan must be reinterpreted—not as a historical testimony that links new ritual practices to the arrival of Tezcatlipoca or to a people associated with this deity but instead one that is placed within a specific mythical context.

In conclusion, if we consider the structure of the names of Quetzalcoatl and Tezcatlipoca, we see that both are composed of two elements: one that is basically celestial (quetzal and smoke), and one that is terrestrial (the serpent and the mirror).[21] This pairing is undoubtedly a testimony to their mythical activity (separating the heavens from the earth) and the expression of their divine nature, since they inhabited and moved within vertical spaces and were the privileged intermediaries between mortals and the supreme deity. Indeed, in many respects, Tezcatlipoca and Quetzalcoatl are very close to humankind, as they often work on earth among the mortals. This characterization fits with the proposal of Gordon Brotherston (1997 [1992], 335, 349), who defined the roles of twins in Amerindian myths as "intermediaries between cosmic forces of creation and daily history." In a way, Quetzalcoatl and Tezcatlipoca are also close to the Indo-European twins gods or heroes Georges Dumézil (1974, 262; 1994) associates with the third function (fecundity, wealth) and who, in stark contrast with the deities attached to superior functions (those asociated with power and war), willingly mingle with humans. This function of mythic twins, who act as intermediaries between humans and gods, has also been noted among present-day African peoples, who grant these personages a pivotal role in their own mythologies. Thus the "mythical ancestor" twins of the Minyanka of Mali, "in all the rites, incarnate modes of mediation between the God Klé and men" (Heusch 1986, 272, 280).

FIGURE 3.19. Quetzalcoatl realizing a human sacrifice (Codex Borgia 1963, 42).

But let us return to our Mesoamerican heroes. This statement could be qualified, but we must acknowledge that in Quetzalcoatl we recognize the image of the "classic" hero, to whom humans owe not only the creation of life but also the gift of important cultural elements. Yet his name is formed by the names of two animals. In many respects, Tezcatlipoca is closer to "natural" forces, asociated with untamed spaces and night, though his name is composed of two cultural elements: smoke, which comes from the epitome of cultural creations—fire—and the mirror, undoubtedly one of the manufactured objects whose creation is the most exacting. This kind of arrangement shows a cosmogonical pattern in which elements both complete and oppose each other, somewhat like the Chinese yin and yang. Quetzalcoatl and Tezcatlipoca seem to diverge in that the former has a more creative function, while the latter works toward the completion and destruction of cycles (Olivier 2003, 277).

As for the incomplete twin-ness of our two deities, each of them himself could integrate the entire process of twin-ness. Indeed, I have insisted that one of the meanings of Quetzalcoatl is "Precious Twin." In contrast, Tezcatlipoca was equated with a two-faced mirror, with a hole though which the god observed humans, who in turn could see their image reflected in the divine instrument (Durán 1967, 1: 38; Pomar 1986, 59; Sahagún 1997 [1559–61], 95). This play of mirrors between mortals and Tezcatlipoca reaches its apogee in one of Tezcatlipoca's names, Titlacahuan, "We, His Men," which symbolizes the identification of mortals with the mirror god (Olivier 2003, 274). That said, this apparent internal twin-ness of each of the gods was in a perpetual state of imbalance: Tezcatlipoca's was a deforming mirror, which can amplify the differences between our two heroes—young and old, for instance—on each face of the double mirror. As Lévi-Strauss (1991, 302, 304) points out, "To answer the question of twin-ness, the Old World has been in favor of extreme solutions: its twins may be either antithetical, or identical . . . Amerindian thought rejects that notion of a pair of twins between whom a perfect identity would rule."

The impossible twin-ness proclaimed by Amerindian myths is thus well founded in Mesoamerica. In fact, ancient Mexicans, like many other Amerindian peoples (ibid., 163–65),[22] regarded the birth of twins as especially unfortunate. According to Fray Toribio Benavente o Motolinía (1971, 152):

> They also feared that the woman who gave birth to twins, which was rather common in that land, was a sign that either the father or the mother was to die, and the remedy that the cruel demon gave them was to kill one of the twins, so that neither the father nor the mother would die. Those who thus are born two from one womb they called cocoua in that land, which means "serpents," because they say that the first woman to give birth to twins was called couatl, which means "serpent," and from then on they call the twins serpents, and they say they would eat their father or their mother if one of the twins is not killed.[23]

Thus the cooperation, but above all the differences and oppositions, between these two incomplete twins, Quetzalcoatl and Tezcatlipoca, serve as the true mythical engine that powers the various processes of creation in a universe in perpetual motion.

Acknowledgments. I thank Elizabeth Baquedano for inviting me to the Tezcatlipoca symposium, Michel Besson for translating my chapter, and Rodolfo Ávila for doing the drawings.

NOTES

1. In the same way, Marcel Detienne (2000) advocated brilliantly for a broader and "experimental" comparativism in the field of the history of religions.

2. Este [Quetzalcoatl] tenían los yndios por dios del ayre y pintanle los yndios la media cara, de la nariz abajo, de palo, como una tronpa, por do soplaba el ayre.

3. Nohmatca nehhuatl. NiQuetzalcoatl. NiMatl. Ca nehhuatl niYaotl.

4. Y para esta guerra llevaron los chololtecas consigo a su dios Quetzalcoatl, porque como siempre les hablaba el demonio por boca de este ídolo, quisiéronlo tener cerca para saber en toda ocasiones lo que mejor les estuviese y debiesen hacer.

5. A media noche, después de haberle hecho mucha honra de incienso y música, tomábanlo y sacrificábanlo al modo dicho, a aquella misma hora, haciendo ofrenda de su corazón a la luna.

6. Desterró a Quetzalcoatl que en Tulla fué muchos años señor, porque jugando con él a la pelota, se volvió en tigre, de que la gente que estaba mirando se espantó en tanta manera, que dieron a huir, y con el tropel que llevaban y ciegos del espanto concebido, cayeron y se despeñaron por la barranca que por allí pasa, y se ahogaron.

7. Sano de pies y manos, sin mácula ni señal ninguna, que ni fuese tuerto, ni con nube en los ojos; no cojo, ni manco, ni contrahecho; no lagañoso, ni baboso, ni desdentado; no había de tener señal ninguna de que hubiese sido descalabrado, ni señal de divieso, ni de bubas, ni de lamparones. En fin, que fuese limpio de toda mácula.

8. Y estar tan certificado de su muerte, no se averiguó que jamás ninguno de todos los que para esto fueron electos, se hubiese huido ni puesto a salvo, pudiéndolo hacer, pareciéndole cosa indigna para hombres que representaban tan gran majestad como la deste ídolo.

9. Señor, sepa vuestra majestad cómo de aquí a nueve días se le acaba este trabajo de bailar y cantar, y sepa que ha de morir. Y él había de responder que fuese muy en hora buena.

10. Iba cantando y bailando por toda ella para ser conocido por la semejanza del dios, y esto era en lugar de la flautilla que el otro tañía para el mismo efecto de ser conocido.

11. Los tales reyes y caciques, en heredando el reino o señorío, venían a esta ciudad [Cholula] a reconocer obedencia al ídolo della, Quetzalcóatl, al cual ofrecían plumas ricas, mantas, oro y piedras preciosas, y otras cosas de valor.

12. About this primordial double deity, Maarten Jansen (1982, 132) wonders: "It is strange that both individuals have the same calendarical name. Maybe they are twins?"

13. To my knowledge, the theme of the relationship between the Black Tezcatlipoca and the Red Tezcatlipoca—which deserves a thorough study—has not attracted the attention of specialists. We can, for instance, cite the representations of both deities facing each other on the same plate of the Codex Borgia (1963, 21), where, apart from their different colors, they share most of the same attributes.

14. Some good comparative studies could be made with the remarkable mythology of the Dogons from Mali, where twin figures hold a central position (Griaule and Dieterlen 1965). There, too, we find the supreme deity creating two pairs of androgynous twins, then the birth of the ancestors who form pairs of mixed twins. Luc de Heusch (1986, 209), who studied the place of sacrifice in these myths, considers that one of the functions of the sacrificial act is to "slow down that precipitous fall, that brutal transition from a harmonious Unity, as represented by the androgynous features of the twins, to the sterile solitude of maleness."

15. According to Alfredo López Austin (1982, 144), "The supreme command in the political organization of Mexico-Tenochtitlan was shared, though not on an equal footing, between two governors: the *tlatoani* or 'king' and the *cihuacoatl*, a male, but who represented the goddess of the earth. Thus was constituted a relative balance between two opposite sides of power." In the opinion of Nigel Davies (1980, 200), the dual offices of tlatoani and cihuacoatl were derived "from a dualistic relationship between Huitzilopochtli and his sister, the goddess Cihuacoatl."

16. Moreover, Miguel Acosta Saignes (1946, 176) claims that the first appearance of the cihuacoatl as a distinct office in Aztec history was in the time of Motecuhzoma Ilhuicamina with Tlacaellel. However, other specialists insist on the antiquity of this dual system of Aztec government (Davies 1980, 200–201).

17. According to Edwin M. Loeb (1958, 173), "Both Peru and Japan also have the legend that their rulers are descended from cross-heavenly twins."

18. According to Johannes Neurath (2004, 96–98), following previous investigations by Konrad Theodor Preuss (1998 [1925]), twin heroes in the myths of west Mexico's Gran Nayar region could adopt the figures of the Morning and Evening Star, two aspects of planet Venus, within a system of complex transformations.

19. Disimuló [Motecuhzoma] bien el pesar que su corazón tenía por lo hecho, mandando luego secretamente deshacer una ramería de mujeres públicas que ganaban en el Tlatelolco ... serían las casas más de cuatrocientas y así las mujeres, diciendo que por los pecados públicos de aquellas, habían los dioses permitido que viniesen a su ciudad y reino cristianos que pudiesen y mandasen más que él.

20. S'en alla à Tula, où ne savoyt encore que s'estoit de faire sacrifice; et par ainsi, comme il aporta l'usaige du sacrifice, fut tenu pour dieu.

21. In the case of Quetzalcoatl, Henry B. Nicholson (1979, 35) states: "Perhaps the most 'logical' interpretation ... of this union of bird feathers and a slithering reptile would be that the former symbolize the bird's environment, the atmospheric realm, while the latter connotes the snake's milieu, the terrestrial sphere, i.e., Quetzalcoatl may well symbolize the union of earth and sky—which in many cosmologies signifies a creative concept."

22. However, some Amerindian peoples, such as the Totonac, Squamish, Lummi, and Yuman, associated the birth of twins with fertility and prosperity (Ichon 1969, 151; Lévi-Strauss 1991, 164–65; Loeb 1958, 153). George Devereux (1941) has analyzed the ambivalent attitude toward twins among the Mohave Indians. For instance, a testimony asserts that "it was a great and pleasurable surprise to the parents, who expected but one child to receive two instead. They happily announced their great good luck to all concerned" (ibid., 578). In contrast, in what Devereux calls the "secondary pattern," another informant affirms that "when, however, twins are born to them, people think that the twins are just dead people who have come back, and they do not feel so enthusiastic about them" (ibid., 585).

23. Tenían también que la mujer que paría dos, lo cual en esta tierra es muy común, que había de morir el padre o la madre, y el remedio que el cruel demonio les daba era matar el uno de los mielgos, y que no moriría el padre ni la madre. A los que ansí nacen dos de un vientre en esta tierra llámanlos *cocoua*, que quiere decir "culebras," porque dicen que la primera mujer que parió dos se llamaba *couatl*, que quiere decir "culebra," y de aquí es que dicen culebras a los mielgos, y que han de comer a su padre o a su madre, si no matasen uno de los mielgos. Aversion to twins is also attested to in South America, where one of them might be killed; for example, among the Tukano (Reichel-Dolmatoff 1973, 270), the Arawete (Viveiros de Castro 1992, 360n4), the Achuar (Taylor 1993, 659), and the Bororo (Crocker 1985, 49).

4

Tezcatlipoca and Huitzilopochtli
Political Dimensions of Aztec Deities[1]

Emily Umberger

ICONOGRAPHIC STUDIES

In post-conquest scholarship there are two basic approaches to Aztec deities,[2] a term that generally refers to anthropomorphic figures rather than other forms of *ixiptla* (clothed and decorated representations of supernatural beings).[3] The first approach focuses on Aztec ideas about the forces of the supernatural world. In this approach the costume parts and implements of ixiptla are considered for their functions as references to these forces, but that consideration examines neither the complexity of the metaphorical references of costume parts nor their material forms (Hvidtfeldt 1958).[4] The second approach starts with the visual traits and focuses on generalizing their distributions but likewise without examining the metaphors in any detail. Its aim is to determine which traits are diagnostic of particular deities and which are variable traits worn by groups of like deities (see Boone 1989; Durand-Forest 1977; Nicholson 1963, 1971, 1973, 1988; Seler 1960–61, 1990–98; Spranz 1964).[5] Classifications and groupings of deities have been constructed from this information (e.g., Nicholson 1971).

The iconographic approach aims to devise neutral and consistent ways of identifying figures represented in artworks of various forms (written and pictorial) and production dates and from different periods of Aztec myth and history as recorded in a single source. However, neutrality and consistency are mistaken goals, as visual expressions are not neutral or consistent. Individual artworks project individual messages, which must be understood in themselves before being brought together

DOI: 10.5876/9781607322887.c004

with other artworks, even in the same medium. The groups formed, in turn, must be analyzed together before being correlated or compared with other corpora of data. Tenochca artists gave form to messages with great variety and creativity, using culturally specific guidelines that changed from period to period and place to place. These need to be learned through the determination of the contexts surrounding pictures and descriptions—ideational, social, and political contexts, as well as ritual usage and production and display scenarios. Unfortunately, modern studies tend to analyze deity forms without considering the structures of the environment in which their images or descriptions are found.

Eloise Quiñones Keber (1988b, 199) has characterized the problem in the visual arts thus: "Studies of [Aztec] 'picture writing' have frequently focused on iconographic interpretations of [individual] figures, symbols, or 'glyphic' units. Less attention has been directed to the grammar of form, to the morphology and syntax of pre-Hispanic pictorial imagery. How did Aztec pictorial images function singly, in groups or sets or series, and as part of a system?" The rules of syntax and the range of their usage have yet to be recovered through historical reconstruction, and the existence of a universal organizing principle cannot be assumed. Unlike the European friars, the Aztecs seem not to have thought in terms of an encyclopedic list of supernatural beings.

A neutral classification of all Aztec deities may still be a modern desideratum, but it cannot be achieved if elements like time, place, politics, and change that were essential to Aztec thought are not incorporated. So in addition to rethinking how we can organize the materials in ways that reflect original contexts and native systems of thought, we need to acknowledge the western biases behind post-conquest attempts at organization.

The following discussion deals with the interrelationship of the visual images of Tezcatlipoca (Mirror, Its Smoke) and Huitzilopochtli (Hummingbird, Left) and what they reveal about Aztec thought, but it does not attempt comprehensiveness; much has been written about these deities that is not covered here.[6] Rather, this essay consists of some speculations about sculptural imagery, generated principally from study of the Stone of Tizoc (figure 4.1), one of the public monuments of the imperial capital city of Tenochtitlan (Umberger 1998, 2002, 2008, 2). The images on it require linkage to contemporary politics for its intended messages to be understood.

TEZCATLIPOCA AND HUITZILOPOCHTLI IN AZTEC POLITICAL HISTORY

Both Tezcatlipoca and Huitzilopochtli belonged to a class of supernatural beings whose imagery depended on the vicissitudes of political history. Both were patron

FIGURE 4.1. Stone of Tizoc (circa 1484), found in the central precinct of Tenochtitlan, polished andesite without paint, Museo Nacional de Antropología, Mexico City. Courtesy, Instituto Nacional de Antropología e Historia, Mexico City.

deities of cities and states, and as such they functioned differently from deities like Tlaloc and Chalchiuhtlicue, the rain and water gods who had relatively permanent assignments to discreet realms of the cosmos.⁷ This is an important distinction. The patron gods were actors in multiple settings in the past, as well as active political representatives and the principal guises of rulers in the present. Among these deities, relative status paralleled the ranking of their polities within a greater hierarchy, and they changed accordingly. When his town was politically ascendant, the patron god was compared to the sun and occupied primary positions in town history and rituals. The types of positions available were determined by calendrical and metaphorical structures held in common among the inhabitants of Central Mesoamerica, whose lives were dominated by post-Toltec Nahua thought. Upon losing hegemony to another rising sun, the political patron was compared to the moon and stars and put into lesser positions or relegated to the past, where his cycle of power in an earthly historical arena was seen as completed. Of course, at any point in his political career, his relative position and attendant imagery in his home territory could differ from his position within a broader context, where he might be subject to a greater being. In other words, although the hierarchy of patron gods paralleled the political hierarchy, this in turn was viewed from both local and international contexts. In addition, fallen deities had individual fates, as did the rulers who represented them. There were general patterns in their treatment, but the details might vary according to circumstances.

The historical relationship of Tezcatlipoca and Huitzilopochtli follows this pattern in that before Tenochtitlan's rise to imperial dominance in the mid-fifteenth century, Huitzilopochtli was a lesser being while Tezcatlipoca dominated the hierarchies of probably all Nahuatl-speaking polities in the Basin of Mexico. Tezcatlipoca was patron of Texcoco and Azcapotzalco, the capitals of earlier expansionist states, and probably the patron of the Triple Alliance Empire before Tenochtitlan rose to dominance. Tezcatlipoca was the god of multiple cities simultaneously and was represented in those cities by individual sculptures, probably differentiated in appearance. The history of Huitzilopochtli's rise is difficult to reconstruct because the written evidences all date from after the Spanish conquest and reflect the situation immediately before. In addition, these colonial sources all posit something that cannot be supported by material remains—the existence of Huitzilopochtli as a distinct being whose worship by the Mexica dated back to their departure from an invented homeland (see Boone 1991 on the symbolic structure of the story). It is probable that Huitzilopochtli grew out of the version of Tezcatlipoca particular to the Mexica cities of Tlatelolco and Tenochtitlan. He rose in the hierarchy as these cities did, until finally—after the Mexica defeat of Texcoco—the Mexica made him distinct from Tezcatlipoca, redefined their relative realms of power, and made him politically superior. After that there were two Huitzilopochtlis until the civil war between the two cities in 1473, when the Tenochca ruler and his version of Huitzilopochtli defeated the ruler and deity of Tlatelolco (Umberger 2007b).

The fact that Huitzilopochtli's image was not consolidated until late in preconquest history is indicated by sculptures manufactured in Tenochtitlan before about 1460 and after 1480. The Ex-Arzobispado Stone (Padilla, Sánchez-Nava, and Solís Olguín 1989) is one of perhaps seven "stones of the sun"—monumental, decorated sacrificial stones (called both *cuauhxicalli* and *temalacatl*)—that each late imperial ruler of the city commissioned to celebrate his skill as a warrior. The victories depicted on this stone indicate manufacture around 1460 in the reign of Motecuhzoma I. The Tizoc Stone, another great stone of the sun, was created over twenty years later, in 1484. The Tizoc Stone is so named because it bears the image of this ruler accompanied by a hieroglyphic name and wearing Huitzilopochtli's hummingbird headdress. With him is a group of fourteen other victorious figures representing Tezcatlipoca, who was probably the patron of unnamed imperial warrior-officials below the king (figures 4.2 and 4.3). In contrast, on the earlier Ex-Arzobispado monument, all the victors bear the Tezcatlipoca symbols, and none is labeled by a king's hieroglyph or adorned with the hummingbird headdress. The figure that probably represents the ruler of the time is highlighted by a rampant feathered serpent behind him, but he is dressed like the other Tezcatlipocas (figure 4.4, left). The same idea, that Tezcatlipoca once occupied the superior position later taken by Huitzilopochtli, is evident in a similar scene of conquest carved on a rock at Peñon de los Baños, formerly an island called Tepetzinco. In this vignette of unknown date, the victor above the date 1 Flint has only the power attributes of Tezcatlipoca (figure 4.5). It is true that Tenochca kings took the identities of various deities according to occasion and ritual dates in the 260-day calendar (Umberger 2002, 2008, figures 7: 14–15), but in the calendar of late Aztec times, the date 1Flint pertained to Huitzilopochtli, not Tezcatlipoca. So the multiple deity roles of the ruler probably do not explain the differences in ruler imagery between the two sacrificial stones. The closeness of appearance of the monuments in general indicates an almost identical ceremonial context.[8] The likely explanation is that the early sacrificial stone and the Tepetzinco relief were created before the promotion of Huitzilipochtli to the top position and his assumption of the date 1 Flint.

The possibility that Huitzilopochtli did not appear in sculptures before the 1460s does not mean that he appeared from nowhere; nor does it mean that the general structure of the charter myth describing his rise was invented at the same late date. It means rather that Huitzilopochtli, whatever his previous identity and rank, probably replaced a version of Tezcatlipoca in positions where the most prominent god appeared. In addition, in distant, independent polities sharing the same Nahua culture, other patron gods like Camaxtli and Mixcoatl were associated with the date 1 Flint and occupied the role of the hero, perhaps in similarly structured myths.[9]

DEITY IMAGES IN MANUSCRIPTS: THE *TONALAMATLS* AND FRAY BERNARDINO DE SAHAGÚN'S BOOKS

The more specific problem addressed here is the use of deity images from manuscripts to interpret pre-conquest sculptures.[10] The problem is not just a matter of the difference between pre- and post-conquest contexts of creation, as might be supposed. The tonalamatls (books of days for divination) were used as research tools by small groups of priest-historians, who studied and reconceived the past to prognosticate on the foreseeable future. The tonalamatl recorded the days of the *tonalpohualli*, the pan-Mesoamerican 260-day sequence of named days divided into 20 "weeks" of 13 days each. (These weeks were called *trecenas* in Spanish.) Despite the different proveniences and dates hypothesized for the surviving examples of this tradition, the deities represented as regents of the trecenas, their sequence, and their costumes were fixed. So there is a remarkable consistency

FIGURE 4.2. Tizoc as (Tenochca) Huitzilopochtli capturing Matlatzincatl on the Stone of Tizoc. Drawing by author.

FIGURE 4.3. (Tenochca) Tezcatlipoca capturing Tlatelolcatl on the Stone of Tizoc. Drawing by author.

FIGURE 4.4. Two pairs of figures on the Ex-Arzobispado Stone (circa 1460), unpolished andesite, formerly painted; the Tenochca ruler at the time (Motecuhzoma I) is probably the victor with the rampant serpent behind him (vignette on left). Like the other victors on the monument, he is dressed as Toltec-Tezcatlipoca. Museo Nacional de Antropología, Mexico City. Drawing by author.

FIGURE 4.5. One of three relief vignettes on a rock at Peñon de los Baños (destroyed in late modern times) with victor dressed as Toltec-Tezcatlipoca above 1 Flint date. Drawing by author.

among different versions (see Boone 2007; Quiñones Keber 1995; Seler 1960–61, 1990–98; Spranz 1964). This standardized system continued to be used during Aztec times; by this time it was a conservative form. Its long duration and widespread distribution indicate independence from the practices of individual states.

Preliminary research on the deity images in the tonalamatls reveals that they are accurate in the representation of particular costume parts, and are thus reliable in this respect, but that they are questionable as sources for the analysis of assemblages of these costume parts on sculptures. By Aztec times, some of the tonalamatl deities, which Eduard Seler called "calendar gods," were no longer prominent. In addition, the transcendent deity in late Aztec times, Huitzilopochtli, is never depicted in a tonalamatl and the date 1 Flint pertains to Tonacatecuhtli, the sun, as in much earlier times. Moreover, the association of dates with other tonalamatl deities are different from those on state monuments. In other words, it seems that there were two systems of date-deity associations in operation at the same time. One is seen in the traditional tonalamatls that were used for the private and individual decisions of the whole population (see Boone 2007). And the other (as far as we know, not represented pictorially in an updated tonalamatl) reflected recent political changes specific to the Aztecs (this calendar is discussed in Umberger 2002). An interesting manuscript that hints at this more up-to-date system of associations is the Codex Telleriano-Remensis (1995). Here the traditional system is represented in a pictorial tonalamatl, but the glosses include some references to the new associations in the glosses. For instance, the trecena beginning with 1 Reed pictures Chalchiuhtlicue

FIGURE 4.6. First page of Sahagún's *Primeros Memoriales* sequence of important Tenochca deities (after Sahagún 1993 [1559–61], folio 261r). Codex Matritense del Palacio Real de Madrid. Drawing by author.

as regent, while the association of the date 1 Reed with Quetzalcoatl, the deity named by that date in sculptural inscriptions, is mentioned in the gloss below the image of the goddess. Also relevant is Sahagún's (1950–82, book IV) verbal description of the dates and related deities in the tonalpohualli, in that it corresponds with the sculptures, not the traditional tonalamatl.

Sahagún's (1950–82, book I) deity illustrations, which he first conceived in the 1559–61 *Primeros Memoriales* and reconceived in later versions—most important, the Florentine Codex of 1578–85—also need to be considered in relation to the sculpted images of Tezcatlipoca and Huitzilopochtli on the Tizoc Stone.[11] In these images Sahagún had his artists picture a set of deities, the same deities he described in his verbal tonalpohualli, reorganized into a pictorial hierarchy comprehensible

FIGURE 4.7. First page of Sahagún's Florentine Codex sequence of important Tenochca deities (Sahagún 1979 [1575–78], book I: folio 10r). Biblioteca Medicea Laurenziana, Florence. Courtesy, Archivo General de la Nación, Mexico City.

to his anticipated European audience (figures 4.6 and 4.7). Sahagún's information was derived seemingly from a variety of pictorial and oral sources rather than a single pre-conquest pictorial type, like a tonalamatl (for a different hypothesis, see Baird 1993).[12] Perhaps he did not know the tonalamatl images and their ordering, or, if he did, he recognized the limits of their usefulness to convey the gods prominent in Aztec times.

It appears that Sahagún's images were meant for a new purpose—to create simple images for a European audience as explanatory and mnemonic devices. In the process he simplified them, created a new, non-Aztec type of context, and organized them in a linear hierarchy comprehensible to a European audience.[13] The different versions of his hierarchy are closely related, although not identical. Since my interest is the images of Tezcatlipoca and Huitzilopochtli, I am concentrating on the beginning of each series in which they are depicted. The difficulties of using these pictorial images to interpret sculptures are different from those pertaining to the tonalamatls, in that the depictions of costume are very inaccurate. Because Sahagún highlighted the deities prominent in Aztec times, one might think his images are more appropriate, but this is an illusion. In addition to the ignorance of Aztec imagery that they reveal, they are also problematic in their lack of a pre-conquest type of context. Pre-conquest images did not exist outside a ritual or pictorial context, and the costumes worn were closely related to the context. So although evidence shows that the Aztecs did group deities together, for instance, on monuments like the Tizoc Stone, the encyclopedic and summarizing view of Renaissance Europeans was unknown.

In the text in the Florentine Codex (Sahagún 1950–82, book I) accompanying the images, Sahagún makes clear that their order is hierarchical according to his own ideas, with the most important male deities first, followed by major female deities, and then lesser deities of both genders. The order is different in the earlier *Primeros Memoriales* in that the deities are arranged in columns, but it is likewise a European format. Both series place Huitzilopochtli at the beginning and put Tezcatlipoca second.[14] The criteria behind the ordering after the first two deities are unclear, but the placement of the central male gods of the Aztec state at the beginning is very different from native deity arrangements. For instance, in any system with a calendrical structure, the two gods would not be found together but rather with their associated dates. Thus in the tonalpohualli Huitzilopochtli's location was with the date 1 Flint near the center of the count. Likewise, in the fifty-two-year count, 1 Flint was in the exact center; thus that was Huitzilopochtli's place (see Umberger 1981b, 2002). In the year count, Tezcatlipoca's position was in the second year with the invention of fire (his places in the tonalpohualli are discussed later). The fact that Sahagún was addressing a European audience is even more obvious in the annotations of the Florentine Codex, which compare the pre-conquest deities with Roman gods.

Unfortunately, we do not know what the accoutrements chosen for Sahagún's deity series meant because we do not know their original contexts or even whether there was a pictorial context. Therefore, consistency in the functioning of the distinctive costume parts in Aztec period imagery cannot be assumed without good reason. In other words, the modern process of identifying deity figures by a system wherein fixed traits of costumes, accoutrements, and even gender are considered diagnostic may be misleading if conceived too simply. Identity was projected by a variety of signs, and some of the traits we use to identify a being were manipulated to mean something else; in addition, identity itself was not a simple matter.

SCULPTURAL IMAGES OF DEITIES

Among sculptures, there are differences in the ways clothing signaled historical contexts and realms of power (Townsend 1979, chapter 2). In Tenochtitlan the major images of the temple seem to have been carved as relatively undecorated anthropomorphic forms to which real clothing and implements were added and changed according to occasion (as in Spanish processional sculptures). However, on sculptures like the public relief monuments of the Aztec state these elaborations were carved in stone, fixing the imagery to individual moments in time. Yet the imagery could change from ensemble to ensemble and from monument to monument, according to the varied ideas attached to an occasion, the variety of metaphors activated by a sequence of activities, or changes in time. In addition, as will be seen later, a uniform language of costume cannot be assumed to apply even to the apparel of a single figure. The sculptures of the late imperial period remaining to us date from around 1450 to 1521, and the commemorative function of many images can be ascertained and tied to historical events of that period, even for images that look purely mythological (Umberger 1981a, 1007). Their messages were particular to this polity, they were fixed by the Tenochca rulers, and they changed accordingly.

THE TIZOC STONE

The Tizoc Stone, one of the great sacrificial stones with a solar image on top, was created for the Tenochca ruler Tizoc in the last two years before his death in 1486. It was part of an ensemble decorating his enlargement of the Templo Mayor (Great Temple) of Tenochtitlan, and the stone was probably used in the ceremony of dedication of the completed temple in 8 Reed 1487 after his death. Tizoc anticipated the dedication ceremony to be a general celebration of Tenochtitlan's rise to domination over all other Valley of Mexico cities, even allied cities, after the defeat of its final rival, Tlatelolco, in the civil war. Symbolically, the pyramid represented the hill of Coatepetl (Serpent Mountain), where in myth Huitzilopochtli rose to power over his enemy "siblings," the Centzon-Huitznahua (Numerous Southerners?). Although Tizoc did not live to see this ceremony, his anticipation of its format is revealed in the imagery of the monument (see Townsend 1979; Umberger 1998, 2002).

The Tizoc Stone represents the images of rulers dressed as the patron deities of their polities in fifteen pairs, with the victorious representatives of Tenochtitlan grasping the hair of the defeated ruler-gods of other polities of the empire conquered by Tizoc and his predecessors (Barnes 2009, chapter 4; Wicke 1975). The defeated figures are given locative titles derived from the polity of origin by the hieroglyphs next to them (Umberger 2008). Some parts of their dress are individualized, giving the impression that they allude to original costumes before defeat. However, since the monument is a projection of Tenochca ideas of superiority, it is obvious also that in general the costumes of all figures were simplified, standardized, and manipulated in many ways controlled by the Tenochca, and this may extend to many of the traits we see as identifiers in this sense.

The aim, of course, was to convey a message of Tenochca strength backed by divine and cosmic forces and of foreign humiliation and defeat through lack of such support. The costumes are so much a part of the vocabulary expressing these ideas that they may not yield much about the foreign deities themselves. Even some of the individualizing traits may symbolize humiliation in ways not accessible to us or even refer to details of particular conquests.[15] After the parts charged with propagandistic meanings are eliminated, the question is: what remains to represent previous identities? Further, one might ask: were any of these permanent, diagnostic fixtures of individual deities? In the basin center of Aztec culture, some names of principal conquered gods are known to us but not their costuming. Unfortunately, in most cases outside the basin, little is known of the names of political patrons and their clothing and accoutrements. In these outer areas some of the deities had to have been foreign, previously unknown to the Nahua-Aztecs also and very different from theirs.

On the Stone of Tizoc the images of Huitzilopochtli and Tezcatlipoca are displayed prominently, and both are among the defeated as well as the conquerors (see Wicke 1975 for Tezcatlipoca among the losers). Of special interest are contrasts among their images, according to whether they are victors or losers. Also of interest are the ways the two triumphant versions of Tezcatlipoca and Huitzilopochtli overlap in their shared power symbols and costume parts. What do the various evidences say about their relationship to each other, the effects of changing political states on their images, and the concept of diagnostic and variable traits?

MULTIPLE IMAGES OF TEZCATLIPOCA AND HUITZILOPOCHTLI

Two vignettes on the Tizoc Stone well illustrate the issues brought up by the different representations of individual patron gods (figures 4.2 and 4.3). The conqueror in figure 4.2, depicting what is generally considered pair number 1 on the monument, is the only figure on the monument with the hummingbird that is the distinctive trait evoking the name of Huitzilopochtli. He wears it as part of a headdress topped by a spray of long quetzal feathers. The dots around his eyes refer to the face paint seen on images of the god in manuscripts—a black area framed by white circles around the eyes. The line in the *Primeros Memoriales* (where it is worn by another god, Painal) that describes it, "mixçitlalhviticac, moteneva tlayoallj," is translated as "His face is painted with the star design called darkness" (Sahagún 1993 [1559–61], folio 261r; 1997 [1559–61], 95), the starry sky mask for short. The glyph next to him, a striped leg, is the only personal name on the monument (its etymology is unclear, but see Umberger 1999, 77–78, 91, 95nn2, 4). The figure is the ruler Tizoc dressed as the supernatural patron of Tenochtitlan and wearing also the power attributes of the god Tezcatlipoca: the smoking mirror on the temple area of the headdress and the leg stump from which emanates a plume of smoke. Finally, he wears a circular back device with another spray of long feathers and carries in his right hand a shield, banner, and *atlatl* (dart thrower).

With his left hand Tizoc grasps the hair of a captive accompanied by a hieroglyph in the form of a net, *matlatl* in the Aztec language, which gives his locative title rather than a particular name. The figure and glyph together yield the word *Matlatzincatl*, a title probably referring to the ruler-god of an area dominated politically by the Matlatzinca ethnic group before it became an Aztec imperial province. The principal conquests in this area were accomplished in the mid-1470s during the reign of Tizoc's predecessor, Axayacatl, the king who defeated Tlatelolco; but Tizoc participated in the conquest as a military officer, consolidated the victories, and overthrew rebellious polities there as part of his required coronation battles. For this reason he is depicted as the conqueror of that area. The Matlatzincatl carries darts in his left hand and in his right hand a staff Charles Wicke (1975) identified as the *tlachialoni,* or device for seeing, often associated with Tezcatlipoca (Sahagún 1993 [1559–61], folio 261r; 1997 [1559–61], 95n12). Unfortunately, this device is damaged in the detailing of the upper part, so the identification is uncertain, but it is probably a mace. On his head the Matlatzincatl wears a headband, also damaged, topped by the *aztaxelli,* a feather decoration like a badminton shuttlecock worn by people letting their own blood or prepared to die as sacrificial victims (Umberger 1999, 83–85, 96n15; Wicke 1975). This motif is part of the headdresses of all captives on the Tizoc Stone.

The second scene (figure 4.3), pair 12 on the monument, depicts an unnamed conqueror, like Tizoc, representing Tenochtitlan and with the same distinctive smoking leg stump and a smoking mirror at the temple of the head. The mirror is thought to be a diagnostic trait pointing to the name Tezcatlipoca. His clothing, like that of the remaining victor figures, is identical to Tizoc-Huitzilopochtli's except for the lack of the hummingbird headdress (his is a typical Toltec headdress composed of shorter upright feathers topped by a panache of long feathers) and the starry sky mask. Added are the darts in the hand holding the shield and atlatl. This unnamed Tezcatlipoca conquers a figure accompanied by a glyph identifying him as the Tlatelolcatl, the ruler-god of Tlatelolco. Under the aztaxelli, his headdress is composed of a layered section covering the head, a hanging of feathers in back, and another panel with spots hanging on the side. The figure also wears the starry sky mask seen on Tizoc-Huitzilopochtli, and, as is well known, a version of Huitzilopochtli was the god of Tlatelolco before the war between the two Mexica cities. Thus in the two scenes there is the possibility of two Huitzilopochtlis, one victorious and the other defeated, and two Tezcatlipocas, one victorious and the other defeated. There are only two Huitzilopochtli figures on the monument, the two described, but there are many more Tezcatlipoca figures, including the remaining thirteen conquerors identical to the one in the second vignette and other versions among the conquered, if Wicke's (1975) identifications of their accoutrements are correct, plus some that may be identified as the older deity through other means.

Both the Matlatzincatl and Tlatelolcatl figures are named only by locative glyphs. So we might conclude that specific rulers were not the intended references but rather the royal line, *tlatocayotl*, from which the rulers of the city were descended. Behind this is a concept like that among the Maya wherein a specific ruler was a replacement for his predecessors of the same line (for instance, Schele and Miller 1986, 265–66). The fourteen identical Tezcatlipoca conquerors lack both personal names and locative titles. Again a specific person is not intended but rather probably an important office in the imperial hierarchy, and their political affiliation with Tenochtitlan is understood (Tizoc is the only named person).

On the monument, all figures are human and the human body is important as a distinctive type of frame for the costume parts. In the past the figures themselves have been ignored because of their generic appearance, the primary question about human forms having been the degree of portraiture present. However, the human body and its parts had metaphorical and metonymical associations too, and the meanings of decorations were intimately related to the parts decorated (Houston and Cummins 2004; López Austin 1988). I will not pursue this line of investigation here; still, it can be said that the references—especially in the case of patron deities—are to actors in the human world, and there are many correspondences

FIGURE 4.8. (Tenochca) Huitzilopochtli and (Tenochca) Tezcatlipoca/Titlacahuan on the Stone of Tizoc. Drawing by author.

between the human body and the polity, as made clear by metaphorical expressions (e.g., Durán 1994 [1581], 254). More relevant here are questions of whether depictions represent historical personages, generic human roles, deities, or some combination. Differences that point to an emphasis on one of these are sometimes made obvious by the context, for instance, the presence of personal name hieroglyphs referring to historical beings.

Nevertheless, someone identified in this way cannot be defined as human in our modern, secularized sense of the word. A ruler wearing the garb of his patron god was a living ixiptla taking on the powers of the deity. If a specific name is lacking, usually it is the office or position that is referred to, not a particular occupant. When personal name glyphs are added, the reference is made more specific (see also Barnes 2009). On the Tizoc Stone the hieroglyphic label of the figure on the left in figure 4.2 names him as the historical Tizoc. Nevertheless, the figure has only a stump at the end of the left leg, whereas the actual person was not missing a leg. This naturalistic representation of a leg stump emanating smoke, a deity attribute rendered as if it were reality, indicates that the figure, despite the name glyph and the costume-like appearance of the rest of his garb, had supernatural powers. So he is not a human being in our sense. He is the divinely sanctioned occupant of an office (see also Read 1994).

THE VICTORIOUS GODS (FIGURE 4.8)

It is obvious that I accept the validity of the hummingbird symbol as a diagnostic trait of a being named Huitzilopochtli; similarly, I see the smoking mirror as the trait of Tezcatlipoca. In both cases the name itself is evoked. Are all figures with hummingbirds and smoking mirrors Huitzilopochtli and Tezcatlipoca, and, conversely, do all representations of these gods wear the traits? As will be seen, defeated versions of Tezcatlipoca and Huitzilopochtli on the Tizoc Stone do not have these power symbols. Is this a matter of a lack of power or a change in name or both? What is the nature of the relationship between trait and being? If there are multiple traits pointing to different deities, as in the case of Tizoc-Huitzilopochtli, who wears both hummingbird and mirror, is the figure a composite of these beings or a single being? The distribution of traits on this and the other figures on the Tizoc Stone points to the following. For the victors, the traits refer to specific powers, and the deity with multiple powers should be identified as the most recent in the sequence of beings linked to the symbols. The conclusion is that this being has "inherited" or adopted through victory the powers of predecessors. The sequence of patron deities of importance to the Tenochca was detailed in their politically specific accounts of pre-imperial history and reiterated in the varied calendrical cycles.[16] Although chronological order may not be a universal explanation for the mixing of traits in a figure, I suggest that the two victor types on the Tizoc Stone can be identified as Tezcatlipoca wearing his own symbols of power and Huitzilopochtli wearing his own plus those he adopted/inherited from Tezcatlipoca. This suggestion is based on the history of these closely related beings.

However, not all traits characterized by scholars as diagnostic are diagnostic in the same way as these two. A good example of an accoutrement that is not diagnostic is the "butterfly" breast-plate worn by all victor figures on the Tizoc Stone but that is sometimes seen as a reference to Xiuhtecuhtli (Fire/blue/turquoise Lord) (for instance, Nicholson and Quiñones Keber 1983, 95). In the Codex Telleriano-Remensis tonalamatl (Quiñones Keber 1995, folio 24r) it is worn by a figure with this name (figure 4.9). However, on the Tizoc Stone the butterfly breast-plate appears as part of an ensemble of Toltec costume parts, whose occurrence together points to conscious derivation from sculptures visible at Toltec Tula in Aztec times (figure 4.10) (Umberger 1987b) without direct reference to any particular deity. Its meanings in these two contexts had something in common, but what this was is not known; at any rate, it is not a diagnostic trait of Xiuhtecuhtli.

TEZCATLIPOCA AND HUITZILOPOCHTLI   99

FIGURE 4.9. Xiuhtecuhtli wearing butterfly breast-plate, regent of the right side of Trecena Twenty of the tonalamatl, which begins with 1 Rabbit, Codex Telleriano-Remensis (after 1995, folio 24r). He is labeled "el fuego" rather than Xiuhtecuhtli. Bibliothèque National de l'Assemblée, Paris. Drawing by author.

In some contexts, Tezcatlipoca and Huitzilopochtli appear as equal "brothers" both wearing the smoking mirror attributes, for instance, on the interior of the Great Jaguar Cuauhxicalli (figure 4.11). In the creation stories it is difficult to distinguish the two gods, where Huitzilopochtli is called one of four Tezcatlipoca brothers (Historia de los mexicanos por sus pinturas 1973, 23–24). However, Huitzilopochtli was the youngest brother, which in Aztec thought means he was destined to dominate in the end, just as he did over the Centzon-Huitznahua, another group of older brothers. In political contexts like that on the Tizoc Stone, one might say that Tezcatlipoca, although still powerful and respected, was demoted, and Huitzilopochtli's acquisition of his power traits was the result of an aggressive act. Huitzilopochtli, as top god, adopted or appropriated the power attributes of any god he dominated. This interpretation is inherent in the story of Huitzilopochtli's rise to power at the mythical Coatepetl. After his birth from his mother Coatlicue (Serpent[s], Her Skirt) and defeat of the army of Centzon-Huitznahua, Sahagún (1950–82, book III: 1–5) states that "when he had slain them . . . he took from them their goods, their adornment, the paper crowns. He took them as his own goods, he took them as his own property; he assumed them as his due as if taking the insignia to himself."

The historical background is found in accounts of the steps of Tenochtitlan's rise over Texcoco and the attendant rise of the Mexica patron god over the Texcocan Tezcatlipoca. The combined evidence of several colonial histories shows

FIGURE 4.10. Toltec Atlantean figure wearing butterfly breast-plaque, triangular hip cloth, and upright feather headdress, reassembled and placed on top of reconstructed Mound B at site of Tula, Hidalgo (circa 900–1200). Photograph by author.

FIGURE 4.11. Partially skeletal (Tenochca) Tezcatlipoca and Huitzilopochtli as equals drawing blood from their ears, relief on the bottom of the receptacle of the Great Jaguar Cuauhxicalli (circa 1490–1521), found in the central precinct of Tenochtitlan, Museo Nacional de Antropología, Mexico City. Drawing by author.

how Huitzilopochtli eclipsed the power of this near ally. Although Texcoco and Tenochtitlan had been equal partners in the Triple Alliance Empire at its foundation in 1431 (from the beginning Tlacopan was a junior partner), sometime in the 1440s and 1450s Tenochtitlan became more powerful. The long-lived ruler of Texcoco, Nezahualcoyotl, acknowledged this by staging a faux war and the acts of surrender (Durán 1994 [1581], 125–29). Some modern scholars do not believe this actually happened, but there is no reason to doubt it. As a sign of surrender, Nezahualcoyotl set fire to the principal temple of the city himself, at the time of the Spanish conquest a double pyramid that looked much like that of Tenochtitlan. This last indicates that the Great Temple of Texcoco preexisted the event, and I would guess that the image occupying the temple, presumably Tezcatlipoca, was removed and the temple was refurbished for the installation of Huitzilopochtli. The main temple of Tezcatlipoca at the time of the conquest was in the Huitznahuac section of the city (Pomar 1964, 163). The god's image was probably taken to Huitznahuac after being removed from the principal temple.

The combined evidence in various sources on the Huitznahuac sections of Texcoco and Tenochtitlan indicates that this was a section devoted to conquered gods in both cities. The name of the inhabitants, Huitznahua, is that borne by the enemy god-siblings of Huitzilopochtli, the Centzon-Huitznahua (Sahagún 1950–82, book III: 5). In Fray Diego Durán's (1994 [1581], 26–28) version of the story, Huitznahua[tl] was the leader of the god's enemies together with Coyolxauhqui (Bell[s], Painted). For this reason, the Huitznahuac *calpolli* was the site of the sacrifice of some victims during Panquetzaliztli, the month that celebrated the defeat of the enemy brothers (Sahagún 1950–82, book II: 148). The chief deity of

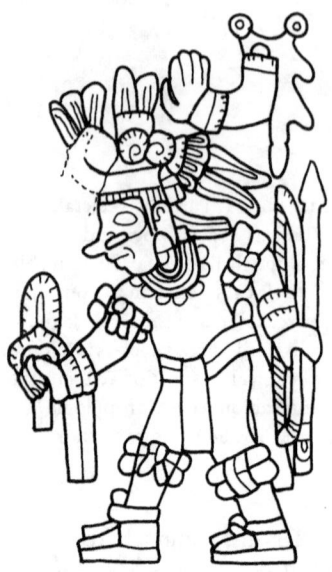

FIGURE 4.12. Another Tezcatlipoca? Acolhuacatl on the Stone of Tizoc. Drawing by author.

Huitznahuac calpolli would have been called Huitznahuatl, among other names, and Huitznahuatl, given its mythical basis, is probably not a flattering term even when borne by a powerful god. It is probably a reference to a once powerful being who led defeated forces, a "sibling" who did not rise to the top or was demoted. The Tenochca conquest of Texcoco itself may be referenced on the Tizoc Stone by the figure named Acolhuacatl, the representative of the Acolhua province—in other words, the ruler of its capital Texcoco (Umberger 2008), perhaps an image of the conquered Tezcatlipoca of that place (figure 4.12).

Despite the obvious demotion of the images of the Tezcatlipoca patrons of enemy polities in late Aztec times, Tizoc's monument makes it clear that the Tenochca version of the god was still powerful and honored as one of Huitzilopochtli's most important colleagues, as indicated by his multiple unnamed forms on the monument. His presence was a result of continuing power, which had much greater time-depth than Huitzilopochtli's, probably even in Tenochtitlan. As indicated at the beginning of this chapter, the date of the consolidation of Huitzilopochtli's persona as different from Tezcatlipoca's is unknown, but it was probably something that happened between the time Texcoco capitulated to Tenochtitlan and the Mexica civil war, which was conceived as a battle between rival Huitzilopochtlis. The imagery of power in sculptures seemingly did not change until after 1460.

The nature of the relationship of the two gods after that is probably best illustrated by their sequence in an important fifty-two-day ceremonial interval in the two hundred sixty-day count, where Tezcatlipoca operated during a period of darkness before Huitzilopochtli rose like the sun (Umberger 1987a, app., 2002). The period extended from 1 Death to 1 Flint. It occurred in every tonalpohualli, of course, but it must have been especially important at the time of the new fire lighting at the beginning of a new fifty-two-year count. On 1 Death Tezcatlipoca, in the form of Titlacahuan (He Whose Slaves We Are), was the master of arbitrary fate, making the formerly rich poor and making rulers into slaves who could be sacrificed (Sahagún 1950–82, book IV: 33–36). The first half of the period was probably a time of darkness, but halfway through it, on the day 2 Reed, Tezcatlipoca took on another identity, Ome Acatl (2 Reed) (ibid., 56), to light the new fire. Then at the end of the period, the day 1 Flint, Huitzilopochtli's day (ibid., 77)—symbolic, one would suppose, of his "solar" rise—initiated a period of light. Here the temporal sequence of the two gods is related to the gradual appearance of light from darkness. It is probable that before Huitzilopochtli's rise to prominence, Tezcatlipoca was associated with the date 1 Flint in a third aspect, his transformation into the being that helped the sun rise. An image of the Sun God seems to rule this day in the tonalamatls, but Tezcatlipoca probably held this position in the Basin of Mexico before Huitzilopochtli.

On the Tizoc Stone, the setting is the time of darkness before the rising of the sun, which the sacrifice of the enemy gods will aid. Thus Tizoc-Huitzilopochtli, who rises with the sun, still has his starry sky mask, and his colleagues in conquest probably represent officers dressed as Titlacahuan orchestrating the reversal of fortunes of once powerful and independent ruler-gods.

THE CONQUERED GODS

As indicated, a figure wearing symbols pertaining to several patron beings may represent the most recent of these because in succeeding the others he inherits their powers. In the case of the losers on the Tizoc Stone, the same type of layering is pertinent but in different ways, because temporally their fates were the opposite of Huitzilopochtli's. As he rose in power, they fell. First, the figure usually has insulting attributes added—for instance, the decorations presented to a ruler at the outset of war, the basic message of which is that he should prepare for death or sacrifice (Durán 1994 [1581], 258). Second, although these attributes may overlay other traits pertaining to his garb as an independent being in his home temple, others may allude to his present state as a step backward in the hierarchy of power to an earlier, lower identity. I have suggested this for the interpretation of the Tezcatlipoca figure on the orange funerary vessel next to the Great Coyolxauhqui Stone on Phase IVB of the Tenochtitlan Templo Mayor. If the image refers to the defeated ruler of Tlatelolco, his depiction as Tezcatlipoca was a demotion, and a serpent atlatl he holds may refer to his former identification with Huitzilopochtli (Umberger 2007b). Third, some traits on a defeated figure, if he were a foreign god unknown in Tenochtitlan, may have been used to reclassify him by pointing out his resemblance to a Nahua-type god like Tezcatlipoca. Of course, the nature of the traits and degree of humiliation conveyed by them would have varied according to the conditions of surrender to Tenochtitlan, which ranged from collaboration to aggressive hostility. Detailed interpretations of the circumstances of a particular capitulation are possible when historical accounts exist, but unfortunately these are known for very few conquered places. They are also more numerous for conquests over other Nahua groups and less so for more distant conquests. In the following I give examples of several of these types, and what they seem to have in common with the victor figures is the action of time in the layering or removal of attributes.

Some traits, like the aztaxelli symbolic of victims destined to be sacrificed, were obviously Tenochca additions to all the defeated figures on the Tizoc Stone. Also obvious is their lack of the Toltec ensemble and the power implements, the lack of which indicates that they are like Chichimecs and commoners (Umberger 2008). Some traits pertain to all figures, victors and victims alike—for instance, the rectangular loincloth panels and the sandals—and seem not to have a pointed message. Among the defeated, some necklaces, ties on limbs, and ear frontals are found on multiple figures and might have had metaphorical significance and united smaller groups among the captives in ways I cannot reconstruct. The fact that the items held in the hands had symbolic value, rather than or in addition to their literal values as functional types, is indicated by mismatches among them. This is seen in two figures carrying bows and arrows along with atlatls (for instance, figure 4.11) and the figure carrying the device for seeing with a set of darts (figure 4.2). In the case of the first two, no single figure in an Aztec army would carry both an atlatl and a bow; one carried either one or the other to hurl darts or arrows, respectively (Hassig 1988, chapter 6 and 97–99). In the case of the third, the figure does not carry a weapon to hurl the darts, neither an atlatl nor a bow.

The atlatl is a special case, as it is carried by all victors and most of the vanquished and thus does not differentiate them. As a weapon of the nobility presumably inherited from the Toltecs, it may indicate that the vanquished originally had the same noble heritage as the victors. If so, then a general implication is that through defeat in warfare, once noble and independent captives were converted into non-Toltecs, meaning Centzon-Huitznahua in myth, Chichimecs in the past, and political subjects/commoners, even slaves and sacrificial victims, in the present. It also implies that the same weapons, when used unsupported by supernatural powers, were ineffective.

FIGURE 4.13. Three Huitzilopochtlis: Tizoc as (Tenochca) Huitzilopochtli on the Stone of Tizoc, Tlatelolcatl-Huitzilopochtli on the Stone of Tizoc, and Painal from the *Primeros Memoriales* (the last is a detail after Sahagún 1993 [1559–61], folio 261r). Drawing by author.

FIGURE 4.14. Three Tezcatlipocas: (Tenochca) Tezcatlipoca/Titlacahuan on the Stone of Tizoc, Matlatzincatl-Coltzin-Tezcatlipoca on the Stone of Tizoc, and Tezcatlipoca from the *Primeros Memoriales* (the last is a detail after Sahagún 1993 [1559–61], folio 261r). Drawing by author.

In the more traditional iconographic method of deity identification, as demonstrated by Wicke (1975), the specific deities on the Tizoc Stone are identified by comparison with colonial manuscript images. Wicke used Sahagún's *Primeros Memoriales* to identify the figures from Matlatzinco and Tlatelolco by matching individual traits (Sahagún 1993 [1559–61], folio 261r). In figures 4.13 and 4.14 the victors on the monument—Huitzilopochtli and Tezcatlipoca—are on the left, defeated images of the same god are in the middle, and the *Primeros Memoriales* deities Wicke used are to the right. Wicke identified the Matlatzincatl as a form of Tezcatlipoca from the device he holds in his hand and the lines indicating facial paint (the monument has no color, so that dimension cannot be used). He identified the Tlatelolcatl as Painal because of the starry sky mask he has in common with that god in the *Primeros Memoriales*, which the image of Huitzilopochtli seems to lack (probably a combination of artistic and scribal mistakes, see note 11). Painal (Hasty One) is said to have been a deputy or substitute for Huitzilopochtli (Sahagún 1950–82, book I: 3), and for this reason, I believe, he wears the mask. Aside from the face paint, this figure has no other distinctive traits in common with the figure on the Tizoc Stone.

Whether all of Wicke's observations are correct is not the question here, but I do feel the emphasis is wrong in that it requires a choice among possibilities that might all have been alluded to in the image. The discussion of the costumes of individual figures needs to be elaborated to give a sense of the relationships among beings in Tenochca thought before understanding what was intended by the depiction. I suggest that a corrective approach to decoding the iconography of the Tizoc Stone uses colonial texts to identify at least some of the conquered figures. The results are especially enlightening in respect to Tenochca manipulations. Historical accounts clearly state that the patron god of the Matlatzinca bore the name Coltzin (Respected Grandfather in Nahuatl) and that the patron god of the Tlatelolca was a second Huitzilopochtli (e.g., Durán 1994 [1581], 270). But if this is true, why are the images wearing traits Wicke linked to other deity names?

The resolution of seeming contradictions like these may differ from case to case. The first case, the Matlatzinca being, is a god from outside the Basin of Mexico that was probably foreign to the Aztecs, and the second case, that of the Tlatelolca god, involves the god of a near neighbor of the Tenochca that shared a nearly identical culture. The sources on the Matlatzinco area are confusing and contradictory, so the recreation of the first example is particularly hypothetical and depends on José García Payón's (1936, 193–95) reconciliation in his reconstruction of the history of the Aztec conquests there.

Coltzin, the god of the Matlatzinca of the Valley of Toluca, was the god of a collaborating lord who received special privileges after his capitulation. Like other enemy deities, Coltzin's image was brought to Tenochtitlan, but, unlike most of them, he was accompanied by his priests; and the former ruler of Calixtlahuaca, Chimaltecuhtli, was brought to Tenochtitlan to live for four years. He carried with him the sacred fire from Calixtlahuaca to the adoratorio of his people in Tenochtitlan. Apparently, he was also allowed to offer a sacrificial victim to his god (Coltzin?) in his new home (Chimalpahin Cuauhtlehuanitzin 1965, 107, 217; Durán 1994 [1581]). It is even possible that the god and his retinue were set up in their own barrio, Tlamatzinco, rather than with the other conquered deities in the prison-temple called Coatlan. Because Matlatzinca culture was seemingly very different from Tenochca-Nahua culture and Coltzin was a god not previously known to the Tenochca (Sahagún 1950–82, book II: 171–72), it is possible that he was called Tlamatzincatl and reclassified in Tenochtitlan as "another Tezcatlipoca,"[17] as Sahagún characterized him. Sahagún's observation, I suggest, may not mean he was described as a version of Tezcatlipoca at home; rather, it could mean that in Tenochtitlan he was reconceived as like Tezcatlipoca in being the high god of his polity.

In contrast to the scenario created by the existence of a collaborating lord among the Matlatzinca, the Tenochca war with the Tlatelolca was a true civil war between two adjacent Mexica polities that had different images of Huitzilopochtli and almost identical cultures in other respects. The battles fought between them were very fierce, and upon defeat the Tlatelolca Huitzilopochtli was taken from his temple to Tenochtitlan, where he was both honored and humiliated through demotion (Umberger 2007b). I suggest that the Tlatelolcatl on the Tizoc Stone represents the Huitzilopochtli of Tlatelolco as defeated and demoted. But the question arises of what he had in common with Painal, the Tenochca deity who likewise shared a number of Huitzilopochtli's traits, such as the starry sky mask. Sahagún (1950–82, book I: 3) describes Painal as an imitator, representative, and subordinate of Tenochca Huitzilopochtli whose rapid movements stirred up the dust. Both the quick movement and the dust were signs of a faulty character in Mexica thought (see Burkhart 1989, 60–62, chapter 4), not that of a ruler. So the defeated Huitzilopochtli of Tlatelolco could well have been called Painal also in Tenochtitlan, having lost his independence and even the name of the high god. I suggest, in fact, that the image is just one of many variations of the defeated Tlatelolcatl in Aztec imagery (Umberger 2008, 99–101, figure 3.17).

Thus among the four figures in the two vignettes on the Tizoc Stone, there is the possibility of two Huitzilopochtlis—the one Tizoc represents and the one the Tlatelolcatl represents—and two Tezcatlipocas, the one the Matlatzincatl represents and the one the anonymous official-conquerors represent. They are dressed so differently that one would not expect them to represent the same gods. In the cases of the losers, neither figure has the diagnostic traits of the deities they represented before conquest: the hummingbird of Huitzilopochtli and the smoking mirror of Tezcatlipoca that were also the instruments of their powers.

CONCLUSION

An approach that considers the effects of time and place is needed to account for differences in imagery that relate to the waxing and waning of political power. There is a large difference between the changing identities of Tezcatlipoca during the calendar cycles within Tenochtitlan itself and the different images identified with the same supernatural from other towns. On the Tizoc Stone one aspect of Tezcatlipoca is represented in the fourteen Tenochca victor figures, but the others are defeated, and their costumes are manipulated to show their humiliation. In other cases this identification may have been imposed after defeat by the Tenochca. Some parts are readily seen manipulative additions or subtractions, as shown earlier, but others may refer to the particulars of the story of conquest, different types of deals struck with the conquered, or a new demoted state. In other words, despite the unifying characteristics even among the captives, each of these figures and the defeats they represent had different stories.

A variety of approaches and data—that is, the visual approach of Wicke combined with the historical and political data presented here—reveals the importance of context and complexities inherent in the costuming of the anthropomorphic ixiptla depicted in Aztec art. The different data give different types of information that are not necessarily mutually exclusive. However, to use this information, we need to be more conscious of the origins of source materials and the rules behind compositions. This is true of both textual and pictorial materials and of pre- and post-conquest remains; none of these can be automatically excluded or automatically accepted. The greater comprehensiveness of multiple approaches will lead to more refined analyses of costume traits and their relationship to a being's identity. Some traits evoke a name and seem truly diagnostic of the being with that name, some are power implements alluding to supernatural domains, some allude to class, some link figures to the past and former identities, some constitute obvious insults, and some place a being in a generic category.

Despite this knowledge of the complexities of costume parts and their variability in different contexts, what should we call the deity images in political artworks like the Tizoc Stone? Do their costumes evoke particular names? The Tlatelolcatl is a former Huitzilopochtli, with the starry sky mask but without the hummingbird headdress that would indicate this name. Both of these attributes are also worn by Painal, whom I identify as the Tlatelolcatl Huitzilopochtli in ceremonies that put him in subservient positions to the Tenochtitlan version.[18] If the hummingbird headdress was meant to evoke the name Huitzilopochtli, does its lack mean the being was called Painal because of the traits that are present? Whatever they called him, the (educated) Nahuatl-speaking viewer would have known that he was formerly another Huitzilopochtli and that Painal referred to his continuing presence in Tenochtitlan as a subordinate of the victorious god. (We must consider that Aztec period viewers' aims and knowledge were not the same as ours, and the decoding of these complexities of iconographic language is only possible with written accounts.) Because the figure is labeled by a hieroglyph as Tlatelolcatl, I consider this to be the being's primary identification on the monument, and the costume parts are hints to a plethora of other ideas and identities. Thus one can still say that a figure's identity is a sum of its parts, including its costume parts, but there was no single a-historical identity of the type sought by Sahagún and his modern successors.

NOTES

1. I wrote this chapter in 2007–8, so relevant recent references have not been included.

2. I use the word *deity* to designate the costumed anthropomorphic figures in Aztec art; they are probably all ixiptla of different sorts (Hvidtfeldt 1958).

3. Here the term *Aztec* refers inclusively to the inhabitants of the Basin of Mexico during the Middle and Late Postclassic periods of Mesoamerican history. Individual ethnic terms are used to refer to smaller groups among them. The term *Mexica* is especially difficult to use, as it changed through time. In many contexts it refers to the inhabitants of both Tenochtitlan and Tlatelolco before the civil war between them in 1473. After that the Tenochca called themselves Mexica and called the Tlatelolca, Tlatelolca. I use the terms *Tenochca* and *Tlatelolca* to make this same distinction. Mexica is not appropriate when applied to the empire until that group became dominant after 1473. It is safer to refer to it as the Aztec empire because for its first four decades it was an alliance among three powers with different ethnic names.

4. *Metaphorical* is used loosely here to mean figurative. The subject of Aztec figurative thought is more complicated than I am indicating, as it seems to involve a complex of metonymical and syntagamatic relationships linking the symbolism of costume parts to the personage wearing them as well as to metaphorical references.

5. The art historian Richard Townsend (1979) is unusual for having combined these two strains; he studied the forms as well as metaphorical references of costume parts, but he has not pursued this beyond initial observations. Neither he nor anyone else has explored the effects of Aztec period events on the apparel of deities.

6. On Huitzilopochtli, also see Boone 1989; Conrad and Demarest 1984; Hunt 1977; Nicholson 1988; Seler 1990–98; Zantwijk 1976, among others. On Tezcatlipoca, also see Carrasco 1991; Nicholson 1954, 1958, 2001; Olivier 2003.

7. Townsend (1979) also discusses this distinction. I agree that the patron figures are more closely related to human leaders, but I do not see a human hero-leader as a necessary predecessor to the god in a simple historical ancestry of the type suggested in colonial sources (for instance, Sahagún's [1950–82 (rev. ed.), book I: 1] comment that Huitzilopochtli was "just a man"). The problem is a simplistic notion of the historical process behind the formation of a deity's persona and the universal application to all patron deities. A patron deity embodied the supernatural powers and aspects of behavior of the ideal human leader (and for this reason he was like a man), but any resemblance to actual leaders resulted from the dialectics of historical change, where their individual lives helped reshape the ideal (see Umberger 2002 on the dialectics of Aztec historical thought). Huitzilopochtli's persona at the time of the Spanish conquest was the result of multiple transformations and reconceptions, just as the understanding of past events was reconceived according to later happenings. The attributes of some leaders more than others may have reshaped his image, but this did not necessarily happen at the beginning and does not mean we should think of patron gods as deified versions of historical figures. If some are, there is no way of determining which ones from the existing (colonial) sources. It is a "chicken and egg" argument. By the way, some nature deities like Tlaloc and Chalchiuhtlicue may have had more political power in the past, for instance, at Teotihuacan.

8. Barnes (2009) is studying changes in the representation of kings on these and other sculptures during the same period—specifically the lack of royal hieroglyphs before Tizoc's time—and ties them to other ideational changes and historical circumstances.

9. The Historia de los mexicanos por sus pinturas (1973, 23–24) states that Huitzilopochtli was the youngest of four Tezcatlipoca brothers, the oldest being the Red Tezcatlipoca called Camaxtli by the Huexotzinca and Tlaxcalteca. Later it says, "These gods had these and many other names, because they were named according to the thing that they were attending to, or assigned to. And because each town gave them different names, [also] according to its language . . . they were called by many names" (ibid., 24). Evidence of the use of the date 1 Flint for the roles pertaining to the patron god of different towns is behind Sahagún's (1950–82, book IV: 77) mention that 1 Flint was the ceremonial day of Camaxtli among the Huexotzinca, as it was of Huitzilopochtli among the Tenochca.

10. On the problems of using manuscripts to interpret sculptures, see Boone 1980; Nagao 1985; and Pasztory 1987, among others.

11. On Sahagún's deity images, see Baird 1993 and elsewhere; Boone 1989; Nicholson 1988; Peterson 1988; Quiñones Keber 1988a, 1988b, 1997; Robertson 1959, chapter 4; Sahagún 1997 (1559–61), notes by Nicholson; Seler 1998 (1908).

12. Whether he was familiar with the images in tonalamatls is unknown. He would not have been familiar with the deities on monuments and their associated dates. In fact, no one in Early Colonial times studied these in any detail.

13. Even if one believes Aztec costumes contained relatively simple diagnostic clues to identity, Sahagún's depictions and descriptions are anomalous. His deities lack the traits

scholars commonly associate with individual beings. His Tlaloc lacks the goggles usually represented, his Tezcatlipoca lacks the smoking mirror, and his Huitzilopochtli lacks the hummingbird. This last was a mistake, as can be demonstrated by looking at the rest of his series. I suggest that his zoomorphic back-hanging was meant to represent a hummingbird rather than a *xiuhcoatl* (Fire Serpent) and that it is mistakenly labeled (see also Boone 1989, chapter 2; Nicholson 1988; Sahagún 1997 [1559–61], 93–94, notes). This probability is indicated by the back-hanging on folio 262v (ibid.), which is labeled likewise as a xiuhcoatl and depicted differently from Huitzilopochtli's. It is a true xiuhcoatl, and Huitzilopochtli's represents a different animal, most likely a badly drawn hummingbird. Neither image has the veristic appearance of Prehispanic art because, despite the non-European aspects of his style, the artist (and Sahagún) did not know the appearance of a number of items of deity costumes. This is not surprising. In the mid-sixteenth century some items of pre-conquest clothing continued to be used (Umberger 1996b), but deity garb was not. See the increasingly fantastic images of Huitzilopochtli in Boone's (1989) study.

14. He also placed Painal with Huitzilopochtli and Tezcatlipoca because he focused on Painal in the ceremonies as Huitzilopochtli's deputy, and he locates Painal with the highest-ranking gods at the beginning of the list only because of this. He was not truly important in Tenochtitlan.

15. Janice Lynn Robertson (2005) has suggested the possibility of the latter to account for differences among glyphs of conquered places in the Codex Mendoza.

16. For accounts of how the Aztecs worked out the reiteration of history in the fifty-two-year count and the two hundred sixty-day count, see Umberger (1981b, 2002). In both counts the powerful patron gods of the past, Quetzalcoatl and Tezcatlipoca, preceded Huitzilopochtli, the most recent to be associated with the sun. I have not developed this idea of sequencing in the monthly calendar, but the obvious climax is the month of Panquetzaliztli near the end of the year, when Huitzilopochtli rose to power and killed his enemies. The ceremony was a reenactment of the story of the god's rise at Coatepec and defeat of all other gods. Given the antiquity of the calendrical structures on which these sequences were based, the details had to have differed from period to period and from polity to polity.

17. The evidence that leads to this hypothesis is found in Sahagún (1950–82, book II: 171–72) and Torquemada (1969/1975–83 [1613–15], 2: 151–52), added to that of Durán and Chimalpahin cited in the text. Torquemada says the Matlatzinca god was called Tlamatzincatl, and Sahagún describes a section of Tenochtitlan dedicated to the god Tlamatzincatl, whom he calls "another Tezcatlipoca." Thus I think it is possible that upon transference to Tenochtitlan the god's name was changed by reversing the first two syllables, that he was classified as similar to the Aztec god who had been the patron deity of many, if not all, Aztec towns before Huitzilopochtli's rise, and that he was installed in his own section with his temple, *calmecac* (priestly school), and sacrificial stone. These are problematic assertions because the reversal of syllables in a name is otherwise unknown in the Nahuatl

language (Louise Burkhart, personal communication, 2007); however, it merits further investigation.

18. My present hypothesis, based on the notion that Painal represents the Tlatelolco Huitzilopochtli in Tenochtitlan, is that varied images represent him at different stages in ceremonial reenactments of the historical events leading to and following his downfall.

5

Tezcatlipoca as a Warrior

Wealth and Bells

Elizabeth Baquedano

This chapter examines Tezcatlipoca as a warrior and the use of gold as a symbol of power and status. Both qualities were present in the cult of Tezcatlipoca. The descriptions given by the Spanish chroniclers of the sixteenth century emphasized the use of gold in his distinctive iconographic features, as will be seen. Likewise, warrior gods carry gold, gold symbols, and metal objects such as bells. The Mexica kings were also representative of the warrior class and made lavish use of gold jewelry. It is clear, therefore, that warfare, rulers, and Tezcatlipoca go hand in hand, especially as he was identified with rulership and royal descent.

One of the most important aspects of Tezcatlipoca is that of a warrior god; Yaotl (Enemy) is the name given to him in this guise. Fray Bernardino de Sahagún (1950–82, book I: 68) compared him to Jupiter but also to Lucifer: "This wicked Tezcatlipoca, we know, is Lucifer, the great devil who there in the midst of Heaven, even in the beginning, began war." He was therefore responsible for war.

Sahagún's informants (ibid., 5; book III: 12) refer to him as Yaotzin and Necoc Yaotl, which translate as "Enemy" and "Enemy on Both Sides," respectively. Tezcatlipoca's ambivalent character is implied through the term *Necoc Yaotl*. Tezcatlipoca was invoked under that name to assist warriors in their martial endeavors. Wherever there was war, Tezcatlipoca was responsible for initiating the conflict—the "Enemy on Both Sides" created hostility, though his purpose was not to side with either faction but instead to ignite war. Fray Diego Durán (1971, 109–10) mentioned that his arm was extended in such a way that he seemed always ready to throw his *atlatl* (spear-thrower).

DOI: 10.5876/9781607322887.c005

According to Burr Cartwright Brundage (1979, 85–86), Tezcatlipoca's "enemy part in war was more important than the part played by Huitzilopochtli. His real role was in representing the Mexica who were war like, not in representing war itself."

The parents of children who went to the Telpochcalli school dedicated their sons to their Lord of the Smoking Mirror, who was then known as *Telpochtli* and *Yaotl* (names of the Smoking Mirror), among others (Sahagún 1985, 11). One of the main functions of the Telpochcalli was to provide military training for young students. It was at the Telpochcalli where the Eagles and the Ocelotls were born and made, wrote Sahagún.

Cristóbal del Castillo (1991, 128–29) also described the benefits of war: "And those who devote themselves to war will have no limit, nothing will hamper them, they will do what they want and all their ambitions will be fulfilled: in all places they will take women, nobody will oppose them; everything will be for them, all the good things, all the pleasing things, the flowers, the tobacco, songs, all things."

TEZCATLIPOCA'S DEPICTIONS AS A WARRIOR

Tezcatlipoca is often depicted as an armed warrior holding arrows and a shield (figure 5.1). However, the Spanish chroniclers often described a mirror (*tezcatl*) that appears on Tezcatlipoca's temple or in place of one of his feet. The tezcatl is the god's most significant trait, which often appears with the symbol for smoke. When the smoking mirror is absent, either a pectoral gorget(?) (*anahuatl*) or his staff *tlachialoni*— the "seeing instrument," or mirror, that allowed Tezcatlipoca to see all that took place in the world—was used as a substitute. The banded facial painting is also essential in determining the identity of the god. Using codices, Guilhem Olivier (2003, 56) has listed and quantified the iconographic elements that identify Tezcatlipoca as a warrior (table 5.1).[1]

War and death are inexorably linked in ancient Mexico. Tezcatlipoca is thus connected with killing related to war. War captives killed in public rituals were shown with balls of feathers, as was Coyolxauhqui. Hence, as part of his iconography, Tezcatlipoca carries feather balls (*yuiteteyo*) decorating his headdress, but they can also be seen on his shield (e.g., Durán 1971, 331, plate 9). Olivier (2003) has found this iconographic symbol in twenty-one representations (see table 5.1).

The flag (*pantli*), normally made of paper, is another symbol of warriors and death. This flag is a component of Tezcatlipoca's shield (figure 5.2) in a figurine from the Cleveland Museum of Art.

TEZCATLIPOCA AS A WARRIOR 115

FIGURE 5.1. Tezcatlipoca as a warrior (Durán 1971, 331, plate 9).

THE USE OF GOLD IN TEZCATLIPOCA'S REPRESENTATIONS

Tezcatlipoca is perhaps the god that wears the most gold, if we are to believe the descriptions by the Spanish chroniclers. The use of certain types of gold objects was restricted to certain deities. For example, Sahagún mentioned that the gods carried

TABLE 5.1 Iconographic elements that identify Tezcatlipoca as a warrior.

Iconographic Elements	Number of Occurrences
Tezcatlipoca wears the warrior's hairstyle ("crew cut," tzotzocolli)	22 representations
Heron feather headdress (aztaxelli), typical of warriors	26 representations
Jaguar-skin ornaments on his legs (Tezcatlipoca was the protector of jaguar warriors)	9 representations
Tinker bells on calves or ankles	22 representations
Carrying a shield (chimalli)	22 representations
Carrying arrows or lances	16 representations
Holding a spear-thrower (atlatl)	6 representations
Holding a feathered staff weapon	10 representations
Feather balls (yuiteteyo)	21 representations
Flint knife (tecpatl)	4 representations

items made of gold, and some of the items were unique to certain gods, such as Tezcatlipoca's tlachialoni.

The Dominican friar Diego Durán (1967, 1: 37) wrote that Tezcatlipoca had gold earplugs in the form of a hook and gold shell earplugs. This is confirmed in Juan Bautista de Pomar's (1975, 9) Relación de Tezcoco. In the Codex Ramírez (1980, plate 21) there are representations of bells suspended from his ears (figure 5.3).

Tezcatlipoca wore a breast ornament that was also made of gold, and two gold bracelets adorned his arms as well. According to Durán (1967, 1: 38), Tezcatlipoca had a mirror made of gold: "Tenía una chapa redonda de oro muy relumbrante y bruñida, como un espejo, en aquel espejo veía todo lo que se hacía en el mundo llamado itlachiayan, su mirador." He also described Tezcatlipoca's fan: "a fan of precious feathers, blue, green, and yellow. These emerged from a round plate of gold, shining and brilliant, polished like a mirror." This is the object that allows Tezcatlipoca to see people: "It has a hole through which he watches people" (Tlachielonj yn imac icac centlapal, coyunqui, ic teita, in Sahagún 1997 [1559–61], 95). Pomar (1986, 54) describes a cape of eagle feathers strewn with gold leaves and a fabric whose ends were elegantly finished and which seemed to be used as a loincloth. Tezcatlipoca can be seen as a warrior in Anders, Jansen, and Reyes (1994, 3) holding a flint knife in each hand (figure 5.4). The Lord of the Smoking Mirror is represented here wearing knee bands with gold bells hanging from them. The same kind of decoration can be seen on his wrists.

FIGURE 5.2. A: figure of a warrior; B: figure of a warrior (reverse); both courtesy, Cleveland Museum of Art.

FIGURE 5.3. Representation of Tezcatlipoca, Codex Ramírez (plate 21).

FIGURE 5.4. Tezcatlipoca holding two flint knives, Anders, Jansen, and Reyes (1994, 3).

Sahagún (1950–82, book II: 69) also described the items that were put on Tezcatlipoca's impersonator during the feast of Toxcatl: "Then on both sides, on his upper arms, he placed golden bracelets, on both sides, on his wrists, and then he went placing his bells on both sides, on his legs. All gold were the bells, called *oyoalli*. These [he wore] because they went jingling, because they went ringing; so did they resound."

Sahagún's (1992, 116–17) informants reported "campanillas, cascabeles y cascabeles redondos" (pear-shaped bells, bells, and round bells). Durán (1967, 1: 38) gives the number of bells that were put on Tezcatlipoca's effigy—twenty golden rattles, placed on the feet (a los cuales llamaban sonajas de los pies).

Joseph de Acosta (1973, 2: 319–20) left a detailed description of the Lord of the Smoking Mirror and the uses of gold, which I quote at length:

> They call this idoll Tezcatlipuca; he was made of blacke shining stone like to Iayel, being attired with some ornamental devises after their manner; it had earerings of golde and silver, and through the nether lippe a small tube of cristall, in length halfe a foote: in the which they sometimes put greene feather, and sometimes an azured, which made it resemble sometimes an emerald and sometimes a turquois: it had

the haire broidered and bound vp with a haire-lace of golde burnished, at the end whereof did hang an eare of golde, with two firebrands of smoake painted therein, which did signifie the prayers of the afflicted and sinners that he heard, when they recommended themselves vnto him. Betwixt the two eares hanged a number of small herons. He had a iewell hanging at his necke, so great that it covered all his stomacke: vpon his armes bracelets of golde: at his navill a rich greene stone: and in his left hand a fanne of pretious feathers, of greene, azure, and yellow, which came forth of a looking glasse of golde, shining and well burnished, and that signified that within this looking glasse he sawe whatsoever was doone in the world. They call this mirror or plate of golde Itlacheaya, which signfies his glasse for to looke in. In his right hand he held fore dartes, which signified the chastisement he gave vnto the wicked for their sinnes.

The ethnohistorical descriptions quoted here support the fact that Tezcatlipoca was literally clad in gold from his hair and ears to his wrists and ankles; even his clothes were embellished with gold. I have confirmed the places where gold is represented through a close inspection of codices, as well as through the limited finds of archaeological objects.

TEZCATLIPOCA'S PRIVILEGED RELATIONSHIP WITH ROYAL POWER

Tezcatlipoca's cult was particularly identified with royalty. Richard Townsend (1992, 109) mentions that Tezcatlipoca is the object of the longest and most reverent prayers in the rites of kingship. Political and religious leaders were required to have military skills, considered a prerequisite to be elevated to the throne.

Together with the Lord of the Smoking Mirror, the king bore the title Telpochtli. The ruler became associated with Tezcatlipoca in both his title and his qualities. Tezcatlipoca was the god of kings. So closely was Aztec rulers' prestige identified with Tezcatlipoca that when they died their faces were sometimes covered with the mask depicting him. Is the British Museum example the skull mask of one of Tezcatlipoca's representatives on earth?

The cult of Tezcatlipoca was preeminently centered at Texcoco, where it was particularly associated with the royal house. The rulers and warriors were heavily attired with gold, as in Sahagún (1979 [1575–78], book VIII: 28). The presence of gold on both Tezcatlipoca and the rulers is not accidental. In a society where class distinctions were followed very strictly, the nobility (*pipiltin*) used powerful and propagandist symbols to display wealth, and gold was one of those symbols. Indeed, I contend that gold was possibly the most precious material used by the Mexica.

Warfare entitled warriors to receive various benefits, including high social status as well as a number of material benefits in life and the afterlife. Those who died on the battlefield or on the sacrificial stone went to the dwelling of the Sun, Tonatiuh Ilhuicac. This was considered a place of glory, wealth, and joy (Sahagún 1950–82, book III: 49).

SYMBOLISM AND FUNCTION OF BELLS

According to Dorothy Hosler (1994, 233), bell sounds and the sounds of composite bell instruments played a major role in at least three sacred contexts: in ritual celebrating human and agricultural fertility and regeneration; in warfare, where bell sounds could protect warriors; and in the sacred paradise, created through song and sound.

The Sound of Bells: Fertility and Regeneration

Hosler mentions that the deities most frequently associated with bells represent fertility, life, and regeneration: "In Mesoamerica rain, water, storms, thunder, lightning, rattlesnakes, and new vegetation appear as symbols of fecundity and new life. Bell sounds replicate the sounds of thunder, rain, and the rattle of the rattlesnake" (ibid., 235).

The *Cantares Mexicanos* has endless examples in which bell sounds shaped the experience of the sacred with metaphorical associations of bird songs, bell sounds, and singing: "My songs are shrilling like gold bells" (Bierhorst 1985, 259).

The Sounds of Bells: Warfare

Given that Tezcatlipoca was considered a warrior god, it is therefore necessary to study the iconography of other warrior gods such as Huitzilopochtli. Both of these gods are often depicted in codices and sculptures wearing bells. Hosler (1994, 241) has stated that bells and other rattling sounds not only attract rain but also protect those engaged in warfare. Bells worn by warriors in Aztec sculpture are depicted in detail, with one example the sitting warrior (figure 5.5) from the Museo Nacional de Antropología e Historia (no. 156-11-3277), and they seem to replicate bells made of metal.

Coyolxauhqui—Huitzilopochtli's malevolent sister—is not only depicted with bells on her cheeks, but her very name is derived from bells (coyolli). The colossal greenstone head (Museo Nacional de Antropología 10-11641/10-220913) exhibits the gold symbol on her cheeks, and the relief found at the Templo Mayor shows

FIGURE 5.5. Sitting warrior, Museo Nacional de Antropología e Historia (no. 156-11-3277).

bells on both her cheeks and her wrists. The mask representing Coyolxauhqui in the Peabody Museum of Archaeology and Ethnology, Harvard University (no. 28-40-20), displays one significant element missing on the colossal head—the band

FIGURE 5.6. Relief depicting Coyolxauhqui, Templo Mayor.

incised across the nose linking the bells on the cheeks. Bells are without doubt a very important iconographic trait of the goddess, and the incised band linking the bells is also a diagnostic trait, as it appears on the Templo Mayor relief sculpture depicting Coyolxauhqui (figure 5.6).

Huitzilopochtli, the patron of warriors, had as his insignia ankle bells. Sahagún (1950–82, book III: 3–4) recorded that in Huitzilopochtli's cosmic battle with his 400 brothers, the latter arrayed themselves as if for war, binding little bells to the calves of their legs. Nonetheless, Huitzilopochtli killed them using his serpent of fire. The event is commemorated in myth and translated by Miguel León-Portilla (1969, 47):

> In vain they tried to rally against him,
> in vain they turned to attack him,
> rattling their bells,

FIGURE 5.7. Copper shield; according to Solís Olguín, associated with the symbolic mirrors called Tezcacuitlapilli that warriors wore on their backs (Solís Olguín 1991, 205, figure 310).

and clashing their shields
Nothing could they do,
Nothing could they gain,
With nothing could they defend themselves.

Hosler (1994, 241) mentions that the reference to slapping their shields coincides with a statement by Durán (1967, 2: 167), who described Huastec warriors fighting with the Aztecs as wearing bells that made "a strange sound" (un ruido extraño) attached to their shields or at their shoulders. There seems to be a mistake in the translation, as Durán wrote: "Y los huastecos arremetieron a ellos con un ruido de cascabeles de palo. Que traían por orla de las corazas y otros, con cascabeles de metal grandes, que traían a las espaldas y a los pies, con los cuales hacían un ruido extraño."

Bells, therefore, were large when attached to the warrior's back (not the shoulders, as pointed out by Hosler); the other type of bells was attached to their feet, placed around their ankles. Solís Olguín (1991, 205) has illustrated one such warrior's metal back device (figure 5.7).

Bells were such an important component in warfare that Sahagún recorded poems describing them:

> The smoke of the brazier! There, the clamour of the shields.
> The god of the tinker bells
> There your flowers are spread out, oh Enemy:
> There is clamour of the Eagles and the Jaguars!

It is difficult to determine whether this poem refers to Tezcatlipoca or to Huitzilopochtli, as both were associated with war and wore gold bells. However, Sahagún (1950–82, book II: 69) described how Tezcatlipoca's impersonator placed bells on both legs—all gold bells, called oyoalli. As he ran, they jingled and rang, and thus they resounded.

According to Gerónimo de Mendieta's (1980 [1870], 134) *Historia*: "Los que captivaban en la Guerra se podían ataviar y usar joyas de oro y plumajes con sus pinjantes de oro que colgaban a manera de chias de mitra de Obispo" (Those who managed to capture prisoners in war could wear and carry gold jewelry and feathers with headdresses that hung like bishops' mitres [my translation]).

The missionary friars reported that gold bells were worn by Aztec and other Mesoamerican rulers and also by members of the elite. Aztec dignitaries wore jewels and gold bells bound to their calves and ankles. For example, Durán (1967, 2: 301) reported that when the Aztec ruler Axayacatl died, Nezahualcoyotl, king of Texcoco, gave the newly elected ruler, Tizoc, a crown of green stones and gold; he then pierced his nose and put in a nose plug, and in his ears he put round green earplugs surrounded by gold, two glittering bracelets, and gold bells for his ankles (my translation). Durán (ibid., 297) also mentions that when Axayacatl died in 1481, bells were brought to Tenochtitlan as one of the tribute items (figure 5.8).

The Relación de Michoacán shows the Tarascan ruler wearing bells around his ankles (Tudela 1977, 251) and states that at his death he was buried with bells of gold. Gold and warfare seem to go hand in hand. The Codex Mendoza (Berdan and Anawalt 1992, folio 46r) lists a variety of gold objects paid as tribute, including gold shields (figure 5.9).

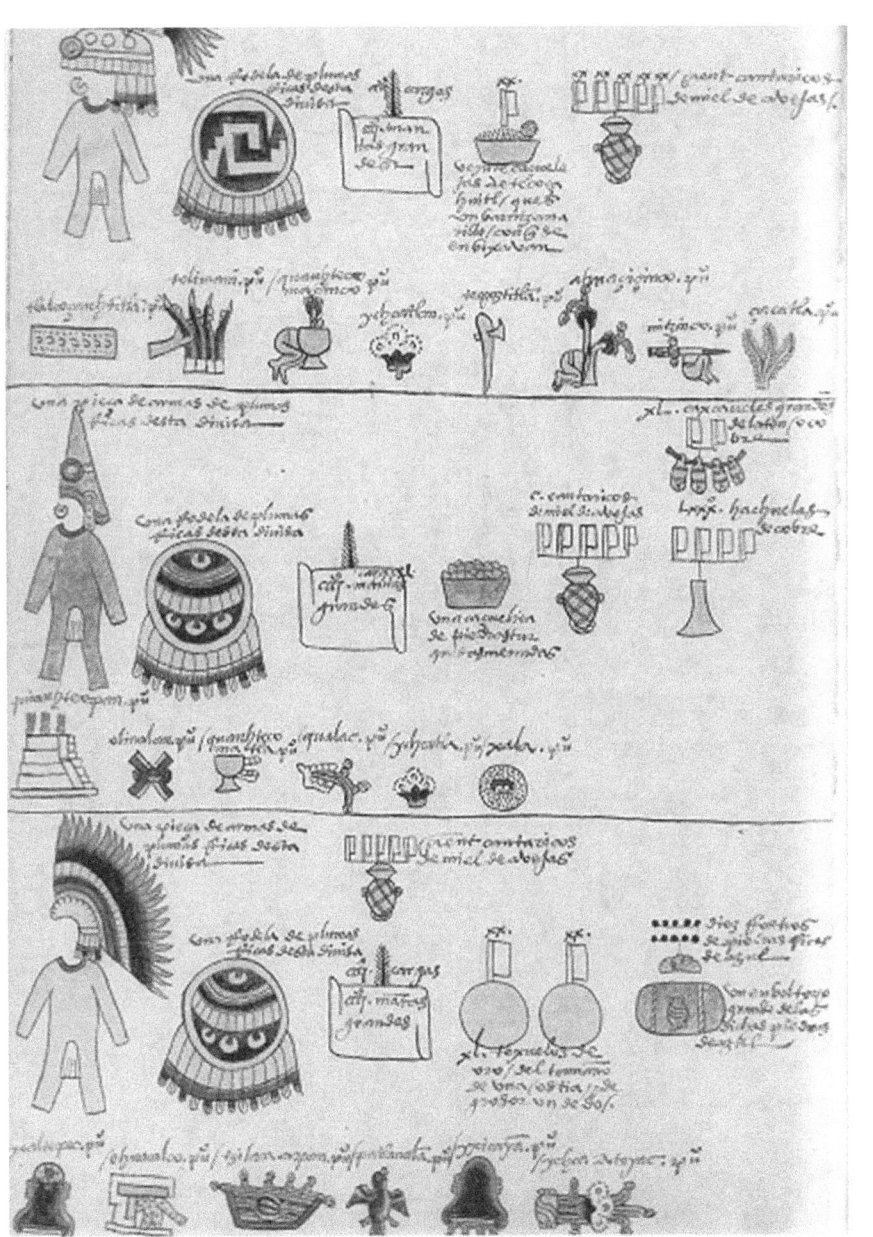

FIGURE 5.8. Tribute list including bells (Codex Mendoza 1541–42, folio 40).

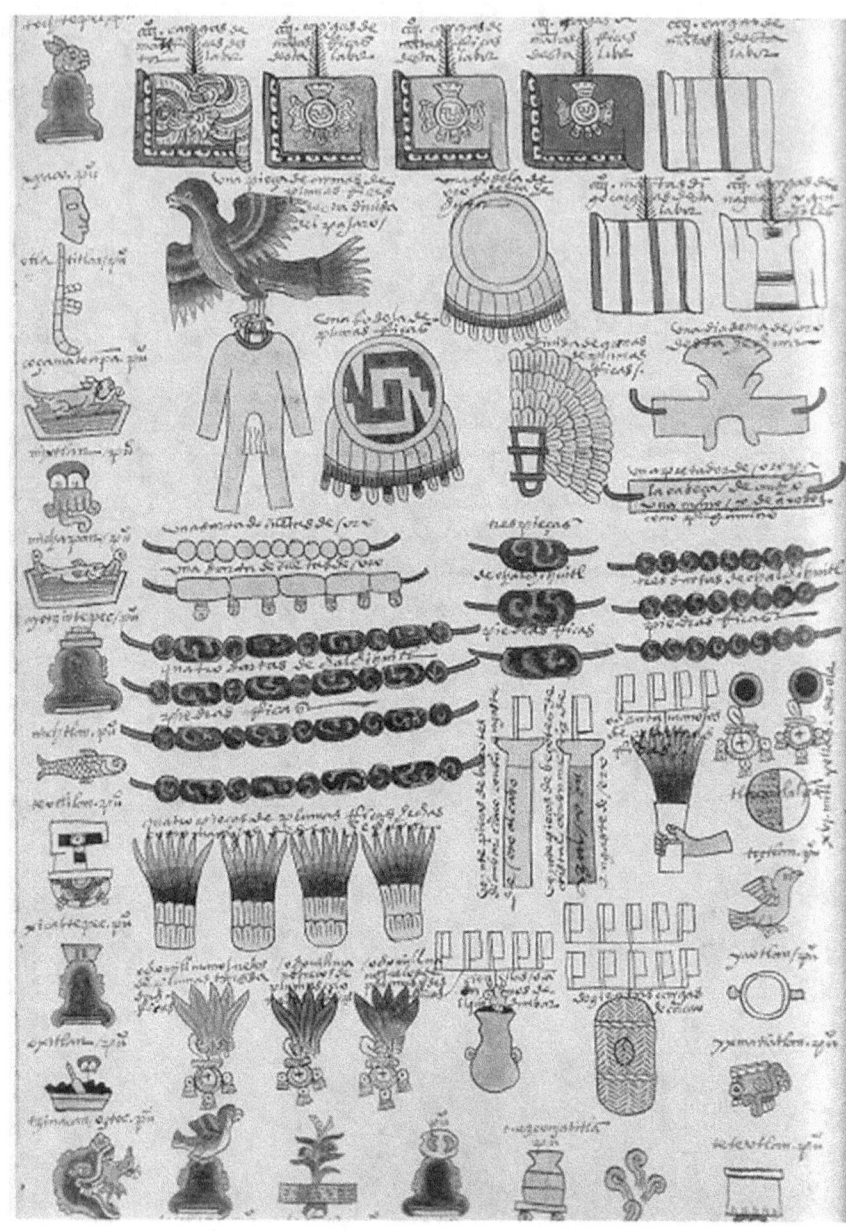

FIGURE 5.9. Tribute list (Codex Mendoza, folio 46).

FIGURE 5.10. Symbol for gold, redrawn from Pasztory (1983, 85).

Warriors enjoyed a privileged position in Aztec society. Sahagún (1950–82, book II: 94) described the use of jewelry, bells, and gold lip plugs by warriors, depending on their rank: "And as for all the men, whether brave warriors [or] youths, their net capes were only black . . . And those who led had only bell-shaped earplugs. And those who had bell-shaped earplugs also had lip plugs. Some were like lizards some were like dogs, some like a broad-leafed water plant, some rectangular. And the youths who already wore [their] hair long [in token of war exploits] had lip plugs which were rounded."

The translation misses an important point, as the Spanish text incorporates the description of the gold symbol—those who had achieved success in war carried lip plugs with the symbol for gold: "Y los mancebos que habían hecho alguna cosa señalada en la Guerra llevaban unos bezotes redondos, como un círculo, con cuatro circulillos en cruz, dentro de la circunferencia, que era algo ancha" (Sahagún 1969, book II: 177; see figure 5.10).

It is clear that victorious warriors often wore visible signs of prestige in their ornaments (figure 5.11). This proves my point that warriors, Tezcatlipoca, and social status were largely alluded to through gold, a material that signaled success in Aztec society. The Aztecs made more use of gold as they improved their position and as time went on. When the Spaniards arrived in Mexico, they were using gold and the gold symbol in a variety of materials (figure 5.12) and for a variety of intentions: to succeed on the battlefield and to obtain good crops (figure 5.13).

Other Contexts in Which Bells Are Used

Gold, especially compared with jade, is very malleable and well suited to intricate designs. The people of highland central Mexico made a large variety of ornaments in gold, including forms such as bells. These gold artifacts were often placed in, for example, funerary bundles (figure 5.14). The wealthy and successful were fully

FIGURE 5.11. Nezahualcoyotl, Codex Ixtlilxóchitl (1976, folio 106).

FIGURE 5.12. Vessel found at Zultepec, Tlaxcala. Drawing by Natalie Wilkinson.

FIGURE 5.13. Tecuilhuitl festival, Codex Magliabechiano (1970, folio 36v).

equipped at death to continue their existence in the afterlife, as attested to in the Codex Magliabechiano (1970, folio 56r). The number of bells found in the archaeological record in several Mesoamerican sites reflects the importance given to them.

In the Codex Telleriano-Remensis (1964–67, folio 33r) for the year 1458, we see a male figure bearing a precious jade and gold bead necklace and a bundle of green feathers. According to Eliose Quiñones Keber (1995, 218), this signifies the presentation of tribute. The source of this tribute is the town of Xiuhcoac (Place of the Turquoise Snake).

Also in the Codex Telleriano-Remensis (ibid., folio 33v), we see a tribute-bearing figure with green plumes and a gold necklace as well as a shield. The shield seems to be represented with bells around its edge.

Again in the Codex Telleriano-Remensis (ibid., folio 43r), we see the place sign for Huexotzinco (Place of the Small Willow) and a warrior. Quiñones Keber (1995, 231) explains that the line that appears ties him to the place sign of Mexico Tenochtitlan, which specifies the destination of the jade bead and gold necklace he carries.

GOLD BELLS IN THE ARCHAEOLOGICAL RECORD

The excavations of the Great Temple of the Aztecs have yielded a huge amount of information, particularly on religious and political aspects of the Mexica. The

FIGURE 5.14. Funerary bundle, Codex Magliabechiano (1970), folio 56r.

extraordinary finds within the offerings of the Templo Mayor are especially noteworthy. They have thrown light on the role played by the supernatural, especially by Huitzilopochtli and Tlaloc.

Offerings 14 (figure 5.15) and 10 are located on the southern half of the Templo Mayor, Huitzilopochtli's Temple. Two orange burial urns, which seem to form a pair, were found by Eduardo Matos Moctezuma and his team on Huitzilopochtli's Temple. The urns, which have straight walls and rounded bases with ceramic lids, represent deities. They were found in offerings 10 and 14, respectively. According to Nicholson and Quiñones Keber (1983, 95), these ceramic vessels probably come from what is now the State of Campeche.

Leonardo López Luján (2005 [1994], 173) mentions that these urns represent deities in profile, armed with an atlatl and a bundle of darts. The urns found in offerings 10 and 14 contained incinerated human remains. Greenstone and gold beads predominated. Most of these objects showed signs of having been in a fire.

Two projectile points (helicoidal) made of obsidian were found in offering 14, which is important to the discussion here because it depicts an armed deity. The deity is Tezcatlipoca, who appears as a warrior carrying a spear-thrower. Furthermore, inside the urn more warrior attributes, such as spear points of obsidian mixed with gold and other materials, seem to pertain to Tezcatlipoca. War weapons and bells were found inside the urn, which depict the god in this burial urn. This is a good example of the relationship I am trying to establish among Tezcatlipoca, war, and

FIGURE 5.15. Funerary urn depicting Tezcatlipoca, found at the Templo Mayor in offering 14, no. 10-168823.

bells. In addition, Matos Moctezuma (1988, 106) believes an important warrior could have been buried in the urn because it was found on the side of the temple corresponding to Huitzilopochtli: "Because these vessels were located near the relief of Coyolxauhqui, the female warrior of the myth, and on the side of the Temple associated with Huitzilopochtli, the principal Aztec war god, I would argue that the cremations may have been those of outstanding military captains, honoured by interment in the pyramidal base of the Great Temple." These terra-cotta urns are the oldest objects found at the Templo Mayor, Construction Stage II (AD 1390), according to Matos Moctezuma (ibid., 54).

According to Emily Umberger (2007b, 23) the human remains were those of Tlatelolca rulers: "A circumstantial case can be constructed to identify the occupants of the two urns as Moquihuix and Teconal, the Tlatelolca leaders who fell together from the Tlatelolca temple, according to Durán. The primary evidence is the contents of the vessel on the left (Offering 14)."

GOLD WARRIOR FIGURINE FROM THE CLEVELAND MUSEUM OF ART

One of the few extant gold figurines depicting deities comes from the Cleveland Museum of Art (figure 5.2). The gold statuette depicts a standing warrior, possibly Tezcatlipoca or Huitzilopochtli (Baquedano 2005, 366).

One of the most important iconographic characteristics of Tezcatlipoca is the forked heron feather hair ornament, the aztaxelli. This is clearly seen on the head of the figurine, and a ring around this ornament allows the figurine to be worn as a pendant. Tezcatlipoca as a warrior, as is the case here, carries spears and a shield. The feathers of the shield and those of the statue's headdress seem identical, and we can compare this kind of ornament with those of the representation of Tezcatlipoca in Durán's Atlas (Durán 1967, 1: plate 9).

The Cleveland Museum object carries a small flag that seems to come out of Tezcatlipoca's shield. Two arrows emerge from the figurine's shield, and arrows are also illustrated in Durán (ibid.). The earplugs in the Cleveland representation are very similar to those of Tezcatlipoca illustrated in the Codex Magliabechiano (Boone 1983, folio 92r).

I agree with Olivier (2003, 58) that the cord decoration around the head recalls the description by Durán (1967, 1: 37), which mentions a ribbon of polished gold that girded his head. This ribbon was finished by one earring, also of gold, on which were painted smoke motifs (una cinta bruñida de oro, and so on).

On his right hand, the statue carries a spear-thrower in the shape of a Fire Serpent. Large bells hang from the waist and from the spear-thrower, as well as the characteristic bells warriors wore around the ankles. This small gold figurine is a rare and good example of the importance attributed to gold in the depictions of Tezcatlipoca in his role as a warrior.

CONCLUSION

All of these gold and metal objects promoted state religion and functioned as propaganda in a small but powerful way. Warfare was the vehicle through which the

Aztec state acquired wealth and prestige; and Tezcatlipoca, as a major Aztec god depicted with arrows, represented a successful warrior, clad in shimmering gold and full of symbolic power, including that of his sonorous metal bells.

Gold had played a very small part in luxury objects in Mesoamerica until the Late Postclassic period when its use increased considerably, especially among the Aztecs. Most Mesoamerican peoples valued gold but not the way the Aztecs did. We see the symbol for gold as an emblem of power used in a variety of media: in large sculptures such as Coyolxauhqui and small objects such as terra-cotta vessels. Gold as a symbol was also used in a variety of media: in codices, shells, pottery, and similar items.

I have suggested elsewhere (Baquedano 2005, 367; 2011) that gold was as important as jade or turquoise before the Spanish conquest, not less important as many scholars have long insisted. As an example, Esther Pasztory (1983, 250–52) claims that "gold, which was secondary in importance, was called teocuitlatl, 'excrement of the gods,' and was not usually a metaphor for beauty."

It is therefore revealing that important gods are depicted wearing gold or the gold symbol. We cannot continue to say that gold ranked second after jade or turquoise. It is time we began to use the new excavations and finds to continue to discover and decode the meaning of materials among the ancient Mexicans.

I have tried to show in this chapter that gold was used as propaganda, designed to convey messages about how the elite wanted to be viewed—as rich and powerful. Certain gods like Tezcatlipoca reinforced precisely that message.

Acknowledgments. I thank Natalie Wilkinson for the drawing of the vessel found at Zultepec and for her invaluable help in organizing the volume. I would also like to thank Alison Oldham for her editorial suggestions. I gratefully acknowledge the Cleveland Museum of Art for its kind permission to reproduce the photographs that appear in this chapter.

NOTE

1. The codices listed by Olivier are Borgia, Vaticanus B, Fejérváry-Mayer, Cospi, Laud, Nuttall, Porfirio Díaz, Aubin, Borbonicus, Vaticanus A, Durán Atlas, Ramírez, and Matritense del Real Palacio.

6

Gender Ambiguity and the Toxcatl Sacrifice

CECELIA F. KLEIN

At the time of the Spanish conquest of central Mexico in 1521, the Aztecs in control of the region were staging elaborate rituals in and around their capital Tenochtitlan, located on a small but densely populated island in Lake Texcoco.[1] One of the most important and unusual rites occurred during the Aztec month Toxcatl, when the heart of a young enemy captive chosen the previous year to impersonate the Aztec god Tezcatlipoca, "Smoking Mirror," was removed atop a small pyramid located near a place named Tlapitzauayan. According to the sixteenth-century Franciscan Bernardino de Sahagún, who in 1529 had arrived at the Spanish capital that rose above the ruins of Tenochtitlan, Tlapitzauayan was located on the southern mainland, on a road leading to the city of Iztapalapan, today a suburb of Mexico City known as Ixtapalapa (Sahagún 1950–82, book I: 115; Siméon 1977 [1885], 639).[2]

Although Sahagún never witnessed the Toxcatl rite, he described it at length in his encyclopedic Florentine Codex, in which he included his Aztec informants' vivid description of the ideal victim's physical appearance. This extraordinary passage, written in Nahuatl alongside Sahagún's Spanish translation, takes up over two pages of that massive manuscript (Sahagún 1979 [1575–78], 2: folios 30v–31r). Since it is highly improbable that the Franciscan either asked for or expected such a lengthy and passionate exegesis from his informants, I have always assumed that the subject held special meaning for them. In these pages I propose a possible explanation for their enthusiasm. I will argue not only that the young Aztec impersonator was chosen for his androgynous appearance but also that, during the events leading

DOI: 10.5876/9781607322887.c006

up to the moment of his death, his gender—but not his sex—was symbolically feminized to the point where he transcended the male-female binary altogether. The impersonator's increasingly ambiguous gender, in other words, served as a visual sign of his association with, and ultimate transformation into, the god himself.

I have suggested previously that Sahagún's passage describing the Toxcatl impersonator reads like the rapt portrayal of a man whose beauty approximated that of the ideal unmarried Aztec woman (Klein 2001). Conjuring up for us a vivid mental image of the young impersonator, it lists his numerous physical perfections: his slender build, ideal height, unblemished skin, and straight nose, as well as the absence of injuries and deformities, among other physical assets (Sahagún 1950–82, book III: 66). The impersonator was, reports Sahagún, "like something smoothed, like a tomato, like a pebble, as if sculptured in wood; he was not curly-haired, curly-headed...his teeth were [like] seashells...he was not of hatchet-shaped buttocks; he was not of flabby buttocks; he was not of flabby thighs" (ibid., 66–68).[3] Perhaps most telling were the informant's references to the youth's long hair, which the friar in one place says "fell to his loins." In another place he says it fell "down to the waist" (ibid., 9, 69). To judge by painted manuscripts such as the immediately post-conquest Codex Mendoza, only girls and unmarried women among the Aztecs wore their hair both long and loose. The hair of young Aztec boys, like that of some adult men, was typically cut short just below the ears, while older boys and commoner men who let their hair grow long usually tied it at the nape of the neck (Berdan and Anawalt 1992, folios 60r, 71r).[4]

The theory that the Aztec Tezcatlipoca impersonator may have been chosen for his androgynous appearance is supported by the small paintings that illustrate Sahagún's discussion of the events of Toxcatl (Sahagún 1979 [1575–78], 1: folios 30r–32r).[5] These images, each contained within a rectangular frame, were painted by anonymous male natives already trained in European pictorial techniques and conventions. If we take up the scenes according to their appearance in the text, the first scene, which depicts the young man at the moment when he has just been chosen to represent the deity, shows his hair to be as short as that of the considerably smaller men who surround him (figure 6.1). His slender, perfect body, however, has been placed on the central axis in full frontal view and at arm's length from his companions, whose smaller size surely connotes their subservient status. Moreover, the artist has depicted him as nude except for his loincloth, in contrast to his attendants, who wear capes. Thus while the artist provided neither the hair nor the clothing that would unequivocally identify the impersonator as effeminate, he did emphasize the physical perfection of his body.

The Tezcatlipoca impersonator's physical beauty was probably intended to signify not only that the youth was worthy of representing the god but also that he was

GENDER AMBIGUITY AND THE TOXCATL SACRIFICE 137

FIGURE 6.1. Selection of the Tezcatlipoca impersonator; from Sahagún (1979 [1575–78], 1: folio 31r). Courtesy, Archivo General de la Nación, Mexico City.

worthy of dying on behalf of the ruler and the state. As Guilhem Olivier (2002, 121) has pointed out, according to the seventeenth-century native chronicler Domingo de San Anton Chimalpahin Cuauhtlehuanitzin, Tezcatlipoca had been highly revered in his home city of Chalco as "a great king or lord." Sahagún, as Olivier has also noted, wrote that the Aztec ruler personally dressed the impersonator just prior to his sacrifice. Olivier concludes from this that the Tezcatlipoca impersonator was a substitute for the ruler himself (ibid., 122–23; Sahagún 1950–82, book II: 69). By giving up his own life, according to this logic, the doomed youth made it possible for the ruler to live on for at least another year.

The idea that the Tezcatlipoca impersonator was chosen for his feminine beauty would by no means be unusual given what we know about man-gods and religious art elsewhere in world history. The trope certainly recalls a number of European images of Jesus who, like Tezcatlipoca, held a royal title: King of Heaven. Some of these images depict Christ even well before his crucifixion with a grace, a softness of form, and lightness of skin and sometimes hair that we today, like European artists of the time, typically associate with women. The Byzantinist Thomas Mathews (1993, 121) argues persuasively that as far back as the early Christian era, depictions of Christ "often showed a decidedly feminine aspect which we overlook at our own risk." Citing the Gnostic Gospels, which alternately refer to Christ as Mother, female as well as male, and androgynous, Mathews provides as example the full, beardless face, narrow shoulders, and broad, rounded hips of the Christ in the fifth-century apse mosaic in Blessed David, Thessalonica, whose light hair "falls copiously on his shoulders" (ibid., 18, 138, figure 6.2).[6] This parallels David Freedberg's citation of the eyewitness description of Christ by a Roman named Lentulus as "tall and comely," with "a brow smooth and very calm," a face "without wrinkle or blemish," fair skin, and hair that was smooth and parted in the middle (Freedberg 1989, 210–12, 476n39). As Mathews points out, by avoiding a literal rendering of scripture, which states that Christ's head was shaved prior to his death, early Christian artists could use Christ's long, flowing locks to distinguish him from the other men around him (Isaiah 50:6 and 53:7; Acts 8:32; Mathews 1993, 123, 126).[7]

Late medieval and Renaissance artists often did the same. Many portrayals of Jesus at that time depict him with smooth white skin and long, loose, often light hair that distance him from the often darker, conspicuously ugly (and sometimes bald) men who surround him (figure 6.3). In some paintings, these features combine with Christ's long, flowing robes; in others with a nearly naked, hairless, and softly contoured body to remind us forcefully of Isaiah's biblical pronouncement (Isaiah 63:1–2) of the Messiah as "beautiful" (figures 6.4 and 6.5).[8] Leo Steinberg has contended that the knots and flowing extensions of Christ's loincloth in some scenes of the crucifixion symbolized his phallus (figure 6.6), but it could be just as easily argued that the gauzy fabrics and their curving forms function to feminize him.[9] In scenes of Christ's baptism, as Steinberg and Richard Trexler have pointed out, some late medieval artists either greatly minimized the Savior's genitals or eliminated them entirely (Steinberg 1996, 91–94; Trexler 1993).[10]

The Aztec youth who was sacrificed to the god Tezcatlipoca not only approximated a woman's beauty, however. He also behaved in an unusual fashion. The second of Sahagún's illustrations of the events of Toxcatl refers to his informant's mention that once the youth had been selected, "there was taken the greatest care that he be taught to blow the flute" (Sahagún 1950–82, book II: 68; figure 6.7). Following a period of training, according to Sahagún, the impersonator was allowed to roam about the city for the remainder of the year, closely attended by

FIGURE 6.2. Christ in the vision of Ezekial. Detail of apse mosaic, *Blessed David, Thessalonica* (ca. 1425–50); from Mathews (1993, figure 89). Courtesy, Thomas Mathews.

140 GENDER AMBIGUITY AND THE TOXCATL SACRIFICE

FIGURE 6.3. Albrecht Dürer, *Christ among the Doctors* (1506). © Museo Thyssen-Bornemisza, Madrid; from Mellinkoff (1993, 2: plate VIII.16).

guards, playing his flutes and whistles as he went.[11] Examples of such instruments have been retrieved archaeologically, so we know these flutes were probably made of unfired clay and therefore fragile.[12] In this scene, Sahagún's artist has clad the impersonator in a cape and placed him in the company of two other men, one of whom likewise plays a flute.

Who is this second man with a flute? He may be the youth's music teacher, but he could also be the young man whom Sahagún (1950–82, book II: 76) mentions as having "lived together" with the Tezcatlipoca impersonator. The Dominican chronicler Diego Durán (1971, 126), who like Sahagún gathered native testimony following the conquest, also mentions in regard to Toxcatl a second man, a slave, who he says was, like the principal impersonator, dressed as Tezcatlipoca. We are told little about this other man other than that he lived with the principal impersonator and was eventually sacrificed.

No doubt reflecting our own homophobia, modern scholars writing about Toxcatl never mention this other man, referring only to the four women—each

FIGURE 6.4. Rueland Freuf the Younger, *Betrayal and Arrest of Christ* (ca. 1496); from Mellinkoff (1993, 2: plate IX.17). Courtesy, Stiftsmuseum, Kosterneuburg, Germany.

142 GENDER AMBIGUITY AND THE TOXCATL SACRIFICE

FIGURE 6.5. Giovanni Bellini, *Christ Blessing* (ca. 1500). © 2005 Kimbell Art Museum, Fort Worth, Texas; from Kimbell Art Museum (1987, 167).

named after an Aztec goddess—who were reportedly "married" to the young god impersonator twenty days before his sacrifice (Sahagún 1950–82, book II: 9, 70).[13] Might the impersonator not have been provided with a male sexual partner as well?

FIGURE 6.6. Hans Baldung Grien, *Crucifixion*; from Mellinkoff (1993, 2: plate VII.31). Courtesy, Bayerische Staatsgemäldesammlungen, Staatsgalerie Aschaffenburg, Germany (ca. 1516).

144   GENDER AMBIGUITY AND THE TOXCATL SACRIFICE

FIGURE 6.7. The Tezcatlipoca impersonator playing his flute; from Sahagún (1979 [1575–78], 1: folio 31r). Courtesy, Archivo General de la Nación, Mexico City.

There are a number of references in Sahagún, as well as other chroniclers, to the bisexuality of the god he represented. A shape-shifting transsexual, Tezcatlipoca is said in several Aztec myths to have introduced the Aztecs to what the Spaniards called the "nefarious sin"; in another he changes into a woman to seduce his enemy (Alva Ixtlilxóchitl 1985, 1: 277; Sahagún 1950–82, book V: 171; Torquemada 1975, 1: 34–35; 2: 393; see also Klein 2001, 222). In most of these accounts, the god is accompanied by another man with whom he is explicitly said to have had sexual relations.[14] Indeed, Tezcatlipoca was addressed as "wretched sodomite" by those whose fortunes had been reversed, including those suffering from hemorrhoids and other diseases of the anus (Klein 2001, 219).[15]

Sahagún's text tells us that at the end of the year, the impersonator's "wives" left him at the place named Tlapitzauayan, whereupon he went forward to ascend the

GENDER AMBIGUITY AND THE TOXCATL SACRIFICE 145

FIGURE 6.8. Sacrifice of the Tezcatlipoca impersonator; from Sahagún (1979 [1575–78]), 1: folio 30v). Courtesy, Archivo General de la Nación, Mexico City.

pyramid steps "by himself . . . of his own free will" (Sahagún 1979 [1575–78], 1: 115).[16] His guards also stayed behind, as the rite required that his sacrifice appear to be voluntary. This parallels Jesus's willingness to accept his own suffering and pending death without protest or resistance. However, what the two men did in the moments leading up to their deaths differed significantly. Sahagún says that "as he was taken up a step, as he passed one [step], there he broke, he shattered his flute, his whistle." I have assumed that this act was highly significant because in the accompanying illustration, which alludes to what the doomed impersonator did as he climbed the steps, the native artist made a point of showing the pyramid steps and the floor below littered with the impersonator's broken instruments (figure 6.8). Indeed, the flutes get as much of the viewer's attention as the victim does (Klein 2001, 223–24).[17]

What did these broken flutes signify to viewers of, and participants in, this ritual? Olivier has pointed out that flutes were played at times of war, the hunt, and homage to the sun and that, according to Sahagún, a newly installed ruler referred to himself as Tezcatlipoca's "backrest" and "flute" (Olivier 2002, 118–22, 2003, 214–26). By breaking the flutes, Olivier reasons, the youth signaled his imminent death, the cessation of his ability to communicate with the god on behalf of the ruler, and the need for the Aztecs to select a new impersonator (Olivier 2002, 122–23; Sahagún 1950–82, book VI: 43, 45). Ethnographic reports from Melanesia, as well as South America, however, have noted the association of flutes with the male sex and in some places specifically with the phallus.[18] There is evidence that this was the case in pre-conquest central Mexico as well. In Nahuatl the word for flute, *tlapitzalli,* contains the root *pitz,* which also appears in an adjective, *pitzaoac,* "thin," used by Sahagún's Nahua informants to describe the penis (ibid., book X: 39; see also Karttunen 1992 [1983], 197). The French ethnographer Jacques Galinier, who worked for many years among Otomí speakers living in the Sierra de Puebla, tells us that the Otomí today, whose ancestors lived among the Aztecs in pre-conquest times, associate both the flute and the whistle with the penis. Galinier (1984, 54) notes that the Otomí word *pita* refers not just to a flute or whistle but to the male sex organ as well. Significantly, the Nahuatl word *tlapitzalli* forms the root of Tlapitzauayan, the place where the Tezcatlipoca impersonator stayed briefly before being sacrificed. Whereas Tlapizauayan can be translated as "Place of the Flutes," *pitzauayan* can also mean "to speak in a high voice, to sing like a woman" (Siméon 1977 [1885], 387).[19]

By breaking his flutes, according to this logic, the impersonator underwent a symbolic castration. This may further relate to the fact that in pictorial manuscripts painted outside the Aztec capital before the Spanish conquest, Tezcatlipoca is often depicted with a missing foot that typically has been replaced by the smoking mirror that gives him his name (figure 6.9). I have proposed elsewhere that the missing foot in these images was a sign of the god's ambiguous gender (Klein 2001, 224).[20] Galinier (1984, 45) reports that the Otomí today associate a missing leg or foot with emasculation and effeminacy. An Otomí word for foot, *kwa,* also means penis, while some surviving Aztec flutes terminate in a foot.[21] Other field reports reveal that associations among the male sex organ, flutes, whistles, and the leg and foot exist among other Mesoamerican groups as well. Victoria Bricker (1973, 113), for example, reports for the Tzotzil Maya at Chamula, located in Chiapas, a link between the phallus and a missing or injured foot or leg.

GENDER AMBIGUITY AND THE TOXCATL SACRIFICE   147

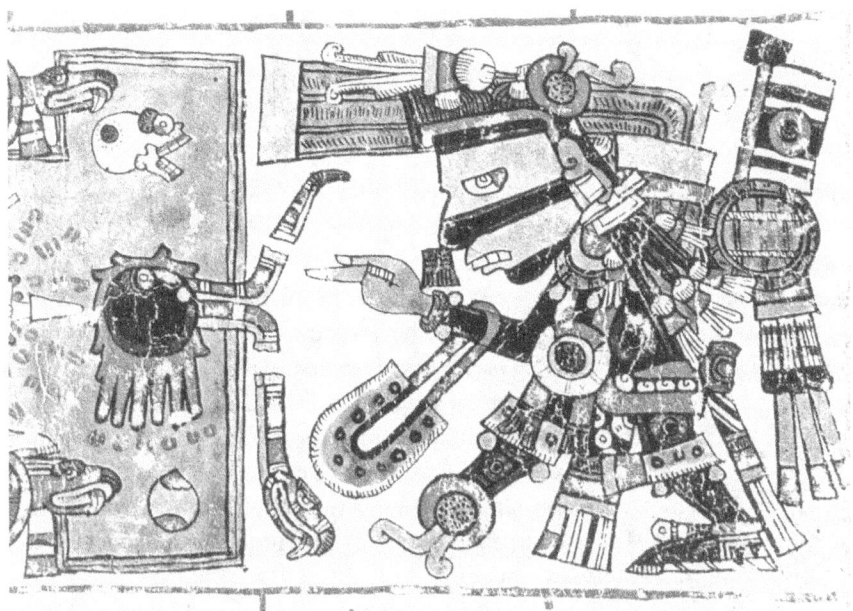

FIGURE 6.9. Tezcatlipoca, Codex Borgia; from Nowotny (1976, 21). Courtesy, the Akademische Druck- ü. Verlagsanstalt, Graz, Austria.

This does not mean, however, that the victim at his death was understood to have turned into a woman. Neither Sahagún nor any other Colonial period source ever says that the impersonator was literally castrated either before or following his sacrifice.[22] This is significant, given visual evidence that the Aztecs did castrate at least some of their enemies. Most of the known Aztec stone and clay statues of a man dressed in a flayed human skin lack a penis; in some cases, the testicles are missing as well.[23] There is no indication that a penis was ever present on most of these statues, which rules out the possibility that they were broken off by prudish clerics in the years following the conquest.[24] The statues are usually interpreted as representations of the Xipe Totec, "Our Lord the Flayer," an Aztec god of war depicted in sixteenth-century pictorial manuscripts wearing a flayed skin, but I have suggested elsewhere that they are commemorative "portraits" of the so-called Xipeme, men known to have temporarily worn the flayed skins of sacrificed war captives on behalf of the latters' captors.[25] Regardless of which interpretation one favors, there can be no doubt that the skins these figures wore came from a former enemy who had been castrated. The fact that the Toxcatl impersonator was perceived throughout his ordeal as biologically 100 percent male is further indicated by the fact that, shortly before his death, his hair was bound up like a warrior's (Sahagún 1950–82, book II: 70). Warfare in Aztec Mexico was, for the most part, a male occupation.

Nonetheless, the impersonator's broken flutes surely symbolized an intensified feminization of his gender. I deduce this from the increasing presence of visual traits and behaviors on the youth's part that, then as now, would have connoted the generative nurturing powers and physical and spiritual beauty normally associated with women. For artists who largely communicate without the aid of spoken language, whether European painters or Aztec officials in charge of scripting and staging calendrical ceremonies, gender signs can be effective means of expressing qualities and states of being that have nothing to do with their subject's reproductive organs or choice of sleeping partner. As Joan Scott (1988, 45) has noted, gender signs "are not always literally about gender itself."[26] Steinberg has made us well aware that it was particularly in medieval and European depictions of those most fateful moments at the end of Christ's life that we see the use of signs of feminine beauty to mark the remarkable physical and spiritual transformations taking place in the Savior's body. The same artistic logic and artistic process were at work in the rituals leading up to the Toxcatl sacrifice.

This comparison of the Toxcatl victim to the crucified Jesus is not without some historical justification, for there are hints that Toxcatl came to be associated with Holy Week in the Early Colonial period. Sahagún (1950–82, book III: 9) wrote that Toxcatl, which in his words was "the most important of all the [Aztec] feasts," was "like Easter, and fell near Easter Sunday—a few days after." This is particularly interesting given Sahagún's mention, noted earlier, that Tlapitzauayan was "near the Iztapalapan road, which goes to Chalco" (Sahugún 1982 [1977], 1: 155).[27] At Tlapitzauayan, Sahagún adds, the youth "turned toward the city."[28] Further down the same page he mentions a "second station" at Ixtapalapan where the same gods were honored, in all likelihood the Tlapitzauayan to which Sahagún refers. From there the impersonator traveled to the place of his sacrifice, described by Sahagún as a small, poorly embellished *cu*, or pyramid, located at a deserted place on the side of a road "about a league or so from the city" (ibid.).[29] Richard Blanton has located what may be the remains of this temple at a site just east of Ixtapalapa, not far from the present-day town of Tlapitzahua(c).[30]

This may be significant because Ixtalpalapa is adjacent to Huixachtecatl, the hill now known as the Cerro de la Estrella, or "Hill of the Star," where prior to the conquest the Aztecs drilled New Fire at the end of every Aztec fifty-two-year cycle, or "century." The New Fire ceremony marked the successful transition from the previous cycle to a new one, a transition fraught with tension and fear. Today, the crucifixion of Christ is reenacted every year on Good Friday at the top of this same hill, which still bears the ruins of Aztec ceremonial structures at its summit. Although the inhabitants of Ixtapalapa today make much of the fact that their Semana Santa, or Holy Week, reenactments culminate at the very site where New Fire was drilled in pre-conquest times, Trexler (2003, 68–70) has shown that the custom of reenacting the crucifixion of Christ at Ixtapalapa cannot be documented prior to the 1880s.[31] Nonetheless, it may be significant, given Sahagún's association of Toxcatl with Easter and Tlapitzahuan with Iztapalapan, that Ixtapalapa has come to be known for the annual reenactment of Christ's sacrifice.

Although we have no documentary evidence of a post-conquest association of Christ's death with that of the Tezcatlipoca impersonator, there is an undocumented legend that the local Ixtapalapan shrine known as the Santuario de Santo Sepulcro, which today houses a wood statue representing Christ as El Señor de la Cuevita, "Our Lord of the Little Cave," overlies a pre-conquest temple for Tezcatlipoca.[32] The local Holy Week reenactments of the crucifixion for which Iztapalapa is so famous today took place for a time at the Santuario and always involved a procession of El Señor de la Cuevita (ibid., 70–71).[33] El Señor de la Cuevita is said to have saved the townfolk from a disastrous cholera epidemic in 1833, which may explain why the annual Feast of the Holy Cross at Ixtapalapa begins, on May 3, with offerings of thanks to him (Rodríguez 1991, 43, 74, 96).[34] The date is significant: although Durán (1971, 100, 426) wrote that Toxcatl began on May 19 or 20, Susan Milbrath (1998, 2005, personal communication, 2008) argues that it ran from May 7 to May 27, and Rafael Tena (1987, 109) puts the first day of Toxcatl as early as May 4.[35] The last date is one day later than May 3, the day that now marks the start of the festival cycle of the Holy Cross throughout much of Mexico. This raises the possibility that in the Colonial period, at Ixtapalapa the Catholic Feast of the Holy Cross was superimposed upon, and in some way conflated with, Toxcatl. If this was the case, the sacrificed Tezcatlipoca impersonator may have come to be associated with the Holy Cross itself.[36]

Johanna Broda (1999, 124–32) notes that the Feast of the Holy Cross, or Santa Cruz, in Mexico retains many features of the pre-conquest Aztec month festival Huey tozoztli, which immediately preceded Toxcatl. Like Huey tozoztli, the Feast of the Holy Cross is related to agricultural fertility and the petition for rain (Olivera 1979, 156). Mercedes Olivera, however, in her study of the ceremony of the Holy Cross in the Nahuatl-speaking *municipio* of San Nicolás Citlala in eastern Guerrero, relates the Feast of the Holy Cross directly to Toxcatl (Olivera 1979, 156).[37] This is particularly interesting because the female-gendered Santa Cruz (Holy Cross) of San Nicolás Citlala is sometimes addressed as male; its gender, as was that of the Tezcatlipoca impersonator, is ambiguous.[38] Moreover, like Toxcatl, the Feast of the Holy Cross marks the imminent end of the winter dry season, a time when farmers in particular were anxiously hoping for the beginning of the summer rainy season and the rebirth of vegetation. Toxcatl's pivotal position at the end of the dry season explains the meaning of its name: "Something Dry" (Heyden 1991, 188, citing Durán). In San Nicolás Citlala, Santa Cruz is believed to provide the town with nourishment by intervening with the master of rain, an overtly indigenous supernatural. Shortly after the ceremony, the townspeople sow their seeds. Moreover, the importance of the Feast of the Holy Cross as the introduction of the rainy agricultural season is widespread. As Broda (1999, 125) notes, "In the Basin of Mexico and adjacent areas there still exists the notion that on May 3 '*se abre el temporal*,'" meaning that "the agricultural cycle of dryland farming as well as the rainy season 'are opened.'"

The church's frequent synchronization of Catholic festivals and saints' days with indigenous feasts throughout Mesoamerica in the Colonial period is amply documented. Clergy and mendicants used native religious beliefs, including beliefs in Aztec deities, to help assimilate the indigenous population to Catholicism. Tezcatlipoca was one of the deities most frequently used for this purpose. This is seen in Sahagún's *Colloquios*, written in 1564, which Louise Burkhart (1988, 67) says was an attempt to recreate the discourse about religion that had occurred in 1524, just three years after the conquest. Composed by Sahagún's Nahua assistants—who had been educated at the Colegio de Santa Cruz in Tlatelolco—and informed by four of the friar's elderly Nahua informants, the *Colloquios* reflects, in Burkhart's words, "an unusually high degree of Nahua participation" (ibid., 66). In the text, Tezcatlipoca, perceived by Spanish mendicants as "the major Nahua god," is invoked as—in Burkhart's words—"the closest Nahua parallel" to the Christian God (ibid., 70). Forms of address applied to Tezcatlipoca in earlier times are used in the *Colloquios* to refer to God the Father (ibid., 68).[39] In this way, according to Burkhart, the Aztec deity helped to "ease the transition from old to new" (ibid.). Viviana Díaz Balsera (2005, 49, 70) points out that this process of acculturation guaranteed that the old deities and beliefs were not completely eliminated by the new religion and that "Tezcatlipoca would live on in the lands of Anahuac sometimes as Lucifer and sometimes as God the Father, the One by Whom All Live." More important, Díaz Balsera (ibid., 94) sees in colonial sources a perceived parallel between the requisite sacrifice of Aztec god impersonators such as the Toxcatl victim and the Christian God's need to sacrifice his son. Art history confirms this association. Carol Callaway and Pedro Escalante Gonzalbo, among others, have shown on iconographic grounds that Mexicans of the colonial era understood Christ's death in terms of what they remembered, or had been told, about pre-conquest human sacrifice (Calloway 1990, 211; Escalante Gonzalbo 2002). It would not be surprising to learn that, during the years following the conquest, memories of the sacrificed Tezcatlipoca victim had mutated into memories of the sacrificed Jesus.

Regardless of whether there was a strong historical connection between the Toxcatl sacrifice and the crucifixion, it remains a fact that, particularly in southern Europe, medieval and Renaissance painters often expressed Christ's heightened vulnerability prior to and at Calvary by means of his pale skin, lack of developed musculature, *contrapposto* pose, and—particularly in the north, outside of Italy—absent or minimized genitalia (figure 6.10). To the south, the High Renaissance Italian artist Raphael depicted a more mundane vision of the resurrected Christ, using a different but by now familiar set of female gender signs (Béguin and Garofalo 2001, plate 18). Similar artistic tropes, often including feminine-looking garments, were used in Renaissance Spanish and colonial New World sculptures and paintings of the crucifixion toward similar ends. As Trexler (1993) has pointed out, here it is often the clothing Christ wears that conveys the message of his transcendent status. We see an example in the elaborately embroidered garment covering the groin of the graceful, white-skinned statue of the Christ of Ixquimilpan painted by the eighteenth-century Mexican artist José de Ibarra, where the legend at the bottom of the painting reads "Faithful portrait of the most beautiful image of our Crucified Lord"[40] (my translation; figure 6.11).[41] Trexler has noted that in Mexico and the Spanish Southwest today, as in Spain, statues of Christ on the cross are often dressed by women in women's slips or petticoats, no doubt to honor them by attributing to them a feminine beauty. At the Catholic shrine of Chimayo in New Mexico, the wood statue of Christ crucified known as *Christ of Esquipulas* has been dressed on occasion in the past in what appears to be a woman's apron or pinafore (figure 6.12).[42]

As Mircea Eliade has shown, world history is full of examples of beliefs in bisexual, androgynous divinities and founding ancestors.[43] Many of them appear in art as sensuous, graceful, and gender-ambiguous figures.[44] However, as we have seen, male deities and religious participants who bear feminine attributes cannot necessarily be seen as anything but fully sexual males. Eliade (1990 [1986], 502–6) noted that a man who ceremonially dons the clothes of a woman is normally not believed to have become a woman; rather, he realizes the union of the sexes to return to primordial unity. Similarly, Ana Mariella Bacigalupo (2004, 504–5, 514, 516) has described Mapuche male spiritual practitioners, or "shamans," in Chile as "co-gendered," since they combine male and female powers and can move between masculinity and femininity, but she emphasized that they are not hermaphrodites, homosexuals, or transvestites and are never believed to turn into women. Mathews (1993, 138) concluded something similar regarding the apocryphal Gospel of Thomas's references to the union of male and female in Christ as a "neutralization of sexuality." For Mathews, gender here is a metaphor "intended to work on a philosophical level to express unification of the two sides of the human personality, somewhat like Jung's *animus* and *anima*" (ibid.).

FIGURE 6.10. Fray diGiorgio Martini, *Christ Stripped at Calvary* (ca. 1497); from Torriti (1977, 406). Courtesy, Pinacoteca Nazionale di Siena.

FIGURE 6.11. José de Ibarra, *Cristo de Sta. Teresa* (ca. 1750); from Egan (1993, 64). Museo Nacional de Virreinato, Tezpotzatlan, Mexico/Instituto Nacional de Antopología e Historia. Reproduction authorized by the Instituto Nacional de Antopología e Historia, Mexico City.

FIGURE 6.12. *Christ of Esquipulas*, Chimayo, New Mexico. From photo by Custom Craft, Albuquerque, NM (ca. 2000).

Steinberg (1996, 16, 233) likewise clearly understood that Christ's graven and painted feminine traits served a strictly semiotic function. However softened by feminine attributes he may appear in art, Jesus, Steinberg has continually insisted, remained throughout his life and death a fully sexual male. Artistic feminizing of Christ's figure was intended to connote not a negation of his sexuality but what Steinberg called an "asexuation," a status expressing, in his words, "an ideal of manhood without blight of sex" (ibid., 247). In art, in other words, gender ambiguity signals Christ's ascent from the mundane material world to the spiritual realm and oneness with divinity without negating his biological maleness. Steinberg explained this by concluding that "being more, Christ cannot be less than a man" (ibid., 242).

However, if Sahagún's informant's long and loving description of the physically perfect Toxcatl impersonator and his broken flutes has anything to teach us, Steinberg's emphasis was slightly off the mark. The true function of Christ's ambiguous gender in scenes of the events leading up to and through his crucifixion and its aftermath was clearly similar to that of the carefully selected and choreographed ancient Tezcatlipoca impersonator who died to protect the Aztec ruler and ensure the rains. The Aztec impersonator's long hair, smooth skin, and broken flutes were not intended to reassure those who witnessed the rites of Toxcatl that "being more, he could not be less than a man." As we have seen, they functioned instead to send a clear visual message to everyone that, in the end, the youth had become much more than just a man.

NOTES

1. This chapter is a slightly modified version of a paper included in a festschrift titled *Public Life, Gender, and Private Conduct across the Early Modern and Modern World: Essays in Honor of Richard C. Trexler*, edited by Peter Arnade and Michael C. Rocke for publication by the Centre for Reformation and Renaissance Studies at the University of Toronto (2008). I am very grateful to the centre for permission to include it in this volume. The chapter could never have been written without the ongoing help of the late Dick Trexler, who provided inspiration, information, advice, and moral support throughout the project. Additional assistance came from Ruth Mellinkoff, whose knowledge of medieval painting and openness to unconventional topics is unparalleled. I am also extremely grateful to my research assistants Angélica Afanador and Janet Stephens, who tirelessly fed me books and articles, and my colleague Joanna Woods-Marsden for helping me identify Renaissance sources and setting me straight on certain matters pertaining to the Renaissance. Thanks, too, to Susan Milbrath and Carolyn Tate, who helped with Mesoamerican calendrical matters, and to Mary Weismantle for references regarding flute symbolism in South America.

2. Siméon, in his 1885 French/Nahuatl dictionary, apparently drew upon this passage by Sahagún when he wrote that Tlapitzauayan was located "together with the city of Iztapalapan, where was sacrificed to the god Tezcatlipoca the youth who had been cared for and honored for a year" (639; my translation). In the remainder of this chapter I use Iztapalapan to refer to the pre-conquest site and Ixtapalapa for the modern community.

3. Olivier (2002, 133n56) notes that the youth chosen to represent the god Quetzalcoatl at Chollolan (today Cholula) was also selected for his flawless beauty; see Durán (1994 [1581] 1, 63).

4. This codex, now in the Bodleian Library in Oxford, England, was painted ca. 1541–42 in Mexico City. There are a few exceptions to this rule in the Codex Mendoza; see folios 68r, 69r, and 71r for images of several men wearing their hair at shoulder length and unbound. On folio 71r, however, in the scene of punishment of adulterers, the hair of the two adulterous women is considerably longer than that of the single male youth whose unbound hair falls just to his shoulders. The hair of the other three adulterous men is even shorter, falling just below the ears. Warriors were entitled to a special cut or hairdo indicative of their particular military status.

5. Six of these illustrations line the left sides of the two pages that describe the impersonator's bodily perfections. They are slightly out of order, however, and the last, which appears on a separate page further on in the manuscript (folio 32r), matches those on folios 19v, 20r, and 20v, which depict impersonators of the god Xipe Totec in relation to the festivities that took place during the month of Tlacaxipehualiztli. It is obvious that this last illustration was intended to illustrate the previous chapter and became misplaced.

6. For the relevant apocryphal passages, see Pagels (1989 [1979]). Mathews (1993, 115, 139) notes that legend had it that the artist had started out to represent the Mother of God and mysteriously changed the subject overnight to an image of Jesus. The inscription below refers to the unnamed patron by a feminine noun, suggesting that the patron was a woman. Mathews raises the question of whether Christ's appearance was designed to correlate with the viewer's (in this case the patron's) gender and expectations (ibid., 138–39). Similarly, Trexler (1993, 109) suggests that Christians "might feminize the gender of crucifixes to suit the gender of their devotees."

7. See also Marrow (1979, 68–69) on this point and Trexler (1993, 112n2). Mathews notes that Greek and Roman artists had used the same trope to signal divinity. He also sees breasts in some early Christian artworks depicting Christ (Mathews 1993, 12). If these really are breasts, then they represent rare instances of artists representing Christ's biological sex as both male and female. The body of an androgyne is simultaneously and equally male and female—that is, it displays biological, rather than cultural, signs of both sexes. As Wendy Doniger O'Flaherty points out, "To say that God is androgynous is very different from saying that God is an androgyne." See Doniger O'Flaherty (1980, 283–84); Eliade (1990 [1986], 305). For androgyny in Greek art, see Meeks (1974). For androgyny in Aztec religion, see Gonzalez Torres (1995).

8. Margery Kempe (1985), in the fifteenth century, intuited that Christ's body had been perfect in every respect—white, delicate, and beautiful. As Trexler (1993, 108) notes, the Bible states that Christ was naked at his crucifixion.

9. For additional images of Christ crucified with a flowing loincloth, see Steinberg (1996, figures 102, 103, 284); Mellinkoff (1993, 2: plates VII.26, VII.28). For a critique of Steinberg's emphasis on Christ's masculinity, see Bynum (1982, 1991).

10. For paintings that minimize or leave out Christ's genitals, see Mellinkoff (1993, 2: plates III.4, III.37, IX.24). See also Marrow (1979, 68–69).

11. Much has been made, by those who like to romanticize Aztec human sacrifice, of the youth's seeming freedom to roam at will during this time. Sahagún (1950–82, book II: 69) contends, however, that the victim was closely followed not only by eight servants but also by four "constables" whose duty presumably was to ensure that he would not flee. Durán (1971, 126) identifies all twelve of these attendants as guards who were present "to prevent him from fleeing." According to him, "These guards were always alert, their eyes upon him. If [the man managed] to fall, the negligent guard took his place" (ibid.).

12. For illustrations of Aztec ceramic flutes, see Guggenheim Museum (2004, nos. 247, 248).

13. On the impersonator's four "wives," see Durán (1971, 126).

14. See Klein (2001, 220–21), for a discussion of the evidence that Tezcatlipoca was bisexual.

15. One of Tezcatlipoca's names was Moyocoyatzin, "Capricious One." The god's embodiment of the fickle, uncontrollable nature of fate doubtless underlay his bisexuality.

16. Sahagún says here that the pyramid was called Tlacochcalco, but further on in the same work (Sahagún 1979 [1575–78], I: 155) he omits the proper name of the pyramid. See also Sahagún (1950–82, book III: 10, 71), where he also gives an alternate spelling for the site: Tlapitzauhcan.

17. Three of the illustrations to Sahagún's text that are clearly out of order depict a standing man dressed in what look like white longjohns cut off at the elbows and knees and a tall headdress with green plumes at the top. The black stripes painted across the person's face, together with the *tlachialoni* (magic mirror) held in his hand, identify the costume as Tezcatlipoca's. The images must refer to an event the text says occurred shortly after the impersonator had learned to play his flute. Sahagún says that at this time the Aztec ruler Moteuczoma adorned the impersonator with lavish and costly garments and ornaments, pasting his head with feathers and painting his face black.

18. An example of flutes associated with the male sex appears in Herdt (1981, 233, 268, 271, 283); with the phallus, in Reichel-Dolmatoff (1971 [1968], 112, 115). Herdt (1981, 268) states that for the Sambia of New Guinea the flute represents the phallus not as the penis itself but as "a metaphor and sign for it." As does Herdt (ibid., 283) for the Sambia, Reichel-Dolmatoff (1971 [1968], 168) notes that Desana flutes are often paired, with a smaller flute

understood as the female counterpart to a larger, male flute. See also Murphy and Murphy (1985 [1974], 119–20) on the phallic meaning of the Mundurucu *karókó*, a long, hollow wooden tube they identify as "clearly a phallic symbol in the classic sense of the term."

19. Siméon (1977 [1885], 639) says the root words of Tlapitzauayan are *pitzaua* and *yan* (place). The former bears the same meaning as pitzauayan (ibid., 387). This differs somewhat from Samuel Martí's claim that the name derives from *pitzhua* and *nitla*; however, Martí's reading of the name is similar to that of Siméon: "significa tocar un instrumento de viento y otras cosas parecidas" (it means to play a wind instrument and similar things); see Martí (1953, 154).

20. It is curious that sixteenth-century manuscripts painted in the Aztec capital do not depict Tezcatlipoca with a missing foot. The reason for this is unclear, but it may be relevant that all extant pictorials from this area postdate the conquest and manifest considerable European artistic and cultural influence. The situation was probably different prior to the conquest. The pre-conquest Codex Borgia, which was probably painted by Nahuatl speakers living just to the east of Lake Texcoco in present-day Tlaxcala or Puebla, contains several images of Tezcatlipoca with a foot that is either missing and replaced by a smoking mirror or "caught" in something and thus hidden from view; see Nowotny (1976, plates 17, 21, 69 for the former; plates 3, 14 for the latter). Similarly, a fragmented pre-conquest stone relief from the Aztec capital depicts the earth deity apparently giving birth to Tezcatlipoca, whose left foot appears to be still inside the earth's womb and thus out of sight; see Nicholson (1954, 1967).

21. See, for instance, Guggenheim Museum (2004, no. 232). Another example of an Aztec flute in the form of a disembodied leg with a foot is on display in the American Museum of Natural History in New York.

22. The victim was, however, decapitated after his heart had been removed, and the head was threaded onto a skull rack for display (Sahagún 1950–82, book II: 10, 71).

23. For illustrations of Aztec statues of men wearing flayed skins, see Antiguo Colegio de San Ildefonso (1995, figures 108, 109).

24. Some ceramic figurines of a man wearing a flayed human skin do have a penis. Unfortunately, since most Aztec figurines have not been recovered under scientific conditions, it is impossible to know whether they are authentic or were produced for the modern market.

25. I have also argued this for Aztec stone carved masks of a face wearing a flayed skin; see Klein (1986, 143, 161n18 and 23). William Barnes (2009) thinks these statues are portraits of rulers in battle dress, since some rulers were said to lead their armies into battle dressed as Xipe Totec. I think this is highly unlikely. On the flaying of war captives dedicated to Xipe Totec and the wearing of their skins by men referred to as the Xipeme, see Sahagún (1950–82, book II: 4, 54, 57–60).

26. Scott cites a number of scholars whose pioneering work on gender transformed our understanding of the relation of gender concepts to the body.

27. In this account, written only in Spanish, Sahagún adds that the impersonator was transported to Tlapitzauayan from a place called Tepepulco, which we know was located on a small island just off the southern shore of Lake Texcoco, close to Tlapitzauayan. This detail is omitted from the Florentine Codex. Umberger (1996a, 256) notes Alvarado Tezozómoc's mention that the Aztec emperor Ahuitzotl, upon his return from his conquests in Oaxaca, "went to spend the night in Tlapitzahuayan where there was a temple of Tezcatlipoca"; see Avarado Tezozómoc (1975, 547).

28. It is possible that the city referred to was Chalco, as Durán states that Tezcatlipoca was its principal deity, but Sahagún's statement that Tlapitzauayan was near the road to Iztapalapan suggests otherwise (see note 1; see also Durán 1967, 2: 366).

29. Spaniards (mis)used the Caribbean word *cu* or *cue* for pyramid. As noted, Sahagún (1950–82, book I: 115) elsewhere says this pyramid was named Tlacochcalco, which translates as "House of Darts." In the capital, this name was given to buildings reserved for royalty and the nobility, including the military elite. Tezcatlipoca's association with rulership may explain why the building where his impersonator died was called Tlacochcalco.

30. Blanton (1972, 141, figure 50) named the site Ix-A-35; see also Umberger (1996a, 256). Blanton found no remains at the nearby site IX-A–34, which is partially overlaid by Tlapitzahua(c).

31. In Trexler's (personal communication, 2005) opinion, the modern reenactment of the crucifixion at the Cerro de la Estrella bears no direct historical relation to the preconquest New Fire ceremony. Trexler (2003, 92) notes that according to Santiago Guerra, in an interview published in *El Universal* in 1979, the play came to Ixtapalapa from Chimalhuacan in the nineteenth century. The reason given for the move was that the Cerro de la Estrella was considered an ideal place to stage the crucifixion. Nonetheless, Trexler (ibid., 24–63) documents a tradition of passion plays that occurred elsewhere in Mexico at a much earlier date.

32. Today, the original statue of El Señor de la Cuevita lies in a glass bier elevated high above the main altar of the Santuario. In the back of the church a more recently carved statue reclines at eye level in a manmade "cave." Rodríguez (1991, 94) says the original arrived in Ixtapalapa on May 3, 1833, along with three "brothers" (copies), one of which is at Amecameca, one in Totolapan, and the third in Tepalcingo. All four statues, according to her, are copies of a statue in Oaxaca. A more recent Web account of the arrival of El Señor de la Cuevita, which purports to represent "an ancient legend," makes no mention of either the "brothers" or a pre-Columbian shrine to Tezcatlipoca, claiming instead that the statue had been brought to Ixtapalapa in 1687, apparently alone, from the Oaxacan town of Etla to undergo restoration in Mexico City. In this version of the story, the statue disappeared shortly after its arrival at Ixtapalapa but was eventually found, rooted and immovable, in a cave. This was taken as a sign that Jesus wanted the statue to stay in Ixtapalapa. The proud townspeople built a hermitage behind the cave and later erected the Santuario over it.

33. The reenactment of the crucifixion is documented as taking place at the Santuario and its atrium in 1867 and again in 1921; see Trexler (2003, 92–93). Trexler thinks the switch to the Cerro de la Estrella occurred after 1867 and then briefly reverted back to the Santuario in the early twentieth century. Francis Toor witnessed a reenactment of the crucifixion in 1930 that took place not at the Cerro but at the Santuario. That performance followed an eight-year lull, which Trexler thinks is attributable to a legal prohibition against priests conducting religious rites out of doors (ibid., 92, 244n23).

34. This was also reported on the website of the VII Vicaría Episcopal, San Pablo Apóstol, in an essay titled "Semana Santa en Iztapalapa."

35. All of these dates are in the Julian Calendar, which was not replaced by the Gregorian Calendar until 1582. In the sixteenth century the Gregorian Calendar ran ten days ahead of the Julian Calendar. Thus events that transpired on May 4 in the Julian Calendar took place, in the years immediately following 1582, on May 14.

36. Farther south, the Feast of the Holy Cross coincides with the first zenith passage of the sun. Carolyn Tate (personal communication, 2005) suggests that in central Mexico the feast was moved back to coincide with Toxcatl.

37. At San Nicolás Citlala, the ceremony honoring Santa Cruz falls prior to the official Feast of the Holy Cross, between April 24 and May 2.

38. This kind of "gender switching" has long roots in Mesoamerica. The Classic period Maya maize deity, for example, could be manifested as either male or female; see Carolyn Tate (1999, 94). Moreover, certain dance movements and references to ambiguous gender documented for Toxcatl survive today in ceremonies conducted during or close to Holy Week. Sahagún (1950–82, book II: 74) mentions two "masters of youths" who, following the death of the Tezcatlipoca impersonator, began what he describes as "the dancing for the women." These men, he adds, "danced leaping; they danced just in the fashion of women" (ibid., 75). On offering priests who also danced at this time, he writes: "It was said: 'They make the Toxcatl leap'" (ibid.). These leaping dance movements are usually performed by transvestites; see Klein (2001, 207, 229).

39. Burkhart notes that Nahua forms of address such as *tloque nahuaque* and *ipalnemohuani*, which are used to refer to Tezcatlipoca in Sahagún's Florentine Codex, refer to God in the *Colloquios* and Sahagún's *Arte Adivino*. I have previously argued that Tezcatlipoca may have mutated after the conquest into the highland Maya cult figure variously known as Maximon, Mam, and San Simón (Klein 2001, 211–28).

40. "Verdadero Retrato de la Hermosisima Imagen de Nro. Señor Crucificado . . . que se Venera en el Convento antiguo de Señoras Carmelitas de alla de la Ciudad del México."

41. The painting is one of at least three copies by Ibarra of a no longer extant corn-paste crucifix housed near Ixmiquilpan in the state of Hidalgo. Today it can be seen in the Museo Nacional de Virreinato in Tepozotlan, Mexico.

42. I am greatly indebted to Richard Trexler (personal communication, 2004–5) for pointing out the female garments often placed on statues of Jesus on the cross in Latin America and at Chimayo; see also Trexler (1991) on this subject.

43. Among Mesoamericans, the practice of addressing as "Mother-Father" the most powerful pre-conquest male deities and ancestors, like present-day male political and religious leaders, is well documented for both the conquest period and the present; see Klein (2001, 186–89). Mathew Looper (2002) has argued that the Classic period Maya recognized a third gender, neither male nor female, for which he borrows the label "Two-Spirit People" used by Native Americans north of Mexico.

44. See, for instance, the Chinese torso of Bodhisattra in Kimbell Art Museum (1987, 124).

7

The Maya Lord of the Smoking Mirror

Susan Milbrath

One way to better understand Tezcatlipoca, a paramount god among the Aztecs, is to study his counterpart among the Maya. Both Kawil and Tezcatlipoca are represented with a smoking mirror and a serpent foot, and both share associations with the celestial realm and royalty (figures 7.1, 7.2; Milbrath 1999, 230–31). The name *k'awil* or *k'awiil* in Classic Maya glyphic texts usually includes a mirror glyph (T617a) with volutes of smoke (Macri and Looper 2003, 171; Schele and Miller 1983, 3–22). Often the mirror has a smoking ax, but occasionally this element is replaced by a smoking bone or a flaming torch (figures 7.3–7.5). In imagery of the Classic and Terminal Classic periods, an undulating serpent sometimes replaces one of Kawil's feet (figure 7.1; Freidel, Schele, and Parker 1993, figures 4.8, 4.11). Even though a serpent foot is not seen in Postclassic images of Kawil, his ophidian aspect is manifested by a serpent with the head of Kawil in the Codex Madrid (31b).

Postclassic images of Kawil (God K of the codices) show considerable variation. In addition to a serpent manifestation, he appears in an avian form with bird wings, a beak, and bird claws (figure 7.6). In many Postclassic images he has a long snout with branching elements, sometimes inset with a mirror (Milbrath 1999, figures 6e, 6f). In glyphic contexts, his head is represented with a long snout, fangs, and a smoking element that could be a mirror or an ax (figure 7.7).

Kawil's connection with maize is evident in a number of contexts (Freidel, Schele, and Parker 1993, 194–95; Milbrath 2002, 126; Schele and Mathews 1998, 116–17). Smoke volutes on his mirror sometimes resemble maize foliation (figures 7.1, 7.6,

FIGURE 7.2. Tezcatlipoca with a serpent foot and smoking mirror on his brow in Codex Telleriano-Remensis 3v (after Seler 1960–61, 3: 281, abb. 70).

FIGURE 7.1. Classic period relief of Kawil at Sayil has both the serpent leg and smoking mirror of central Mexican Tezcatlipoca (after Milbrath 1999, figure 6.3h).

7.8; Taube 1992a, figure 32f). Noting Kawil's association with vegetation symbols, especially maize, John Eric Thompson (1970, 289) proposed that Colonial period texts refer to him as Kauil, meaning "surplus of our daily bread [maize]." David Stuart's (1987, 15) phonetic reading of Kawil's name provides support for linking Kawil with maize (Taube 1992a, 78). The Cordamex dictionary defines *k'awil* as food, no doubt a reference to maize, but a secondary definition refers to the Maya word for the great-tailed grackle (*k'au*), a bird especially fond of maize (Milbrath 2002, 126). Perhaps this connection is implicit in a mural from Tulum that shows an avian Kawil with maize symbols (figure 7.6).

Other interpretations of the name *k'awil* suggest references to stone sculptures, flint, and stone ax heads associated with lightning (Freidel, Schele, and Parker 1993, 194–200). Some scholars connect Kawil's imagery with the word for obsidian (*tah* or *toh*; Taube 1992a, 75–76; Tedlock 1985, 365). This suggests a link with Tohil, the Quichean god of lightning and storms who was lord of a ruling lineage at the time

THE MAYA LORD OF THE SMOKING MIRROR 165

FIGURE 7.3. Early Classic Kawil with smoking ax emanating from Akbal mirror brow, Tikal Stela 31 (after Milbrath 1999, figure 6.3u).

FIGURE 7.4. Kawil's forehead mirror with a burning torch (after Milbrath 1999, figure 6.3i).

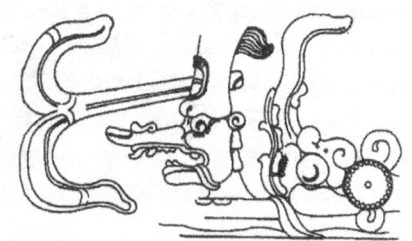

FIGURE 7.5. Kawil's head emerges from jaws of double-headed serpent flanking portrait of ruler on North Palace Substructure, Palenque (after Milbrath 1999, figure 6.3t).

of the conquest. Kawil is similarly connected with both royal lineage and lightning. As Karl Taube (1992a, 76) points out, Kawil's headdress elements—mirrors, fire, burning axes, torches, and cigars—may all allude to lightning.

Like Tohil, Kawil is a royal god linked with ruling lineages. Many Classic Maya rulers incorporate Kawil in their personal names or titles, especially at Tikal (Martin and Grube 2000).[1] The "God K in hand" glyph compound frequently refers to heir designation or accession, when a Maya king assumed power (Stuart, Houston, and Robertson 1999, 175; Taube 1992a, 78). And a glyph compound "Kawil's mirror-in-hand" usually denotes the presentation of Kawil at the time of an heir-designation event (Schele 1984, 304).

Kawil first appears with a mirror and smoking ax in the Early Classic period (figure 7.3). On an Early Classic incised bowl, Chac holds a serpent ax representing Kawil (Taube 1992a, figure 35a). Here Kawil has a smoking mirror on his brow and a smoking ax blade hafted through his mouth. Both his mirror and the ax blade seem

FIGURE 7.6. Kawil's celestial aspect as winged deity on sky band in Late Postclassic mural from Tulum (after Milbrath 1999, figure 6.3b).

to be shiny objects because they have "mirror infixes," a detail that also appears on some images of the Sun God (Milbrath 1999, 88–89, figure 3.8a; Schele and Miller 1983, 20). On Tikal Stela 31, Kawil's mirror is a nocturnal symbol with an Akbal, or darkness, infix and a smoking ax protruding from its center. The dark mirrors represented in Late Classic Maya vase paintings were probably made of obsidian traded to the lowland Maya (Reents-Budet 1994, 83, 322).

In the Late Classic period, Kawil's multiple personalities become evident in studying sets of contemporary monuments. For example, Kawil appears in different forms on the three panels in the Cross Group at Palenque, all of which record the same heir-designation and accession events (Milbrath 1999, 233, figure 3.6b, plates 11, 12; Robertson 1991, 20). Kawil appears as a manikin with a smoking mirror on his brow in the Temple of the Sun. Kawil takes a completely different form in the Temple of the Cross, which depicts a skeletal head with the number nine (*bolon*), alluding to the Bolon Dzacab aspect of Kawil (Schele and Mathews 1998,

FIGURE 7.7. Two variants of Kawil's Postclassic portrait head glyph, Paris Codex 24 and Madrid Codex 77 (after Milbrath 1999, figure 6.3d).

413; Thompson 1970, figures 7b, 7c, 7e, 7f, 7p). The Temple of the Foliated Cross depicts Kawil nestled in a spiral shell with a maize plant in his hand and a bone in place of his smoking ax (Robicsek 1979, 115; Stuart 1978, 167).

Kawil also takes different forms on four Seibal stelae, all marking the same 5 Ahau katun ending in AD 849 (Milbrath 2004, 91; Schele and Mathews 1998, figures 5.10, 5.14, 5.17, 5.21). On Seibal Stela 8, the ruler holds Kawil's head, which has a smoking mirror in front and maize foliation at the rear (figure 7.8). Stela 21 depicts Kawil as a manikin scepter held by the ruler as a royal insignia. On Stela 9, the ruler holds a serpent bar with Kawil positioned at the tail end of the sky serpent. Stela 10 shows the ruler wearing Kawil's smoking insignia, here represented as a tube with maize foliation. These monuments are part of a related set of stelae grouped around a radial pyramid (A–3) dedicated on the previous katun ending (7 Ahau; Schele and Miller 1998, figure 5.7). These multiple manifestations of Kawil evoke links with the many avatars of Tezcatlipoca.

KAWIL AND TEZCATLIPOCA

Kawil's form changes over the span of more than a thousand years, but he almost invariably wears a smoking mirror, also a principal identifying feature of Tezcatlipoca (figures 7.1, 7.3–7.11). Like Tezcatlipoca, Kawil is frequently associated with celestial imagery. Tikal Stela 31 shows Kawil with his lower torso replaced by the sky glyph (figure 7.3). Another Early Classic Tikal monument, Stela 1, depicts a sky serpent with its open jaw carrying a hatchet manikin with a serpent leg, a

FIGURE 7.8. Seibal Stela 8 showing the ruler holding the head of Kawil with smoke volutes that resembles maize foliation (after Milbrath 2004, figure 9).

FIGURE 7.9. Late Classic Kawil with smoking ax or mirror emanating from mirror on brow (Pier C of House A at Palenque; after Milbrath 1999, figure 6.3q).

FIGURE 7.10. Winged Kawil in jaws of coiled serpent with sky band arching overhead on painted capstone from Terminal Classic Temple of the Owls at Chichén Itzá (Structure 5C7; after Milbrath 1999, figure 6.3g).

FIGURE 7.11. Mirror-browed Kawil wearing T510f star (West Court of Palenque Palace; after Milbrath 1999, figure .6.3r).

precursor to Late Classic representations of Kawil as a manikin scepter (Jones and Satterthwaite 1982, figure 1; Proskouriakoff 1993, 16). Late Classic period representations also show Kawil emerging from the jaws of a celestial serpent (figure 7.5) or intertwined with a star glyph (figure 7.11). The Sarcophagus Lid from Palenque represents a sky band surrounding the deceased ruler Pakal II, who wears the smoking mirror of Kawil (Milbrath 1999, plate 10). A sky band arches over a winged Kawil on a Terminal Classic capstone from the Temple of the Owls at Chichén Itzá (figure 7.10). A Postclassic mural pictures Kawil as a bird with a sky-band body (figure 7.6).

Imagery of the Maya ruler wearing Kawil's smoking mirror recalls Aztec rulers represented as deities on the Tizoc Stone. Fourteen figures represent Tezcatlipoca as a conqueror wearing a costume linked with the Toltecs, and the ruler Tizoc also displays attributes of Tezcatlipoca. Emily Umberger (2005) points out that the ruler has supernatural powers because he not only wears Huitzilopochtli's hummingbird headdress but he also has Tezcatlipoca's severed leg issuing smoke.

Setting aside obvious chronological and stylistic differences, some clear links exist between representations of Tezcatlipoca from the central highlands and images of Kawil from the northern Maya lowlands (figures 7.1, 7.2). The smoking brow mirror and serpent foot of Tezcatlipoca in the Aztec Codex Telleriano-Remensis find an earlier precedent in a Terminal Classic relief from Sayil depicting Kawil, even though more than five centuries and almost a thousand miles separate the two images.

The smoking or burning serpent foot of both Kawil and Tezcatlipoca may symbolize fire serpents representing lightning (Olivier 2003, 263; Taube 1992a, 75). Guilhem Olivier (2003, 106, 235, 239–40) notes that Tezcatlipoca's smoking mirror foot relates to Tohil's act of creating fire by twisting his foot inside his shoe like a fire drill. In addition, Kawil is widely considered to be related to the Quichean god Tohil, a god of thunder and lightning.

The link between Kawil and Tezcatlipoca has been questioned by Taube (1992a, 75–79), who sees a stronger connection between Kawil and the rain god Chac and his central Mexican counterpart, Tlaloc. Indeed, Chac's lightning serpent sometimes represents Kawil (ibid., figure 35a), while Kawil's manifestation as a manikin scepter closely resembles Chac's lightning serpent (ibid., figures 5c, 6b; Schele and Mathews 1998, figure 5.21; Tate 1992, figures 114, 136, 148, 157). Some images seem to show either a substitution of Chac for God K or composite forms of God K and Chac (Taube 1992a, figure 37). In my opinion they are similar because they share similar realms. Chac controls rainfall using the power of thunder and lighting generated by Kawil, but Chac and Kawil are not one and the same. A number of scholars have concluded that Kawil's closest Mexican counterpart is Tezcatlipoca (Coe 1973; Milbrath 1999; Olivier 2003; Robicsek 1978).

The cults of Tezcatlipoca and Kawil show similarities but also some clear differences in their development over time. Kawil and Tezcatlipoca may share the serpent as an animal avatar, but they do not seem to share any other animal avatars. The bird most closely linked with Tezcatlipoca is the turkey, while Kawil's bird avatar seems to be a grackle. The jaguar and coyote aspects of Tezcatlipoca do not seem to relate to Kawil. Although Tezcatlipoca is not easily identified in central Mexican iconography of the Classic period (Olivier 2003, 86), his two animal avatars are represented in the murals of Teotihuacan. The Classic period netted jaguar is related to Postclassic anthropomorphic images of Tezcatlipoca (Anawalt 1981). Coyotes and jaguars also appear in relief carvings at both Tula and Chichén Itzá.

The cults of Tezcatlipoca and Kawil overlap chronologically in Yucatan during the Terminal Classic period, but these deities are never shown together, a pattern that could suggest that some form of substitution took place at certain sites. The clearest case seems to be at Chichén Itzá, where Kawil is represented on the Osario around AD 1000 on a Maya radial pyramid. Somewhat later, columns in Chichén Itzá's Temple of the Warriors depict five images of warriors with attributes of Tezcatlipoca, an image shared with Tula during a period of direct contact between the two cities (Cobos 2001; Miller 1998; Olivier 2003, plates 10, 11).

Tezcatlipoca's cult was highly developed in central Mexico during the Postclassic period and was most probably introduced to Yucatan from the highlands. Central Mexican images of Tezcatlipoca in the Codex Borgia (17, 21) bear obsidian sandals also seen on a male figure in fragmentary murals from San Angel, a Late Postclassic site in northern Yucatan (Gallereta Negrón and Taube 2005, 104, figures 6.8, 6.9; Milbrath 2013, 43, 61–62, 97). The Codex Borgia is probably from the Puebla-Tlaxcala area, one of three central Mexican centers for worship of Tezcatlipoca (Anawalt 1981, 848; Milbrath 2013, 1–2). Another major center was in the Basin of Mexico, where the Aztecs worshiped Tezcatlipoca in eight different temples (González Torres 1979, 17).

Tezcatlipoca plays a central role in creation mythology, including accounts of the separation of earth and sky, the creation of the Milky Way, and a cosmic conflict where he lost his foot battling with the earth monster. In his comprehensive study of the Aztec Lord of the Smoking Mirror, Guilhem Olivier (2003, 274, 276) concludes that Tezcatlipoca is a master of fate who plays a chief role in forecasting the end of eras and announcing the rise of future lords and the emergence of new "suns" or historical epochs. Fray Bernadino de Sahagún (1950–82, book I: 5) said of Tezcatilpoca that "his abode was everywhere . . . in the land of the dead, on earth, [and] in heaven." Sahagún cites a litany of negatives, noting that he mocked people and brought all the evils that befall men and also sowed discord and provoked conflict. Tezcatlipoca was also a master of transformation, a trickster who had the power to cheat people (Olivier 2003, 30, 270).

Priests and magicians used Tezcatlipoca's smoking mirror of black obsidian in prognosticating the future (Miller and Taube 1993, 164). His obsidian mirror appears in an Aztec account describing a mirror (*tezcatl*) that showed the "stars and fire drill [constellation]," even though it was daytime, and then revealed an omen forecasting the Spanish invasion (Sahagún 1950–82, book VIII: 18). The mirror's role in fortune telling may be linked with astrology, for Tezcatlipoca has a number of astronomical avatars. Olivier (2003, 271–73) notes that there are solar, lunar, and Venus associations for Tezcatlipoca, with the lunar aspect dominant. Other astronomical guises are also apparent because some accounts refer to Tezcatlipoca as "another Jupiter," whereas others link him with Ursa Major, a constellation incorporating the Big Dipper (Nicholson 1971, 412, 426; Olivier 2003, 263).

Astronomical metaphors may be encoded in Tezcatlipoca's avatars. His omnipresent nature may be linked to Jupiter because that planet seems to dominate the night sky and is therefore "all seeing, omnipresent" (Hunt 1977, 145). Tezcatlipoca's transformations in sequential cosmic eras encode observations of Ursa Major and the changing positions of the celestial pole as a result of precession of the equinox, according to Eva Hunt (ibid., 152). Jaguar imagery associated with Tezcatlipoca is related to both the moon and Ursa Major, which both play a role in the cycles of rainfall (Olivier 2003, 95–98, 103, 124, 234–35, 240).

The jaguar aspect of Tezcatlipoca can be traced back to Classic period Teotihuacan, where the netted jaguar is the precursor to later Aztec images that show Tezcatlipoca wearing a netted cape (Anawalt 1996, 198, figure 19).[2] This suggests a connection with Maya lunar imagery because the Classic Maya moon god is a lunar jaguar, and a net features prominently in Maya folktales of the moon (Milbrath 1999, 41, 120–45, figures 4.2–4.5).

Another manifestation of Tezcatlipoca, Itzlacoliuhqui-Cinteotl, is linked with the planet Venus and maize (Olivier 2003, 117). The blindfolded Itzlacoliuhqui, an avatar of Tezcatlipoca playing the role of Venus in the Dresden Codex (50), refers to the planet in retrograde motion, moving "backward" in the sky (Thompson 1960, 220, 1972, 69). Venus undergoes retrograde as it shifts from the Evening Star to the Morning Star, so the retrograde period has a natural association with the newly risen Morning Star.

Different manifestations of Tezcatlipoca play the role of attacker and victim in two Venus almanacs, an apparent conflict that finds an explanation only in the multiple astronomical personae attributed to Tezcatlipoca. Tezcatlipoca's blindfolded avatar represents the Morning Star spearing his victim in the Dresden

THE MAYA LORD OF THE SMOKING MIRROR   173

FIGURE 7.12. Tezcatlipoca, Codex Borgia 54, depicting the Black variant of Tezcatlipoca (after Seler 1960–61, 1: 652, abb. 48).

Codex Venus almanac, but a closely related almanac from central Mexico shows the black Tezcatlipoca as the victim of the Morning Star (figure 7.12; Seler 1963, 2: 121). This same role is played by Kawil, who is speared by the Morning Star on page 46 of the Venus almanac in the Dresden Codex (Kelley 1976, figure 28; Thompson 1972).

The Dresden Codex provides some keys to identifying Kawil's role as the victim of the Morning Star. Although Thompson (ibid., 67) suggested that the Venus god spearing his victim in the Dresden Codex refers to celestial conjunction, the imagery may actually depict celestial opposition. In all the scenes, the Venus god kills his victim using a long-distance projectile weapon (*atlatl*), a detail also seen in the Codex Borgia Venus almanac (figure 7.12). Reconstruction of dates associated with the Venus almanac in the Dresden Codex provides evidence that Venus spearing a victim symbolizes celestial opposition (Milbrath 1995, 1999, 176). To rise victorious, the Morning Star has to hurl his dart to the opposite side of the sky, killing celestial gods on the western horizon and forcing them into the underworld. The heliacal rise date on page 46 (5 Kan 7 Xul) corresponds to January 26, 1221 (O.S), when the Morning Star rose to the east and Jupiter was visible at the opposite side of the sky in retrograde motion just above the western horizon. On Dresden Codex 46, the victim Kawil seems to represent Jupiter in retrograde. This link between Kawil and the planet Jupiter is supported by study of Classic period monuments, which demonstrate a strong link between the imagery of Kawil and the retrograde of the planet Jupiter (Milbrath 1999, 2002, 2004, 2005).

Retrograde motion is a characteristic of the planets that distinguishes them from the sun and stars because they seem to move "backward" for a period of time (Aveni 2000, 84–88; Milbrath 1999, 53–54). Retrograde is bracketed by two stationary points when the planet seems to stand still for a few days or more (table 7.1). The "departure" from the stationary point cannot be easily detected for a period of time, which in the case of Jupiter can range from three to fourteen days (Aveni and Hotaling 1994, S37, 40n50). These "limits of detectability" for Jupiter's motion make the precise period of retrograde somewhat difficult to predict. Nonetheless, with the aid of the Long Count calendar, the Maya became adept at estimating the periods of retrograde motion. The central Mexican calendar was not so precise, so the planets moving in retrograde may have been seen as unpredictable. Tezcatlipoca's association with the "backward" motion of planets may be linked with his nature as a trickster in central Mexico.

Tezcatlipoca's lunar connection may also be part of the astronomical trickster metaphor. The moon moves "backward" from west to east over the course of a month. Because the moon's cycle cannot be measured in equal intervals of days, the lunar month alternates between twenty-nine and thirty days. The moon also confounds the annual calendar because the year can include a thirteenth month, sometimes considered ominous (Milbrath 1999, 28). If the moon happens to cross the ecliptic at the time of a full moon or a new moon, an eclipse may occur (ibid., 48, figure 2.2b). The Aztecs considered solar eclipses, which invariably occur at the new moon, especially dangerous (Milbrath 1997), and Tezcatlipoca's lunar association no doubt contributed to his aspect as a trickster.

Kawil's serpent imagery might allude to a lunar connection because the moon is widely associated with serpents (Milbrath 1999, 145–47, figure 4.9). Even if future studies indicate that Kawil is closely connected with the moon, we have no evidence that he is a trickster, perhaps because we lack the extensive ethnohistorical sources available for Aztec deities. Kawil makes only brief appearances in the Chilam Balam books, the Ritual of the Bacabs, and in Friar Diego de Landa's

TABLE 7.1. Retrograde of Jupiter and Saturn in relation to Early Classic katun endings.

8.11.0.0.0 13 Ahau katun end 7/10/258
    Saturn retrograde 7/2/258 to 12/9/258*
    [═══S1═KE═══════════════S2═══]

8.12.0.0.0 11 Ahau katun end 3/27/278
    Saturn retrograde 3/14/278 to 8/1/278*
    [═══S1══KE══════════════S2═══]

8.13.0.0.0 9 Ahau katun end 12/12/297
    Saturn retrograde 11/14/297 to 3/29/298*
    [═══S1══════KE═══════════S2═══]

8.14.0.0.0 7 Ahau katun end 8/29/317
    Saturn retrograde 6/26/317 to 11/10/317
    [═══S1══════════════KE══S2═══]

8.15.0.0.0 5 Ahau katun end 5/16/337
    Saturn retrograde 3/2/337 to 7/21/337
    [═══S1═══════════KE═══════S2═══]

8.16.0.0.0 3 Ahau katun end 1/31/357
    Jupiter retrograde 2/1/357 to 6/5/357
    [═══S1KE════════════════S2═══]
    Saturn retrograde 11/22/357 to 4/6/358
    [═══S1═══════════KE══════S2═══]

8.17.0.0.0 1 Ahau katun end 10/18/376
    Jupiter retrograde 10/11/376 to 2/7/377
    [═══S1=KE═══════════════S2═══]
    Saturn retrograde 6/27/376 to 11/11/376
    [═══S1═══════════════KE═══S2═══]

8.18.0.0.0 12 Ahau katun end 7/5/396
    Jupiter retrograde 5/30/396 to 9/27/396
    [═══S1══════KE═══════════S2═══]
    Saturn retrograde 3/3/396 to 7/22/396
    [═══S1═══════════════KE══S2═══]

8.19.0.0.0 10 Ahau katun end 3/22/416
    Jupiter retrograde 1/24/416 to 5/26/416
    [═══S1══════KE═════════S2═══]
    Saturn retrograde 11/23/416 to 4/8/417
    [═══S1══════════════════KE══S2═══]

continued on next page

Table 7.1—*continued*

9.0.0.0.0 8 Ahau katun end 12/5/435
    Jupiter retrograde 10/2/435 to 1/29/436
    [══S₁═══════════KE═══════S₂══]
    Saturn retrograde no longer overlaps with katun end

9.1.0.0.0 6 Ahau katun end 8/25/455
    Jupiter retrograde 5/20/455 to 9/17/455
    [══S₁═══════════════KE═══S₂══]

9.2.0.0.0 4 Ahau katun end 5/12/475
    Jupiter retrograde 1/15/475 to 5/18/475
    [══S₁═════════════════════KE═S₂══]

9.3.0.0.0 2 Ahau katun end 1/27/495
    Jupiter retrograde 9/22/494 to 1/18/495
    [══S₁═════════════════S₂══KE═]

9.4.0.0.0 13 Ahau katun end 10/15/514.
    Retrograde of Jupiter or Saturn no longer overlaps with katun end

Note for tables 7.1–7.3: All dates in Julian Calendar. Maya dates in 584,283 correlation. Katun end date marked by KE. Dates for first (S1) and second stationary (S2) points of retrograde from Jean Meeus (n.d.), except for first three marked * from Anthony Aveni [personal communication, 2005]). Five-day intervals of retrograde marked by =, and the brackets on both ends of retrograde symbolize a brief period during which the planet's movement is not easy to detect (LOD, or Limits of Detectability): for Saturn up to twenty days; for Jupiter up to fourteen days.

account. Landa describes Bolon Dzacab's role in the New Year rituals, and he is also represented in the yearbearer pages of the Dresden Codex (ibid., 227; Thompson 1972, 90–91; Tozzer 1941, 140–42). His role in the yearbearer ceremonies is one he shares with the Sun God (God G) and Itzamna (God D), a benevolent creator god. Even though the New Year is a liminal time of change, Landa's description of the ceremonies indicates that they were stately and controlled. Indeed, with the Long Count calendar and the katun cycle, the passage of time was orderly and predictable. Lunar cycles and planetary retrograde were part of this stately progression of time; hence Kawil's role in calendar ceremonies was probably not visualized as that of a trickster.

Although Kawil's role in the lunar cycle awaits further analysis, he is clearly associated with planetary retrograde. This is seen on Classic period monuments depicting Kawil that bear dates correlating with Jupiter's retrograde motion (Milbrath 1999, 233–40, 2002, 2004, 2005). Monuments with Kawil images at Tikal, Seibal, Palenque, and Yaxchilan all have dates coinciding with retrograde motion of Jupiter.

At Seibal and Tikal, a number of stelae depict Kawil on katun endings that correspond to the retrograde of Jupiter and Saturn (figure 7.8; Milbrath 2004). Other monuments at Tikal associate images of Kawil with dynastic rituals that coincide with Jupiter's retrograde. At Yaxchilan, Kawil imagery is more closely associated with dynastic rituals coordinating with Jupiter's retrograde; although there are a number of katun records on monuments (Stelae 2, 18, 27, Lintel 31), they do not represent Kawil (Milbrath 1999, table 6.1). This is also the predominant pattern at Palenque (ibid., 233–34). The strong link between Kawil and Jupiter's retrograde at Tikal, Palenque, and Yaxchilan is discussed in the next section.

Preliminary analysis of Kawil monuments at Naranjo, Machaquila Aguateca, and Ek' Balam seems to show a similar pattern. Two Kawil monuments from Ek' Balam bear dates that conform to this pattern (Lacadena García-Gallo 2005, 65, 68). Stela 1 shows the ruler displaying a Kawil manikin scepter on 10.0.10.0.0 (January 16, 840), a date coinciding with Jupiter's retrograde period (10/28/839–2/15/840, Meeus n.d.). An avian image of Kawil appears on an Ek' Balam capstone with a Calendar Round date (June 5, 775) that corresponds to Jupiter's retrograde period (5/12/775–9/10/775, ibid.).

Some of the best examples of the correlation with retrograde periods are monuments that bear only one or two dates. For example, a stela in San Francisco's Fine Arts Museum has an image of Kawil emerging from the jaws of a "Vision Serpent" (Miller, Martin, and Berrin 2004, plate 46). The dedication date (1 Ajaw 3 Zip, 9.16.10.0) coincides with Jupiter's retrograde period, and a second date (9.16.9.7.5) corresponds with Saturn's retrograde.

Kawil plays an important part in the Long Count calendar, which records a number of repeating sequences of time, including the katun cycle and a cycle of 819 days, both of which appear to be linked to cycles involving Jupiter and Saturn (Milbrath 1999, 240–41, 2002). Kawil is specifically named in an 819-day cycle that shares a common factor (21 days) with the synodic periods of Jupiter and Saturn, a pattern discussed by John Justeson (1989, 103), who notes a high frequency of Jupiter and Saturn events associated with 819-day counts. Preliminary analysis does not show a strong correlation between 819-day events recorded on monuments and the period of Jupiter's retrograde, so presumably some other correlation involving Jupiter or Saturn is involved. The 819-day phrases often name Kawil in the fifth position (Kelley 1976, 57–58, figure 17). A companion glyph (T739) in the fourth position is also used in Glyph Y of the Supplementary Series, where it is governed by a seven-day cycle that may be a planetary week (Yasugi and Saito 1991). This patterning certainly calls for further study because Kawil's role in the Maya katun cycle and the 819-day count links him with larger cycles of time associated with the concept of world ages (Milbrath 1999, 240, 2004).

FIGURE 7.13. Palenque Triad, Kawil shown as GII, shown full figure in reclining posture, representing counterpart of Kawil (Temple of the Foliated Cross at D2; after Milbrath 1999, figure 6.3n).

As a subdivision of the Long Count calendar, the katun cycle measures spans of time that exceed 5,000 years. Such long cycles of time evoke a link with the world eras in the mythology of Tezcatlipoca. Indeed, Kawil is specifically named as one of the primordial celestial family. Kawil appears as GII of the Palenque Triad in mythological texts recording the birth of three celestial brothers in a previous era. The Temple of the Foliated Cross gives GII's birth date in 2697 BC (1.18.5.4.0 1 Ahau 13 Mac). Glyphs representing GII are like those naming Kawil, but they show the full figure in a reclining posture resembling a fetal position (figure 7.13). Henrich Berlin (1963, 93) named this god GII because he is always the second listed in texts identifying a triad of three brothers; however, his mythic birthday makes him the youngest. Palenque texts indicate that the Sun God is the middle brother and Venus is the eldest (Schele 1976, 10). A modern Mopan tale also designates these two deities as the elder brothers and identifies the youngest brother as Mars or Jupiter, a role played by Kawil (GII) in Palenque's mythological texts (Milbrath 1999, 231–32).

JUPITER AND MAYA RULERS

Kawil may represent Jupiter as the planet of kings (ibid., 248, 2002, 142). In Classic Maya dynastic history, at least five Tikal rulers bear the Kawil title; and Calakmul, Naranjo, and Dos Pilas each have three rulers with this royal title (Martin and Grube 2000). In contrast, the Kawil title is not associated with the rulers of Caracol, Tonina, Piedras Negras, and Palenque—sites that have repeated references to solar titles. Rulers at these cities were apparently seen as the earthly incarnation of the sun (Milbrath 1999, 83–87). Copan showed a preference for the solar title early on but switched to the Kawil title in the Late Classic, when three kings adopted this honorific name. The Kawil title and imagery of Kawil in the monuments do not necessarily overlap. For example, Yaxchilan does not use Kawil as a royal title, but images of Kawil abound in monumental sculpture.

The most ancient image associating Kawil with a living ruler is Tikal Stela 31, a monument dedicated in AD 445 (figure 7.3; Coggins 1990, 85). This monument provides evidence of an early interest in Jupiter's retrograde (Alexander 1992, table 1; Milbrath 1999, 239). The Initial Series dedicatory date (9.0.10.0.0 7 Ahau 3 Yax; October 16, 445) corresponds to a time when Jupiter was approaching its second stationary point (November 23, 445; Meeus n.d.).[3] The ruler's headdress depicts Kawil emerging from a sky symbol, combining two elements that appear separately in his name (Siyah Chan Kawil or Siyaj Chan K'awiil II). This ruler was originally known as Stormy Sky, and the Kawil glyph was interpreted logographically as "stormy," seeming appropriate because of Kawil's connection with thunder and lightning. This early representation of Kawil on Stela 31 associated with a Long Count date marking Jupiter's retrograde indicates that the pattern linking Kawil to planetary retrograde may have first developed at Tikal, the Classic Maya city with the longest recorded history.

Another early Tikal monument (Stela 1) depicts Kawil as a hatchet manikin (Jones and Satterthwaite 1982, 10, figure 1). Stela 1 is tentatively dated to either katun 6 Ahau or katun 4 Ahau (9.1.0.0.0 or 9.2.0.0.0). Both of these katun endings correspond to the retrograde period of Jupiter (table 7.1). In the Late Classic period, Kawil appears on a number of monuments that record katun-ending dates coinciding with the retrograde of Jupiter, a pattern discussed in the next section.

Other Late Classic monuments at Tikal, Yaxchilan, and Palenque represent Kawil with dates marking the retrograde of Jupiter that are not katun endings. They include Tikal lintels carved in the reigns of both Ruler A and Ruler B (ibid., table 5; Milbrath 1999, 237–38, figure 3.6d, plates 15, 16). On Tikal Temple I, Lintel 3, Ruler A carries the Kawil scepter as an insignia of lineage and authority. One of the inscribed dates, 11 Etz'nab 11 Chen (9.13.3.7.18; August 3, 695), falls in Saturn's period of retrograde motion. A bloodletting event forty days later, on 12 Etz'nab 11 Zac (9.13.3.9.18; September 12, 695), coincides approximately with Jupiter's first stationary point and Saturn's second stationary point (Aveni and Hotaling 1994, table 1; Schele and Freidel 1990, 445).

Palenque also represents Kawil on monuments recording dynastic events that were timed by Jupiter's retrograde period. By studying a pattern of dates at Palenque and plotting Jupiter's position on those dates, Floyd Lounsbury (1989, table 19.1) correlated dynastic events in Kan B'alam II's reign with dates marking Jupiter's retrograde motion. Both Kan B'alam II's heir designation and his accession date were timed by Jupiter's departure from the second stationary point, less than two weeks after the end of retrograde. This "departure" is seen as the first time the planet's forward motion is clearly detected. Although Lounsbury did not identify specific imagery that refers to Jupiter, the three Cross Group panels recording these events all depict images of Kawil (Milbrath 1999, 233).

Temple XIV at Palenque also follows a similar pattern, bearing imagery of Kawil and a date that marks Jupiter's departure from the second stationary point. The panel shows Kan B'alam II being offered a Kawil manikin after his death (ibid., 233–34, plate 13). The text opens on the left with a 9 Ik 10 Mol date, followed by a statement that Kawil was displayed under the auspices of the Moon Goddess; then the date is repeated on the right after an interval of almost 100,000 years (Schele and Miller 1986, 272, figure VII.2). The display of Kawil is mentioned again on 9 Ahau 3 Kankin (9.13.13.15.0; October 31, 705), which falls about three years and nine months after Kan B'alam II's death date (3 × 365 days + 260 days). Lounsbury (1989, 250, figure 19.5) links this posthumous date with Jupiter's departure from its second stationary point on 705 October 21 (Meeus n.d.). A lunar event may also be represented because the moon passed by Jupiter on this date. Indeed, Kan B'alam II's deceased mother, who hands him the Kawil manikin, is compared to the Moon Goddess in the texts (Milbrath 1999, 233).

An important image of Kawil appears on the Sarcophagus Lid of the Temple of the Inscriptions at Palenque, a pyramid that houses the tomb of Kan B'alam II's father. An astronomical context is indicated by the sky-band frame and a cosmic tree with a bichephalic sky serpent bearing Kawil. At the base of the tree, King Pakal II appears as an incarnation of Kawil, wearing the god's smoking mirror on his brow (figure 7.14; Milbrath 1999, 234, plate 10; Robertson 1991, 18; Schele 1976, 17). On the edge of the Sarcophagus Lid, an event related to the ruler's death is recorded on the Calendar Round 6 Etz'nab 11 Yax (9.12.11.5.18; August 26, 683). Stuart deciphered the event glyph as stating that "he entered the road" (*och bih*; Schele 1992, 133). It has been suggested that the och bih event refers to Pakal entering a celestial road that represents the Milky Way (Freidel, Schele, and Parker 1993, 76).[4] Heinrich Berlin (1977, 137) notes that this event marks the end of Pakal's reign and may signal either death or apotheosis. Pakal's reclining posture recalls the image of Kawil as the victim of the Morning Star in the Venus almanac on Dresden Codex 46, but the pose also evokes Kawil's birth in the mythological texts referring to birth as GII of the Palenque Triad (figure 7.13). In the case of the Palenque Sarcophagus, the pose refers to both death and birth because the recorded event was the ruler's apotheosis, a form of rebirth in the heavens. Clemency Coggins (1988, 74) interprets the image as the reborn ruler dancing out of his tomb. Pakal's apotheosis was timed precisely to coincide with Jupiter's first stationary point (Milbrath 1999, 234).

It is noteworthy that Pakal II's son, Kan B'alam II, was not inaugurated as the new ruler until Jupiter had departed from its second stationary point four months

FIGURE 7.14. Pakal II's apotheosis as Kawil took place when Jupiter reached its first stationary point in AD 683 (detail of Sarcophagus Lid of Temple of the Inscriptions at Palenque; after Milbrath 1999, figure 6.3p).

after Pakal's apotheosis event. It seems that the priests of Palenque thought the period of Jupiter's retrograde motion was an inauspicious time to crown the new ruler, and they delayed Kan B'alam II's accession until enough time had elapsed to be certain that Jupiter had completed its retrograde loop.

James Fox and John Justeson (1978) suggest that certain astronomical events were of significance when they coincided with historical events, such as the death of a ruler. In contrast, Joyce Marcus (1992, 440) maintains that historical events were sometimes "manipulated" to fit astronomical events. A third alternative is that proposed by Lounsbury (1989), namely, that posthumous events and dynastic rituals were actually timed to coincide with astronomical events. In the case of Pakal's Sarcophagus, the imagery and date indicate that the ruler's spirit ascended to heaven to become one of the gods in accord with astrological portents, when the royal planet Jupiter stood motionless to honor the deceased ruler.

On Copan Stela 11, Yax Pac appears in a guise of Kawil, the only other known portrait of a deceased ruler in the guise of Kawil (Fash 1991, 177, figure 108; Milbrath 1999, 234). According to Linda Schele (1992, 120), Copan Stela 11 records an 819-day passage that refers to the serpent foot as the alter ego of K'awinal (Kawil). Like Pakal II's image of apotheosis, the Copan monument is also associated with the retrograde period of Jupiter. The stela's date corresponds to April 30, 820 (8 Ahau 8 Xul, 9.19.10.0.0), when Jupiter was on the eastern horizon at dusk, approximately at the midpoint of its retrograde loop (February 18 to June 21; Meeus n.d.). Taube (1992a, figure 21) identifies images on Pakal's Sarcophagus and Copan Stela 11 as the "Tonsured Maize God with cranial torch of God K," giving the maize imagery primacy. Nonetheless, the combination of deity traits suggests a complex astronomical metaphor, linking the ruler in death to the planet of kings but also referring to his rebirth embodied in the cycles of the moon and maize. The ruler's guise as Kawil with maize foliation on his brow may encode astronomical metaphors linking Jupiter's retrograde to the cycle of maize and to the moon, which was in conjunction with Jupiter on the date recorded on Stela 11. Pakal in the guise of Kawil also wears a netted skirt characteristic of deities embodying both the moon and maize, but in this case the moon was just about to disappear in conjunction with the sun, evoking the image of death and rebirth associated with the new moon (Milbrath 1999, 155, figures 4d, 4g). Just as the moon is reborn after disappearing in conjunction, the maize seed is buried and reborn when the seed germinates. Metaphorical interpretations are by their nature difficult to prove, so we must turn to statistical analysis for more concrete proof of Kawil's link with Jupiter.

Statistical studies help demonstrate that monuments from Yaxchilan link Kawil to Jupiter events (ibid., 235, table 6.1). The percentage of Jupiter's mean period of retrograde (120 days) plus a 7-day window on either side totals 134 days, representing 33 percent of its synodic period of 399 days. In a random sample of dates using a 7-day window before and after retrograde, you would expect around 33 percent of the dates to coincide with retrograde. When we look at the entire sample of 109 dates for Yaxchilan published by Carolyn Tate (1992), 27 percent of the total fall in Jupiter's retrograde period or within 7 days on either side of retrograde. This figure falls below the expected random frequency. Yet when we narrow our focus to those monuments depicting Kawil, the percentage bearing dates relating to Jupiter's retrograde is relatively high at 53 percent (8 of 15; Milbrath 1999, 235, table 6.1). All of these monuments bear only a single date except Stela 1, which has two dates, both of which coincide with Jupiter's retrograde motion (ibid.). Using a broader 21-day window for the dates, closer to the limits of detectability for Jupiter's retrograde determined by Anthony Aveni and Lorren Hotaling (1994), we find an even stronger correlation because 11 of the 15 Yaxchilan monuments with Kawil imagery have dates that relate to the retrograde periods of Jupiter (Lintels 6, 7, 32, 38, 39, 40, 42, 43, 53, Stela 1, Stela 11; Milbrath 1999, 237). If Saturn's retrograde is considered a substitute event on those dates that do not correspond to Jupiter's retrograde, 13 of the 15 Kawil monuments bear dates coinciding with retrograde motion. This is much higher than the predicted random frequency (a mean of 48 percent) when combining the retrograde periods of both planets (Milbrath 2004, 85).

KATUN ENDINGS AND PLANETARY RETROGRADE

Plotting the pattern of katun endings throughout the Classic period in relation to the retrograde period of all three superior planets reveals a consistent relationship with Jupiter and Saturn during katun endings in relation to the retrograde period (Milbrath 2004).[5] The retrograde of Jupiter and Saturn overlapped with the katun end for a long period of time (tables 7.1, 7.2). We have a large data set, since the most commonly recorded events on Classic period monuments were katun endings

(Justeson 1989, 104). The katun is a basic unit in the Maya calendar of approximately 20 years (20 × 360 days, or 19.71 years). The katun cycle itself may have developed from long-term observations of Jupiter and Saturn because the interval between successive Jupiter-Saturn conjunctions is between 19 and 20 years, the approximate length of the katun (Milbrath 1999, 240).

Study of the Maya katun dates at Tikal, the site with the longest katun history, indicates that when Jupiter was not in retrograde motion at the katun ending, a Saturn event may have been substituted, but when neither planet was in retrograde the katun ending date was generally not recorded (Milbrath 2004). Interest in the retrograde periods of Jupiter and Saturn in relation to katun endings developed during the Early Classic period (table 7.1). As far back as AD 258 (8.1.0.0.0), Saturn's retrograde coincided with the katun end. Saturn's retrograde continued to coincide with the katun ending for the next four katuns. Jupiter joined Saturn in retrograde motion at the katun end by the mid-fourth century at the katun ending in AD 357 (8.16.0.0.0). There was simultaneous retrograde motion of both planets at katun end from AD 357 to 416. By December 5, 435 (9.0.0.0.0), a katun ending 8 Ahau that was also a Baktun ending, Jupiter remained in retrograde motion, but Saturn's second stationary point had slipped back to over three weeks before the katun end. Plotting the katun ending in relation to Jupiter's and Saturn's retrograde in the Early Classic period shows that if the retrograde periods of both planets are considered, the cycle of correspondence between retrograde and the katun ending lasts for a complete katun cycle of thirteen katuns (table 7.1).

A clear link exists between dates on monuments recording the katun endings and the period when the retrograde of Jupiter or Saturn or both marked the katun ending. Kawil is rarely represented in the Early Classic period, but he does appear on one or two monuments that record katun endings. Early katun records appear on Tikal Stela 31, which has one of the earliest known monumental images of Kawil (figure 7.3). Although Stela 31 notes a number of katun endings, the monument is not itself a katun monument because the dedicatory date is not a katun ending. The Initial Series date on Stela 31 (9.0.10.0.0; October 16, 445) correlates with Jupiter's retrograde period and serves as an anchor point for earlier katun endings. Stela 31 records the katun ending on 8.17.0.0.0 (October 18, 376), which correlates with Jupiter's first stationary point, and the katun ending 8.18.0.0.0 when both Saturn and Jupiter were in retrograde motion at katun end (Jones and Satterthwaite 1982, table 5; Milbrath 2004, 86–87, table 1). The stela also records the Baktun ending 9.0.0.0.0, December 5, 435, when Jupiter was in retrograde at the katun end and Mars was approaching its first stationary point. As noted previously, Tikal Stela 1 depicts Kawil on a monument that seems to record a katun ending overlapping with the retrograde of Jupiter (AD 455 or 475; table 7.1).

Tikal Stela 9, dating to AD 475, is the first of a series of Early Classic monuments erected specifically to mark the katun endings that correlate with the retrograde of Jupiter. Stela 9 initiates a new format that depicts the ruler K'an Chitam (K'an Ak) holding a long staff that has been interpreted as a fire drill (Martin and Grube 2000, 37). Similar images appear on Stelae 7, 15, and 27, all recording the katun ending on January 27, 495 (9.3.0.0.0; Jones and Satterthwaite 1982, figures 11, 20, 46, table 5; Milbrath 2004). The fire drill staff creates fire, mimicking lightning that is nature's "fire drill." As such, the fire drill could be a counterpart for later images of Kawil's lightning serpent (the manikin scepter). Kawil is not represented on the katun monuments of the Early Classic period. Indeed, Kawil is rarely represented in Early Classic monumental art. The fire drill staff, the principal insignia of Early Classic katun monuments at Tikal, is later replaced by a variety of images representing Kawil on Late Classic katun monuments (ibid., 87).

Near the end of the Early Classic period, very few monuments with inscriptions were carved at Tikal. The inscriptions of Tikal reflected "troubled times" of political upheaval between AD 508 and 562 (Martin and Grube 2000, 38–40, 104). One of the only katun records from the period at Tikal is Stela 6, dating to AD 514 (9.4.0.0.0), the last in a series representing the ruler with an elaborate staff (Harrison 1999, 95). At this point, Jupiter and Saturn had ceased to mark the katun end, ending a cycle that had lasted for thirteen katuns (table 7.1).

Tikal experienced a complete hiatus in monumental inscriptions during the years AD 562–692, and no inscriptions were recorded at the site for 130 years. During the period of Tikal's silence, other sites recorded numerous monumental inscriptions. Palenque, Yaxchilan, and other cities in the central Maya area document many dates that coincide with Jupiter events on monuments featuring Kawil, but none of these texts are katun endings (Milbrath 1999, 233–34). The so-called hiatus lasted longer at Tikal than at any other site. There are some katun records at Tikal during this period, but not on public monuments (Martin and Grube 2000, 39, 41). For example, an Early Classic ceramic bowl records the katun 5 Ahau (AD 593, 9.8.0.0.0) along with a set of Mexican year signs (Culbert 1993, figure 64c2), suggesting an alternate form of calendar was in place during the hiatus, perhaps one adopted from Teotihuacan. A contributing factor to the hiatus in monumental inscriptions at Tikal could be a loss of faith in the astrological portents of katun ending ceremonies. The hiatus coincided precisely with the period when the katun ending no longer corresponded to the retrograde periods of Jupiter or Saturn (Milbrath 2004, table 1). Apparently, the priests of Tikal had come to expect one of these two planets to be in retrograde motion at katun end, as had been the case for more than 250 years.

During Tikal's hiatus, katun endings were recorded on the Hieroglyphic Stairs at Dos Pilas rather than on stelae. Although Dos Pilas erected a few stela with Kawil images that correspond to the retrograde of Saturn and Jupiter (Stela 14, 15), other Dos Pilas monuments representing Kawil do not seem to record dates that can be linked with the retrograde of Jupiter or Saturn (Milbrath 1999, 234–35). Perhaps this is an indication that priests at Dos Pilas rejected the authority of priests from Tikal and were "marching to a different drummer." In fact, Dos Pilas was established by people who left Tikal and claimed Tikal's emblem glyph, allying themselves with Tikal's enemy, Calakmul (Martin and Grube 2000, 55–57).

Tikal exhibits the greatest elaboration of katun ending monuments, and it is noteworthy that this is where we see the greatest disruption in records of katun endings. Most significant, Tikal initiated new records of the katun endings only when the planets resumed their dance of retrograde motion at the katun end in AD 692 (table 7.2). The katun was recorded again on the katun ending 8 Ahau (9.13.0.0.0) in 692, a date inscribed on Tikal Altar 14 and Stela 30. Commissioned by Ruler A (Jasaw Chan K'awiil I), Altar 14 and Stela 30 are associated with the first in a series of twin-pyramid complexes constructed to celebrate katun endings (3D-98/100; Jones 1969, 110, table 1; Milbrath 2004, 89, figure 4). Although Stela 30 is damaged, the ruler's elaborate headdress might represent Kawil with a smoking tube in his brow (Jones and Satterthwaite 1982, figure 50). A twin-pyramid complex was also constructed for the next katun ending in 711 (9.14.0.0.0), recorded on Stela 16, a katun monument that shows Ruler A wearing a mask with a symbol of a star (Milbrath 1999, 192, figure 5.7, 2004, 89, figure 6).[6] Although Jupiter had not yet entered retrograde motion at the katun end, Saturn was almost precisely at its first stationary point, which would have been considered noteworthy because Saturn's retrograde had marked the katun endings for many centuries during the Early Classic period (tables 7.1, 7.2).

In the Late Classic period, Kawil reappears on katun monuments at Tikal during the epoch when Jupiter's retrograde period coincided with the katun ending (Milbrath 2004). An auspicious interlocking of astronomical events with the katun end occurred during the reign of Yaxkin Chaan Kawil (Ruler B) at Tikal. He appears on Stela 20 wearing a star glyph on his buccal mask and a headdress crowned by Kawil (Milbrath 1999, 237, plate 17).[7] The inscribed date, 2 Ahau 13 Zec, records the first katun ending of his reign (9.16.0.0.0, May 3, 751), coinciding exactly with Jupiter's first stationary point (May 2, 751; Meeus n.d.). Saturn was also in retrograde motion and Mars rose at dawn, while Venus was visible near its maximum altitude. This stela is paired with Altar 8 in Twin-Pyramid Complex P (Group 3D-2), one of the many twin-pyramid complexes devoted to katun ceremonies. The formal elements of the twin-pyramid complex include paired radial pyramids on the east and west sides of a defined plaza area, a nine-door building on the south side, and an enclosure for a stela and altar pair on the north side. Radial pyramids have a long

TABLE 7.2. Retrograde of Jupiter and Saturn in relation to Late Classic katun endings.

9.11.0.0.0 12 Ahau katun end 10/9/652

    Retrogrades of Jupiter and Saturn do not overlap with katun end

9.12.0.0.0 10 Ahau katun end 6/26/672

    Saturn retrograde 6/17/672 to 11/30/672

    [═══S_1═KE════════════════S_2═══]

9.13.0.0.0 8 Ahau katun end 3/13/692

    Saturn retrograde 3/20/692 to 8/8/692

    [═KE═S_1══════════════════S_2═══]

9.14.0.0.0 6 Ahau katun end 11/29/711

    Saturn retrograde 11/29/711 to 4/13/712

    [═══S_1KE═══════════════════S_2═══]

9.15.0.0.0 4 Ahau katun end 8/16/731

    Saturn retrograde 7/19/731 to 12/2/731

    [═══S_1═════KE════════════S_2═══]

9.16.0.0.0 2 Ahau katun end 5/3/751

    Jupiter retrograde 5/2/751 to 8/31/751

    [═══S_1KE═══════════════S_2═══]

    Saturn retrograde 3/22/751 to 8/11/751

    [═══S_1═════KE════════════S_2═══]

9.17.0.0.0 13 Ahau katun end 1/18/771

    Jupiter retrograde 1/1/771 to 5/4/771

    [═══S_1═══KE═════════════S_2═══]

    Saturn retrograde 12/13/771 to 4/28/772

    [═══S_1═══════KE═══════════S_2═══]

9.18.0.0.0 11 Ahau katun end 10/5/790

    Jupiter retrograde 9/6/790 to 1/2/791

    [═══S_1═════KE═══════════S_2═══]

    Saturn retrograde 7/21/790 to 12/4/790

    [═══S_1═══════════KE════════S_2═══]

9.19.0.0.0 9 Ahau katun end 6/22/810

    Jupiter retrograde 4/21/810 to 8/21/810

    [═══S_1═════════KE═══════S_2═══]

    Saturn retrograde 3/23/810 to 8/12/810

    [═══S_1═══════════════KE═════S_2═══]

continued on next page

TABLE 7.2—*continued*

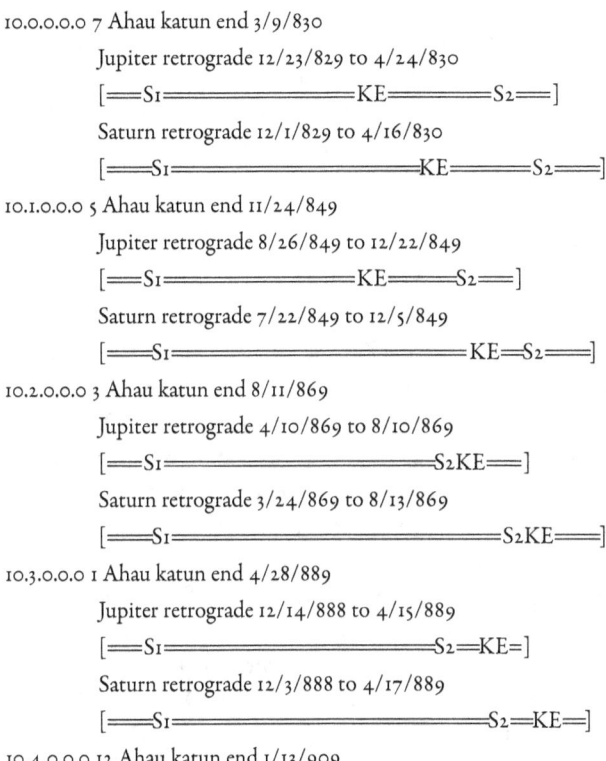

10.0.0.0.0 7 Ahau katun end 3/9/830
    Jupiter retrograde 12/23/829 to 4/24/830
    [═══S1═══════════════KE═══════S2═══]
    Saturn retrograde 12/1/829 to 4/16/830
    [═══S1═══════════════════KE═══════S2═══]

10.1.0.0.0 5 Ahau katun end 11/24/849
    Jupiter retrograde 8/26/849 to 12/22/849
    [═══S1═══════════════KE═══S2═══]
    Saturn retrograde 7/22/849 to 12/5/849
    [═══S1═══════════════════════KE═S2═══]

10.2.0.0.0 3 Ahau katun end 8/11/869
    Jupiter retrograde 4/10/869 to 8/10/869
    [═══S1═══════════════════════S2KE═══]
    Saturn retrograde 3/24/869 to 8/13/869
    [═══S1═══════════════════════════S2KE═══]

10.3.0.0.0 1 Ahau katun end 4/28/889
    Jupiter retrograde 12/14/888 to 4/15/889
    [═══S1═══════════════════════S2═KE═]
    Saturn retrograde 12/3/888 to 4/17/889
    [═══S1═══════════════════════S2═KE═]

10.4.0.0.0 12 Ahau katun end 1/13/909
    Retrogrades of Jupiter and Saturn do not overlap with katun end

Note: For an explanation of format see table 7.1.

history dating back to the Preclassic period, when they seem to be specifically linked with astronomical observations involving the seasonal cycles (Aveni, Dowd, and Vining 2003).

The period AD 692 to 869 coincides with a heightened interest in katun monuments at Tikal, as evidenced in the specialized complexes constructed to house these monuments. Some of Tikal's Late Classic katun monuments depict Kawil on dates that coincide with the retrograde of Jupiter or Saturn, but the condition of other katun monuments makes the iconography difficult to analyze (table 7.2; Milbrath 2004). Stela 22, marking the katun ending in AD 771, represents two small figures wrapped in volutes floating above the ruler, representing a new form of imagery that becomes more common on the later katun monuments in the Peten (ibid., 91, figure 7). These two "cloud riders" may symbolize Jupiter and Saturn in retrograde motion, now positioned fairly close together (less than 30 degrees distant), but the imagery is too effaced to recognize the deities represented. Tikal Stela 11, dating to AD 869 (10.2.0.0.0), also shows two "cloud riders" looming over the ruler, but again the imagery is effaced (ibid., figure 10). The katun ending in AD 869 must have been especially spectacular because Jupiter and Saturn were precisely at their second stationary points and positioned only 5 degrees apart.

The last katun records in the entire Peten area date to AD 889 (10.3.0.0.0), a 1 Ahau katun ending recorded on two monuments carved only with glyphs at Uaxactun (Stela 12) and Jimbal (Stela 2). Xultun Stela 10, also recording this katun end, is the last known monument depicting Kawil in the central Peten, here represented as a serpent-footed manikin scepter (Proskouriakoff 1993, 188–89, 192).[8] The katun ending 1 Ahau on Stela 10 is an Initial Series date followed by a distance number totaling precisely twenty-four synodical revolutions of Jupiter (Thompson 1960, 228). The pattern linking the retrograde of Jupiter and Saturn to the katun end finally came to a close at the end of the Classic period (table 7.2). When the synchronicity of the planetary motions with the katun end ceased, no further katun endings were recorded on monuments in the Peten.

For the next eleven katuns, from AD 909 to 1106, neither Saturn nor Jupiter was in retrograde, but both planets were invariably close together at katun end, their distance apart averaging about seven degrees. At the next katun end in AD 1125 (10.15.0.0.0), Jupiter reached its first stationary point on December 8, about three weeks before the katun end (Milbrath 2004, 94, table 3). The planetary retrograde realigned with the katun end, and both Jupiter and Saturn were in retrograde motion for seven katun endings, from AD 1145 to 1263 (10.16.0.0.0–11.0.0.0.0), dates that overlap with the Venus almanac of the Dresden Codex (table 7.3; Milbrath 1999, 170–73, table 5.2). As discussed previously, Kawil appears as a victim of the Morning Star in this almanac. Kawil is once again prominent in Maya imagery when the katun end again aligned with Jupiter's retrograde period. The earliest of Mayapan's katun stelae (Stela 1) depicts an old enthroned god wearing the headdress of Kawil and an attendant deity who may also have attributes of Kawil. The revival of the stela cult commemorating katun endings commenced with Stela 1, erected at the end of katun 10 Ahau in AD 1185 (Milbrath and Peraza Lope 2003, table 1, figure 30; Schele and Mathews 1998, 204).

The Paris Codex, roughly contemporary with Mayapan Stela 1, represents Kawil's head being carried to different enthroned deities on pages 2 through 11 of the katun sequence (Milbrath and Peraza Lope 2003, 39, figure 31). Bruce Love (1994, 18, figure 3.2) interprets the different deities carrying the head of Kawil as a sequence of katun lords bearing Kawil's royal insignia to a priest or a chief. Alternatively, the scenes could show the transfer of power from one katun lord to another. The katun sequence begins with the katun 4 Ahau on page 1, but this page is too poorly preserved to see any detail. The sequence continues through pages 12 and 13 (katuns 8 Ahau and 6 Ahau), but they are so effaced that we cannot identify the imagery. Considering only the sequence of preserved images of Kawil on pages 2–11, the associated katun dates run from 2 Ahau to 10 Ahau. This could refer to the period running from AD 1263 to 1441 or to the previous katun cycle beginning on AD 987 to 1185, the latter coinciding with a katun date recorded on Mayapan Stela 1. In either case, the sequence of katuns would only partially overlap with a period when Jupiter or Saturn was in retrograde at katun end (table 7.3). If Kawil's appearance on these pages symbolizes planetary retrograde at the katun end, it is not a precise record of such events. The Paris Codex katun sequence probably alludes to a traditional link between katun ending ceremonies and retrograde of Jupiter and Saturn, and the imagery clearly shows that Kawil played an important role in the Postclassic Short Count—a cycle of 13 katuns, a period of 256.25 years (13 × 20 × 360 days or 260 tuns). This may reflect an ancient tradition that linked the cycle of 13 katuns with planetary retrograde, as was the case in the Early Classic period.

The Paris Codex has a number of astronomically significant sections, including a unique sequence of pages that represents a zodiac of thirteen constellations (Bricker and Bricker 1992; Milbrath 1999, 254–58). A tun cycle on the upper section of pages 2–11 may also have astronomical content because the Maya used the 360-day civil year (tun) to correlate the cycles of Mars, Jupiter, and Saturn in the Classic period (Justeson 1989, 102–3, table 7.6). On page 4, Love (1994, 30) identifies a Calendar Round date (5 Akbal 16 Zac) in katun 11 Ahau that must fall in the Classic period. One of the two proposed readings of this date (9.17.16.15.3, August 25, 787) coincides with the retrograde of both Jupiter and Saturn. The other (9.4.13.4.3, October 29, 527) coincides with the retrograde of Saturn and is within 12 days of Jupiter's second stationary point (10/17/527).

Continuing our study of the patterning of katun endings and retrograde, we see that by katun 13 Ahau in AD 1283 (11.2.0.0.0) Jupiter was no longer in retrograde at the katun end, although Saturn's retrograde continued to mark the katun ending up to katun 7 Ahau in 1342 (11.6.0.0.0; table 7.3). The latest surviving katun monument at Mayapan, dating to AD 1283, marks the end of the cycle linking the katun end to Jupiter's retrograde (Stela 6; Milbrath and Peraza Lope 2003, table 1). The pre-Columbian katun inscriptions from katun 13 Ahau to 7 Ahau are very scarce, even if we include the problematic Paris Codex sequence. One possible record appears in the Dresden Codex, which records an 11 Ahau date on page 60, which begins a katun sequence that no longer survives because of the loss of the last pages of the codex (Thompson 1972, 78–79). It seems unlikely that a Classic or Terminal Classic

TABLE 7.3 Retrograde of Jupiter and Saturn in relation to Postclassic katun endings.

10.14.0.0.0 5 Ahau 3/1/1106
    Retrogrades of Jupiter and Saturn do not overlap with katun end
10.15.0.0.0 3 Ahau katun end 11/15/1125
    Retrogrades of Jupiter and Saturn do not overlap with katun end
10.16.0.0.0 1 Ahau katun end 8/2/1145
    Jupiter retrograde 8/7/1145 to 12/3/1145
    [═KE=S1══════════════S2══]
    Saturn retrograde 8/15/1145 to 12/28/1145
    [=KE═══S1══════════════S2══]
10.17.0.0.0 12 Ahau katun end 4/19/1165
    Jupiter retrograde 3/24/1165 to 7/25/1165
    [═══S1═══KE══════════S2══]
    Saturn retrograde 4/13/1165 to 9/2/1165
    [═══S1=KE═════════════S2══]
10.18.0.0.0 10 Ahau katun end 1/4/1185
    Jupiter retrograde 12/29/1185 to 5/1/1186
    [═══S1=KE═════════════S2══]
    Saturn retrograde 12/24/1184 to 5/10/1185
    [═══S1═KE═════════════S2══]
10.19.0.0.0 8 Ahau katun end 9/21/1204
    Jupiter retrograde 7/27/1204 to 11/22/1204
    [═══S1═════════KE═════S2══]
    Saturn retrograde 8/17/1204 to 12/29/1204
    [═══S1═══════KE════════S2══]
11.0.0.0.0 6 Ahau katun end 6/8/1224
    Jupiter retrograde 3/14/1224 to 7/15/1224
    [═S1═══════════KE══════S2══]
    Saturn retrograde 4/14/1224 to 8/3/1224
    [═══S1═════════KE══════S2══]
11.1.0.0.0 4 Ahau katun end 2/24/1244
    Jupiter retrograde 11/20/1243 to 3/20/1245
    [═══S1═══════════KE═══S2══]
    Saturn retrograde 12/26/1243 to 5/12/1244
    [═══S1═════════KE══════S2══]

continued on next page

TABLE 7.3—*continued*

11.2.0.0.0 2 Ahau katun end 11/11/1263
    Jupiter retrograde 7/16/1263 to 11/11/1263
    [═══S1═══════════════════KES2═══]
    Saturn retrograde 8/19/1263 to 1/1/1264
    [═══S1═══════════════KE═════════S2═══]

11.3.0.0.0 13 Ahau katun end 7/29/1283
    Jupiter retrograde no longer overlaps with katun end
    Saturn retrograde 4/17/1283 to 9/5/1283
    [═══S1═══════════════KE═════S2═══]

11.4.0.0.0 11 Ahau katun end 4/15/1303
    Saturn retrograde 12/28/1302 to 5/14/1303
    [═══S1═══════════════KE═════S2═══]

11.5.0.0.0 9 Ahau katun end 12/31/1323
    Saturn retrograde 9/4/1323 to 1/16/1324
    [═══S1═══════════════════KE══S2═══]

11.6.0.0.0 7 Ahau katun end 9/17/1342
    Saturn retrograde 4/18/1342 to 9/6/1342
    [═══S1═══════════════════════S2══KE═]

11.7.0.0.0 5 Ahau katun end 6/4/1362
    Saturn retrograde 12/29/1361 to 5/15/1362
    [═══S1═══════════════════════S2═══KE]

11.8.0.0.0 3 Ahau katun end 2/19/1382;
    retrogrades of Jupiter and Saturn do not overlap with katun end

Katun 11 Ahau date is intended because the codex contains a number of historical dates, but none of them is a katun date. Since Thompson suggests that the pages are katun prophecies representing future events, the katun 11 Ahau could refer to AD 1303, coinciding with Saturn's retrograde period (table 7.3). The same text has a 10 Yaxkin date that cannot occur with the katun ending 11 Ahau, indicating that this notation must be an error or an alternate form of calendar. As the Postclassic period came to a close, there was an apparent shift in the calendar. This adjustment was necessary because the katun endings no longer synchronized with the retrograde periods of Jupiter or Saturn. New calendar paradigms were established that placed a greater emphasis on the solar year (Aveni 2004, 161).

In the Late Postclassic period, there seems to have been an increased interest in the tun as an approximation of the solar year.[9] Murals from Mound 1 at Santa

Rita in Belize, probably contemporary with murals from Tulum that date after AD 1300, depict a series of astronomical deities associated with a sequence of tuns, each marking a period of 360 days that roughly corresponds to a year (Milbrath 1999, 230). The tun sequence is broken at one point by a 1 Ahau date associated with an image of Kawil. In a previous publication, I suggested this was a katun ending date related to a pattern linking 1 Ahau katun endings to Jupiter events during the Classic period (ibid.). Alternatively, since katun endings no longer coincided with the retrograde of Jupiter or Saturn in the Late Postclassic, a Venus event may be the reference point. This date could be linked with the rise of the Morning Star because the mural shows Kawil with his hands tied behind his back, a victim destined for sacrifice, the same role Kawil plays in the Dresden Codex Venus almanac where 1 Ahau is a canonical heliacal rise date in the Postclassic period (ibid., 166–67, figure 5.3a). According to a layout of the Dresden Codex Venus Tables developed by Lounsbury (1983), a 1 Ahau heliacal rise was predicted on December 20, 1324 (1 Ahau 3 Xul, 11.5.2.0.0), which was only a day away from the actual heliacal rise date (Aveni 1992, table 3.2, adjusted for 584,283 correlation). On this date, Jupiter was in retrograde, a few weeks away from its second stationary point (1/11/1325; Meeus n.d.). At this time, the rising Morning Star was located opposite the planet Jupiter, which set about two hours before the rise of the Morning Star. Two other 1 Ahau heliacal rise dates appear on page 50, and one of these also extends the predictions into the fourteenth century. The latest prediction proposed for the 1 Ahau 3 Xul is the sixtieth Venus Round falling ninety-six years after January 1221 (65 VR = 104 years − 8 years = 60 VR; figure 3.10, table 3.4 in Bricker and Bricker 2007). Again, this date corresponds to a period when Jupiter was in retrograde (1/14/1317–5/17/1317; Meeus n.d.). In either case, the 1 Ahau date could refer to Venus rising on 1 Ahau and sacrificing Kawil, symbolizing Jupiter at the opposite side of the sky in retrograde motion.

KAWIL AND TEZCATLIPOCA IN THE CONTEXT OF ASTRONOMICAL IMAGERY

Kawil undergoes numerous transformations over a period spanning more than a thousand years, but his imagery consistently has celestial associations, including sky bands, sky glyphs, and stars. Kawil's mirror may represent the planet Jupiter as an orb shining in the night sky. Kawil's association with Jupiter's retrograde period is revealed in study of monuments that record texts with dated events. Jupiter played an important role, especially in the events recorded in the lives of Classic Maya rulers, many of whom are represented with the insignia of Kawil. Dates associated with images of dead rulers in the guise of Kawil suggest that Jupiter events signaled the apotheosis of Maya rulers at Palenque and Copan. At Yaxchilan, Palenque, and Tikal, royal monuments representing Kawil most often bear dates coinciding with Jupiter's retrograde motion. At Tikal, many of these dynastic monuments record katun endings that coincide with the retrograde of Jupiter and Saturn. Kawil might have more than one planetary aspect, for when a Jupiter event is not apparent on a monument representing Kawil, a Saturn event may serve as a substitute.

Katun monuments seem to cluster in periods when the katun ending corresponded to the retrograde motion of Jupiter or Saturn. This patterning holds true for both the Classic and Postclassic Maya, a finding that deserves considerable emphasis. Indeed, the katun cycle itself may have developed as result of long-term observations of Jupiter and Saturn. Long Count inscriptions in the central Maya area began around the time the retrograde of Saturn first marked the katun end (table 7.1). From 8.11.0.0.0 to 8.15.0.0.0 (AD 258–337), Saturn was in retrograde at each katun ending, and both Saturn and Jupiter were in retrograde motion at the katun end from 8.16.0.0.0 to 8.19.0.0.0 (AD 357–416). For the next 60 years, Jupiter was the only planet in retrograde motion at the katun end, from 9.0.0.0.0 to 9.3.0.0.0 (AD 435–495), a period that correlates with a series of katun monuments at Tikal. Neither planet was in retrograde in the katun endings 9.4.0.0.0 to 9.12.0.0.0 (AD 514–672), a period that overlaps with a hiatus of 130 years in the erection of Maya monuments at Tikal. It is noteworthy that at Tikal, where interest in marking katun endings seems exceptionally well developed, the hiatus period lasted until AD 692, when a katun monument was erected to mark the renewed correlation between the katun end and the timing of retrograde events with Saturn marking the katun end (table 7.2).

Kawil is prominent on Late Classic katun monuments bearing dates that coincide with the retrograde periods of Jupiter and Saturn, but there were also other forms of representing this celestial imagery. In the late eighth century new forms of astronomical imagery developed, most notably the cloud rider deities that probably represent Jupiter and Saturn in retrograde at the katun end.

Classic period representations of Kawil connect him with lineage and rulership. As the god of Maya kings, Kawil evokes parallels with ancient European traditions identifying Jupiter as the planet of kings. There is a natural basis for the association with kings. Jupiter makes a perfect celestial ruler, the counterpart to the good ruler on earth, because the planet seems to dominate the night sky. Jupiter is rarely absent from the sky (with a mean disappearance interval of thirty-two days), its brilliance second only to Venus. Unlike Venus—which makes frequent trips to the underworld and is seen only around dawn and dusk, always relatively close to the horizon—Jupiter can be seen all night long, seemingly producing an "eternal" light. This same eternal presence seems evident in the imagery of Tezcatlipoca that may be linked with Jupiter. His dark mirror symbolized the night sky and possibly also the eternal presence of Jupiter.

Kawil's mirror is linked with smoking axes and burning torches, symbols that may refer to thunder and lightning. As a god of thunder and lightning associated with the planet Jupiter, Kawil shares the same role as Jupiter in ancient Greece and Rome. Perhaps this notion has an explanation in nature, one connected with folklore linking Jupiter to storms. There may be some basis in long-term observations of nature that led to the planet Jupiter being linked to weather phenomena. Through the many different cycles recorded in the Long Count calendar, the Maya linked celestial deities with planetary cycles and the phases of the moon. In the Postclassic period, these cycles were linked to patterns of weather and attendant fortunes of the maize crop (Milbrath 1999, 106–10, 232). As Thompson noted long ago, Maya astronomy is astrology. Instead of personal horoscopes, however, the Maya recorded astronomical cycles in an attempt to predict the weather and other cycles in nature.

Like Kawil, Tezcatlipoca had a connection with planetary cycles and the moon, but his aspect was more capricious. Tezcatlipoca is a lord of fate who seems connected with astrological cycles linked to the motions of the sun, moon, and planets. Whereas Kawil ruled over calendric cycles such as the katun, marking a steady progression of time, Tezcatlipoca's domain was more chaotic and ominous. Without the aid of the Long Count calendar, the Aztecs had more difficulty predicting the celestial motions, an uncertainty conveyed in Tezcatlipoca's aspect as the ultimate trickster linked with fortune telling, magic, and portents of cataclysmic change.

NOTES

1. Stormy Sky (Siyah Chan Kawil or Siyaj Chan K'awiil II) has the earliest known Kawil title in the list of Tikal rulers compiled by Peter Harrison (1999, tables 2, 3). Nonetheless, the Kawil title may be earlier because it appears in the name of an early-fourth-century ruler (Siyaj Chan K'awiil) in the king list developed by Simon Martin and Nikolai Grube (2000, 26).

2. In his analysis of Aztec deity complexes, Henry B. Nicholson (1971, 412, table 3) links Tezcatlipoca to the lunar gods Metztli and Tecciztecatl, while the jaguar aspect of Tezcatlipoca (Tepeyollotl) is seen as an aspect of the earth rather than the moon. Because the earth and the moon are so closely related in Mesoamerica, such a distinction may be more apparent than real (Thompson 1972, 47).

3. The Initial Series date (9.0.10.0.0; October 16, 445) also coincides approximately with the heliacal set of Mars (Alexander 1992, table 1; Milbrath 1999, 239). Other coordinating events include the new moon and Venus approaching its maximum brilliance as the Morning Star. The ruler himself seems to be compared with Hun Ahau, the underworld

sun and Morning Star, while his father seems to be apotheosized as the Sun God overhead (ibid., 85).

4. On this date, Jupiter was in conjunction with the Pleiades, one of the most important constellations in the Milky Way for the Maya (Milbrath 1999, 287). Perhaps och bih is a reference to both the Milky Way and the Pleiades. This glyphic compound includes a glyph that sometimes refers to the Pleiades (Macri and Looper 2003, 61).

5. It is interesting that Mars was almost never seen in retrograde motion at the katun end. During the Early Classic period Mars was in retrograde at the katun ending only twice (AD 278 and AD 435), and the same is true for the Late Classic period, when Mars was in retrograde motion at the katun end in AD 613 and AD 790.

6. Kawil is not represented on Tikal Stela 16, but both Dos Pilas and Naranjo depict Kawil on the katun ending 9.14.0.0.0 (Dos Pilas Stela 14, Houston 1993, figure 3.24; Naranjo Stela 23, Maler 1908, plate 37). These monuments also record dates that correspond to the retrograde of Jupiter, so it is likely that the planet was being observed, even though its retrograde period did not coincide with this katun ending.

7. Ruler B's monuments also record dates that correspond to Jupiter's retrograde on lintels that represent Kawil. Lintel 3 of Temple IV features Kawil in the jaws of a Cosmic Monster arching over the ruler's head (Milbrath 1999, 238, plate 15). Of the four Calendar Round dates on Lintel 3, only the opening inscription, a Lahuntun ending on 3 Ahau 3 Mol (9.15.10.0.0; 741 June 24, 741), relates to Jupiter's retrograde, approximating the planet's first stationary point (7/10/741, Meeus n.d.). The lintel depicts Kawil displaying a mirror glyph in his hand, positioned like the flat-hand mirror compound used to mark Venus positions in the Venus Tables of the Dresden Codex. The same Lahuntun ending, 3 Ahau 3 Mol, also opens the inscription on Lintel 2 from Temple IV. Here Yaxkin Chaan Kawil (Ruler B) holds his Kawil manikin scepter as a Jaguar War God protector looms over him (Milbrath 1999, 238, plate 16). A war event (B8) dates to 7 Ben 1 Pop (February 2, 744; 9.15.12.11.13), coinciding approximately with the midpoint of Saturn's retrograde period, and it may have been visualized as the "departure" from Jupiter's second stationary point (744 January 17, 744; Meeus n.d.). According to Lounsbury (1989, 255), the star war event was timed by Jupiter's departure from its second stationary point. Schele and Grube (1994, 187; 1995, 40–46) note that a solar eclipse in 744 (1/19/744) was a prelude to the star war event recorded on the lintel. Justeson (1989, table 7.8) points out that a number of war events coincide with the retrograde periods of at least one of the superior planets. The last date on Lintel 2 (9.15.15.14.0 3 Ahau 13 Uo; March 5, 747) also falls within retrograde periods of both Jupiter and Saturn.

8. The Xultun ruler holds another manikin in his hand representing the Water-lily Jaguar, a creature that may embody the rainy season moon (Milbrath 1999, 120–24). The katun ending date (4/28/889) aligns with early May in our Gregorian Calendar, associated with onset of rains in many areas of Mesoamerica.

9. A similar emphasis on recording the tun took place in the Terminal Classic period at Chichén Itzá, where Tun-Ahau dates were prominent at a time when the long cycle linking the katun end to the retrograde of Jupiter and Saturn was coming to a close. Tun-Ahau dates are associated with a new type of iconography. Traditional Calendar Round dates also appear with new forms of imagery, as in the Osario, which depicts bird images representing Kawil on a date reconstructed as AD 998 (Graña-Behrens, Prager, and Wagner 1999). Kawil birds are paired with another bird that may represent Chac. Since Chac seems more closely associated with the Venus cult (Milbrath 1999, 199–209), a new astronomical paradigm focusing on Venus may have been developing as early as AD 1000, at the time Jupiter no longer played an important role in the katun cycle. The Venus cult featuring the feathered serpent became increasingly important in the period between AD 950 and 1050, when the northern part of the city was constructed (Cobos 2001, 186).

References

Ackermann, Silke, and Louise Devoy. 2012. "'The Lord of the Smoking Mirror': Objects Associated with John Dee in the British Museum." *Studies in History and Philosophy of Science, Part A* 43 (3): 539–49. http://dx.doi.org/10.1016/j.shpsa.2011.11.007.

Acosta, Jorge R. 1956. "Resumen de los informes de las exploraciones arqueológicas en Tula, Hidalgo, durante las VI, VII, y VIII temporadas, 1946–1950." *Anales del Museo Nacional de Antropología e Historia, Época* 6 (8): 37–115.

Acosta, Jorge R. 1964. "La decimotercera temporada de exploraciones en Tula, Hidalgo." *Anales del Museo Nacional de Antropología e Historia, Época* 6 (16): 45–76.

Acosta, José de. 1973. *Natural and Moral History of the Indies*. Trans. Edward Grimston. New York: Burt Franklin.

Acosta Saignes, Miguel. 1946. "Los teopixque: Organización sacerdotal entre los mexica." *Revista Mexicana de Estudios Antropológicos* 8: 147–205.

Acuña, René. 1984–88. *Relaciones geográficas del siglo XVI*. 10 vols. Mexico City: Universidad Nacional Autónoma de México.

Alexander, Helen. 1992. "Celestial Links to the Ancestors: A Pattern Analysis of Celestial Events on Twelve Dates Recorded on Tikal Stela 31." *U Mut Maya* 4: 8–60.

Alva Ixtlilxóchitl, Fernando de. 1985 [1975]. *Obras históricas*. Ed. Edmundo O'Gorman. Mexico City: Universidad Nacional Autónoma de México.

Alvarado Tezozómoc, Hernando. 1975. *Crónica mexicana*. Ed. Manuel Orozco y Berra. Mexico City: Porrúa.

REFERENCES

Alvarado Tezozómoc, Hernando. 1980 [ca. 1598]. *Crónica mexicana*. Ed. Manuel Orozco y Berra. Mexico City: Porrúa.

Anales de Cuauhtitlan. 1992a. *Codex Chimalpopoca: The Text in Nahuatl with a Glossary and Grammatical Notes*. Ed. John Bierhorst. Tucson: University of Arizona Press.

Anales de Cuauhtitlan. 1992b. *History and Mythology of the Aztecs: The Codex Chimalpopoca*. Trans. John Bierhorst. Tucson: University of Arizona Press.

Anawalt, Patricia R. 1981. "Costume Analysis and the Provenience of the Borgia Group Codices." *American Antiquity* 46 (4): 837–52. http://dx.doi.org/10.2307/280110.

Anawalt, Patricia R. 1996. "Aztec Knotted and Netted Capes: Colonial Interpretations vs. Indigenous Primary Data." *Ancient Mesoamerica* 7 (2): 187–206. http://dx.doi.org/10.1017/S0956536100001401.

Anders, Ferdinand, Maarten Jansen, and Luis Reyes. 1994. *La pintura de la muerte y de los destinos: Libro explicativo del* llamado Códice Laud. Accompanied by a facsimile of the codex. Graz: Akademische Druck- und Verlagsanstalt; Mexico City: Fondo de Cultura Económica.

Anonymous. 1968. "Recent Museum Acquisitions: The Magical Speculum of Dr. Dee (British Museum)." *Burlington Magazine* 110: 42–43.

Antiguo Colegio de San Ildefonso. 1995. *Dioses del México antiguo*. Mexico City: Antiguo Colegio de San Ildefonso.

Arana Álvarez, Raúl M. 1984. "El juego de pelota en Coatetelco, Morelos." In *Investigaciones recientes en el área maya, XVII Mesa Redonda, Sociedad Mexicana de Antropología* 4: 191–204. Mexico City: Sociedad Mexicana de Antropología.

Aveni, Anthony F. 1992. "The Moon and the Venus Table: An Example of Commensuration in the Maya Calendar." In *The Sky and Mayan Literature*, ed. Anthony F. Aveni, 87–101. New York: Oxford University Press.

Aveni, Anthony F. 2000. *Skywatchers*. Austin: University of Texas Press.

Aveni, Anthony F. 2004. "Intervallic Structure and Cognate Almanacs in the Madrid and Dresden Codices." In *The Madrid Codex: New Approaches to Understanding an Ancient Maya Manuscript*, ed. Gabrielle Vail and Anthony F. Aveni, 147–70. Boulder: University Press of Colorado.

Aveni, Anthony F., Edward E. Calnek, and Horst Hartung. 1988. "Myth, Environment and the Orientation of the Templo Mayor of Tenochtitlan." *American Antiquity* 53 (2): 287–309. http://dx.doi.org/10.2307/281020.

Aveni, Anthony F., Anne Dowd, and Benjamin Vining. 2003. "Maya Calendar Reform? Evidence from Orientations of Specialized Architectural Assemblages." *Latin American Antiquity* 14 (2): 159–78. http://dx.doi.org/10.2307/3557592.

Aveni, Anthony F., and Lorren D. Hotaling. 1994. "Monumental Inscriptions and the Observational Basis of Maya Planetary Astronomy." *Journal for the History of Astronomy* 25: 21–54.

Bacigalupo, Ana Mariella. 2004. "The Struggle for Mapuche Shamans' Masculinity: Colonial Politics of Gender, Sexuality, and Powers in Southern Chile." *Ethnohistory* 51 (3): 489–533. http://dx.doi.org/10.1215/00141801-51-3-489.

Baer, Gerhard, ed. 1996. *Ancient Mexican Ceramics from the Lukas Vischer Collection, Ethnographic Museum Basel*. Corpus Americanensium Antiquitatum, Union Académique Internationale. Basel, Switzerland: Friedrich Reinhardt.

Baer, Gerhard, and Ulf Bankmann. 1990. *Altmexikanische Skulpturen der Sammlung Lukas Vischer, Museum für Völkerkunde Basel / Ancient Mexican Sculptures from the Lukas Vischer Collection, Ethnographic Museum Basel*. Corpus Americanensium Antiquitatum, Union Académique Internationale. Basel, Switzerland: Verlag Wepf.

Báez-Jorge, Félix. 1992. "Homshuk y el simbolismo de la ovogénesis en Mesoamérica." In *Antropología mesoamericana: Homenaje a Alfonso Villa Rojas*, ed. Víctor Manuel Esponda Jimeno, Sophia Pincemin Deliberos, and Mauricio Rosas Kifuri, 303–32. Chiapas, Mexico: Instituto Chiapaneco de Cultura, Tuxtla Gutiérrez.

Baird, Ellen Taylor. 1993. *The Drawings of Sahagún's Primeros Memoriales: Structure and Style*. Norman: University of Oklahoma Press.

Baquedano, Elizabeth. 2005. "El oro azteca y sus conexiones con el poder, la fertilidad agrícola, la guerra y la muerte." *Estudios de Cultura Nahuatl* 36: 359–81.

Baquedano, Elizabeth. 2011. "Concepts of Death and the Afterlife in Central Mexico." In *Living with the Dead: Mortuary Ritual in Mesoamerica*, ed. James Fitzsimmons and Izumi Shimada, 203–30. Tucson: University of Arizona Press.

Barber, Sarah B., Gonzalo Sánchez, and Mireya Olvera. 2009. "Sounds of Death and Life in Mesoamerica: The Bone Flutes of Ancient Oaxaca." *Yearbook for Traditional Music* 41: 94–110.

Barlow, Robert H. 1995. "Codex Azcatitlan, Códice Azcatitlan." In *Codex Azcatitlan, Códice Azcatitlan*, ed. Robert H. Barlow and Michel Graulich, 32–153. Paris: Bibliothèque nationale de France and Société des Américanistes.

Barlow, Robert H., and Michel Graulich, eds. 1995. *Codex Azcatitlan: Códice Azcatitlan*. Paris: Bibliothèque nationale de France and Société des Américanistes.

Barnes, William Landon. 2009. "Icons of Empire: The Art and History of Aztec Royal Presentation." PhD dissertation, Tulane University, New Orleans.

Batalla Rosado, Juan José. 1992. "El arte de escribir en Mesoamérica: El Códice Borbónico." Degree Thesis, Universidad Complutense, Madrid.

Batalla Rosado, Juan José. 1993a. "Los *Tlacuiloque* del *Códice Borbónico*: Análisis iconográfico de los signos calendáricos." *Estudios de Historia Social y Económica de América* 10: 9–24.

Batalla Rosado, Juan José. 1993b. "La perspectiva Indígena Prehispánica y el *Códice Borbónico*: Página 31-escena central." *Revista Espanola de Antropologia Americana* 23: 113–34.

Batalla Rosado, Juan José. 1994a. "Datación del *Códice Borbónico* a partir del análisis iconográfico de la representación de la sangre." *Revista Espanola de Antropologia Americana* 24: 47–74.

Batalla Rosado, Juan José. 1994b. "Los *tlacuiloque* del *Códice Borbónico*: Una aproximación a su número y estilo." *Journal de la Société des Americanistes* 80 (1): 47–72. http://dx.doi.org/10.3406/jsa.1994.1525.

Batalla Rosado, Juan José. 1994c. "Teorías sobre el origen colonial del *Códice Borbónico*." *Cuadernos Prehispánicos* 15: 5–42.

Batalla Rosado, Juan José. 1995. "Escritura de tradición Mixteca-Puebla: La escritura Mexica o Azteca." *Estudios de Historia Social y Económica de América* 12: 625–37.

Batalla Rosado, Juan José. 1997. "El palacio real mexica: Análisis iconográfico escriturario." In *Códices, caciques y comunidades*, ed. Maarten Jansen and Luis Reyes García, 65–101. Cuadernos de Historia Latinoamericana, vol. 5. Leiden: Asociación de Historiadores Latinoamericanistas Europeos.

Batalla Rosado, Juan José. 2002a. *Códice Tributos de Coyoacán*. Madrid: Comma/Brokarte.

Batalla Rosado, Juan José. 2002b. *El Códice Tudela y el Grupo Magliabechiano: La tradición medieval europea de copia de códices en América*. Colección Thesaurus Americae, vol. 4. Madrid: Ministerio de Educación Cultura y Deportes.

Batalla Rosado, Juan José. 2007. "The Scribes Who Painted the Matrícula de Tributos and the Codex Mendoza." *Ancient Mesoamerica* 18: 31–52.

Batalla Rosado, Juan José. 2008. "The Mesoamerican Codices: Study Methods." *Itineraries: Journal of Linguistic, Literary, Historical and Anthropological Studies* 8: 43–66.

Béguin, Sylvie, and Cristiana Garofalo. 2001. *Rafaello: Catalogo complete dei dipinti*. Santarcangelo di Romagna, Italy: Octavo.

Benavente o Motolinía, Fray Toribio. 1971. *Memoriales o Libro de las cosas de la Nueva España y de los naturales de ella*. Ed. Edmundo O'Gorman. Mexico City: Universidad Nacional Autónoma de México.

Benson, Elizabeth P. 1998. "The Lord, the Ruler: Jaguar Symbolism in the Americas." In *Icons of Power: Feline Symbolism in the Americas*, ed. Nicholas J. Saunders, 53–76. London: Routledge.

Berdan, Frances F. 2007. "Material Dimensions of Aztec Religion and Ritual." In *Mesoamerican Ritual Economy: Archaeological and Ethnological Perspectives*, ed. E. Christian Wells and Karla L. Davis-Salazar, 245–300. Boulder: University Press of Colorado.

Berdan, Frances F., and Patricia Rieff Anawalt. 1992. *The Codex Mendoza*. 4 vols. Berkeley: University of California Press.

Berlin, Henrich. 1963. "The Palenque Triad." *Journale des Société des Americanistes* 52: 1–99.

Berlin, Henrich. 1977. *Signos y significados en las inscripciones mayas*. Guatemala City: Instituto Nacional del Patrimonio Cultural de Guatemala.

Bierhorst, John. 1985. *Cantares Mexicanos: Songs of the Aztecs*. Stanford, CA: Stanford University Press.

Blanton, Richard E. 1972. *Prehispanic Settlement Patterns of the Ixtapalapa Peninsula Region, Mexico*. Occasional Papers in Anthropology 6, Department of Anthropology, Pennsylvania State University.

Boone, Elizabeth Hill. 1980. "How Efficient Are Early Colonial Mexican Manuscripts as Iconographic Tools?" *Research Center for the Arts Review* 3: 1–5.

Boone, Elizabeth Hill. 1983. *The Codex Magliabechiano and the Lost Prototype of the Magliabechiano Group*. London: University of California Press.

Boone, Elizabeth Hill, ed. 1987. *The Aztec Templo Mayor*. Washington, DC: Dumbarton Oaks.

Boone, Elizabeth Hill. 1989. *Incarnations of the Aztec Supernatural: The Image of Huitzilopochtli in Mexico and Europe*. Vol. 79, book 2 of *Transactions*. New York: American Philosophical Society. http://dx.doi.org/10.2307/1006524.

Boone, Elizabeth Hill. 1991. "Migration Histories as Ritual Performance." In *To Change Place: Aztec Ceremonial Landscapes*, ed. Davíd Carrasco, 121–51. Niwot: University Press of Colorado.

Boone, Elizabeth Hill, ed. 1993. *Collecting the Pre-Columbian Past*. Washington, DC: Dumbarton Oaks.

Boone, Elizabeth Hill. 2000. *Stories in Red and Black: Pictorial Histories of the Aztecs and Mixtecs*. Austin: University of Texas Press.

Boone, Elizabeth Hill. 2007. *Cycles of Time and Meaning in the Mexican Books of Fate*. Austin: University of Texas Press.

Both, Arnd Adje. 2002. "Aztec Flower Flutes: The Symbolic Organization of Sound in Late Postclassic Mesoamerica." *Orient-Archäologie* 10: 279–289.

Both, Arnd Adje. 2005a. "Aerófonos mexicas de las orfrendas del recinto sagrado de Tenochtitlan." PhD dissertation, Department of Ciencias Históricas y Culturales, Universidad Libre de Berlin.

Both, Arnd Adje. 2005b. "Music: Music and Religion in Mesoamerica." In *Encyclopaedia of Religion*, ed. Lindsay Jones, 6266–71. Detroit: Thomson-Gale. http://www.mixcoacalli.com/wp-content/uploads/2007/05/both_music-religion-2005.pdf.

Both, Arnd Adje. 2006. "On the Context of Imitative and Associative Processes in Prehispanic Music." In *Studien zur Musikarchäologie V*, ed. Ellen Hickmann and Ricardo Eichmann, 319–32. Westfalia, Germany: Rahden. http://www.mixcoacalli.com/wp-content/uploads/2007/05/both_2006.pdf.

Both, Arnd Adje. 2007. "Aztec Music Culture." In *Music Archaeology: Mesoamerica*, ed. Max Peter Baumann, Arnd Adje Both, and Julia L. Sanchez, 91–194. Vol. 49, book 2 of *The World of Music*. Bamberg, Germany: University of Bamberg.

Bricker, Harvey M., and Victoria R. Bricker. 1992. "Zodiacal References in the Maya Codices." In *The Sky and Mayan Literature*, ed. Anthony F. Aveni, 148–83. Oxford: Oxford University Press.

Bricker, Harvey, and Victoria Bricker. 2007. "When Did the Dresden Codex Venus Table Work?" In *Cultural Astronomy in New World Cosmologies*, ed. Clive Ruggles and Gary Urton, 95–120. Boulder: University Press of Colorado.

Bricker, Victoria Reifler. 1973. *Ritual Humor in Highland Chiapas*. Austin: University of Texas Press.

Broda, Johanna. 1987. "The Provenience of the Offerings: Tribute and *Cosmovision*." In *The Aztec Templo Mayor*, ed. Elizabeth H. Boone, 211–56. Washington, DC: Dumbarton Oaks.

Broda, Johanna. 1999. "Rain, Rocks and Air: An Anthropological Analysis of Tlaloc Rituals and Political Power in Central Mexico before and after the Spanish Conquest." In *Von der realen Magie zum Magischen Realismus*, ed. Elke Mader, 119–30. Jahrbuch des Osterreichischen Lateinamerika-Instutut. Frankfurt am Main: Brandes und Apsel Verlag.

Brotherston, Gordon. 1997 [1992]. *La América indígena en su literatura: Los libros del cuarto mundo*. Trans. Teresa Ortega Guerrero and Mónica Utrilla. Mexico City: Fondo de Cultura Económica.

Brundage, Burr Cartwright. 1979. *The Fifth Sun: Aztec Gods, Aztec World*. Austin: University of Texas Press.

Buchli, Victor, ed. 2002. *The Material Culture Reader*. Oxford: Berg.

Burkhart, Louise M. 1988. "Doctrinal Aspects of Sahagún's *Colloquios*." In *The Work of Bernardino de Sahagún, Pioneer Ethnographer of Sixteenth-Century Aztec Mexico*, ed. J. Jorge Klor de Alva, Henry B. Nicholson, and Eloise Quiñones Keber, 65–82. Albany: Institute for Mesoamerican Studies, State University of New York at Albany.

Burkhart, Louise M. 1989. *The Slippery Earth: Nahua-Christian Dialogue in Sixteenth-Century Mexico*. Tucson: University of Arizona Press.

Burkhart, Louise M. 1997. "Mexica Women on the Home Front: Housework and Religion in Aztec Mexico." In *Indian Women of Early Mexico*, ed. Susan Schroeder, Stephanie Wood, and Robert Haskett, 25–54. Norman: University of Oklahoma Press.

Bynum, Carolyn Walker. 1982. *Jesus as Mother: Studies in the Spirituality of the High Middle Ages*. Berkeley: University of California Press.

Bynum, Carolyn Walker. 1991. "The Body of Christ in the Late Middle Ages: A Reply to Leo Steinberg." In *Fragmentation and Redemption: Essays on Gender and the Human*

Body in Medieval Religion, 79–117. New York: Urzone/Zone Books. (Reprint of article in *Renaissance Quarterly* 39 (3) [1986]: 399–439.)

Calligaro, T., J.-C. Dran, S. Dubernet, G. Poupeau, F. Gendron, E. Gonthier, O. Meslay, and D. Tenorio. 2005. "PIXE Reveals That Two of Murillo's Masterpieces Were Painted on Mexican Obsidian Slabs." *Nuclear Instruments and Methods in Physics Research: Section B, Beam Interactions with Materials and Atoms* 240 (1–2): 576–582. http://dx.doi.org/10.1016/j.nimb.2005.06.155. http://www.sciencedirect.com/science/article/B6TJN-4GV8SWS-H/2/c439454502d89eb618cbe7f33cd8794b?ccp=y.

Calloway, Carol. 1990. "Pre-Columbian and Colonial Mexican Images of the Cross: Christ's Sacrifice and the Fertile Earth." *Journal of Latin American Lore* 16 (2): 199–231.

Carrandi, Jorge, Daniel Granados Vázquez, and Ricardo Garduño Ramírez. 1990. *Apaxco, Museo Arqueológico: Piezas selectas*. Toluca, Mexico: Instituto Mexiquense de Cultura.

Carrasco, Davíd. 1982. *Quetzalcoatl and the Irony of Empire: Myths and Prophecies in the Aztec Tradition*. Chicago: University of Chicago Press.

Carrasco, Davíd. 1987. "Myth, Cosmic Terror, and the Templo Mayor." In *The Great Temple of Tenochtitlan: Center and Periphery in the Aztec World*, ed. Johanna Broda, Davíd Carrasco, and Eduardo Matos Moctezuma, 124–62. Berkeley: University of California Press.

Carrasco, Davíd. 1991. "The Sacrifice of Tezcatlipoca: To Change Place." In *To Change Place: Aztec Ceremonial Landscapes*, ed. Davíd Carrasco, 31–57. Niwot: University Press of Colorado.

Carrasco, Davíd. 1992 [1982]. *Quetzalcoatl and the Irony of Empire*. Chicago: University of Chicago Press.

Caso, Alfonso. 1958. *The Aztecs: People of the Sun*. Norman: University of Oklahoma Press.

Caso, Alfonso. 1961. "Nombres calendáricos de los dioses." *El México antiguo* 9: 77–98.

Castañeda de la Paz, María. 2006. *Pintura de la peregrinación de los culhuaque-mexitin (Mapa de Sigüenza)*. Toluca: El Colegio Mexiquense and Instituto Nacional de Antropología e Historia.

Castillo, Cristóbal del. 1991. *Historia de la venida de los mexicanos y de otros pueblos e historia de la conquista*, ed. and trans. Federico Navarrete Linares. México: INAH.

Castillo Tejero, Noemí. 1991. "La cerámica policroma Matlatzinca del viejo museo de Toluca." In *Homenaje a Julio César Olivé Negrete*, 297–324. Mexico City: Universidad Nacional Autónoma de México.

Cervantés de Salazar, Francisco. 1985. *Crónica de la Nueva España*. Ed. Juan Miralles Ostos. Mexico City: Porrúa.

Charnay, Desiré. 1888. *The Ancient Cities of the New World, Being Travels and Explorations in Mexico and Central America from 1857–1882*. New York: Harper and Brothers.

Chávez, Gabriel de. 1986. "Relación geográfica de Meztitlán." In *Relaciones geográficas del siglo XVI: México* 2: 51–75. Mexico City: Universidad Nacional Autónoma de México, IIA.

Chimalpahin Cuauhtlehuanitzin, Domingo de Anton. 1965. *Relaciones originales de Chalco Amecamecan*. Trans. Silvia Rendón. Mexico City: Fondo de Cultura Económica.

Chimalpahin Cuauhtlehuanitzin, Domingo Francisco de San Antón Muñón. 2003. *Séptima relación de las différentes histoires originales*. Trans. and ed. Josefina García Quintana. Mexico City: Universidad Nacional Autónoma de México, IIH.

Clark, John E. 1994. "Antiguos instrumentos y ornamentos de obsidiana." In *Cristales y obsidiana prehispánicos*, ed. Carmen Serra Puche Mari and Felipe Solís Olguín, 41–51. Mexico City: Siglo Veintiuno.

Cobos, Raphael. 2001. "Chichén Itzá." In *Oxford Encyclopedia of Mesoamerican Cultures*, ed. Davíd Carrasco 1: 183–87. New York: Oxford University Press.

Codex Borbonicus. 1974. *Codex Borbonicus: Bibliotheque de l'Assemblee nationale Francaise (Y120)*. Commentary by Karl Anton Novotny. Graz, Austria: Akademische Druck- u. Verlagsanstalt.

Codex Borbonicus. 1991. *El libro del Ciuacoatl: Homenaje para el año del Fuego Nuevo; Libro explicativo del llamado Códice Borbónico*. Ed. Ferdinand Anders, Maarten Jansen, and Luis Reyes García. Graz, Austria: Akademische Druck- u. Verlagsanstalt; Mexico City: Fondo de Cultura Económica.

Codex Borgia. 1963. *Codex Borgia*. Ed. Eduard Seler. Mexico City: Fondo de Cultura Económica.

Codex Borgia. 1976. *Codex Borgia. Commentary by Karl Anton Nowotny*. Graz, Austria: Akademische Druck- u. Verlagsanstalt.

Codex Fejérváry-Mayer. 1901–2. *An Old Mexican Picture Manuscript in the Liverpool Free Public Museums*. Ed. Eduard Seler. Berlin: Edinburgh University Press.

Codex Fejérváry-Mayer. 1971. *Codex Fejérváry-Mayer: 12014 M. City of Liverpool Museums*. Ed. Cottie A. Burland. Codices selecti phototypice impressi, vol. 26. Graz, Austria: Akademische Druck- u. Verlagsanstalt.

Codex Ixtlilxochitl. 1976. *Bibliothèque Nationale, Paris, Ms Mex.65–71*. Ed. Jacqueline de Durand-Forest. Fontes rerum mexicanarum 9. Graz, Austria: Akademische Druck- u. Verlagsanstalt.

Codex Laud. 1966. *MS Laud Misc. 678: Bodleian Library Oxford*. Ed. Cottie A. Burland. Graz, Austria: Akademische Druck- u. Verlagsanstalt.

Codex Magliabechiano. 1970. *Codex Magliabechiano*. Ed. Ferdinand Anders. Graz, Austria: Akademische Druck- u. Verlagsanstalt.

Codex Magliabechiano. 1996. *Libro de la vida: Texto explicativo del llamado Códice Magliabechiano*. Ed. Ferdinand Anders and Maarten Jansen. Graz, Austria: Akademische Druck- u. Verlagsanstalt; Mexico City: Fondo de Cultura Económica.

Codex Telleriano-Remensis. 1964–67. *Codex Telleriano-Renensis*. In *Antigüadades de Mexico* 1: 151–338.

Codex Telleriano-Remensis. 1995. *Codex Telleriano-Remensis: Ritual, Divination, and History in a Pictorial Aztec Manuscript.* Ed. Eloise Quiñones Keber. Austin: University of Texas Press.

Codex Tudela. 1980. *Codex Tudela.* Ed. José Tudela de la Orden. Madrid: Ediciones Cultura Hispánica del Instituto de Cooperación Iberoamericano.

Codex Tudela. 2002. *Códice Tudela.* Ed. José Batalla Rosado Juan. Madrid: Ministerio de Educación Cultura y Deportes, Agencia Española de Cooperación Internacional y Testimonio Compañía Editorial.

Codex Vaticano A. 1979. *Codex Vaticanus 3738 ("Cod. Vat. A," "Cod. Rios").* Graz, Austria: Akademische Druck- u. Verlagsanstalt.

Codex Vaticano A. 1996. *Religión, costumbres e historia de los antiguos mexicanos: Libro explicativo del llamado Códice Vaticano A.* Ed. Ferdinand Anders and Maarten Jansen. Graz, Austria: Akademische Druck- u. Verlagsanstalt; Mexico City: Fondo de Cultura Económica.

Codex Vaticanus B. 1902–3. *Codex Vaticanus 3773.* Ed. Eduard Seler. Berlin: Edinburgh University Press.

Codex Vindobonensis. 1992. *Origen e historia de los reyes mixtecos: Libro explicativo del llamado Códice Vindobonensis.* Ed. Ferdinand Anders, Maarten Jansen, and Gabina Aurora Pérez Jiménez. Graz, Austria: Akademische Druck- u. Verlagsanstalt; Mexico City: Fondo de Cultura Económica.

Codex Zouche-Nuttall. 1992. *Crónica mixteca. El rey 8 Venado, Garra de Jaguar y la dinastía de Teozacualco-Zaachila. Libro explicativo del llamado Códice Zouche-Nuttall.* Ed. Ferdinand Anders, Maarten Jansen, and Gabina Aurora Pérez Jiménez. Graz, Austria: Akademische Druck- u. Verlagsanstalt; Mexico City: Fondo de Cultura Económica.

Coe, Michael D. 1973. *The Maya Scribe and His World.* New York: Grolier Club.

Coggins, Clemency C. 1988. "Classic Maya Metaphors of Death and Life." *RES: Anthropology and Aesthetics* 16: 6–84.

Coggins, Clemency C. 1990. "The Birth of the Baktun at Tikal and Seibal." In *Vision and Revision in Maya Studies,* ed. Flora S. Clancy and Peter D. Harrison, 79–97. Albuquerque: University of New Mexico Press.

Conrad, Geoffrey W., and Arthur A. Demarest. 1984. *Religion and Empire: The Dynamics of Aztec and Inca Expansionism.* Cambridge, UK: Cambridge University Press.

Contreras Martínez, José Eduardo. 1994. "Los murales y cerámica policromos de la zona arqueológica de Ocotelulco, Tlaxcala." In *Mixteca-Puebla: Discoveries and Research in Mesoamerican Art and Archaeology,* ed. Henry B. Nicholson and Eloise Quiñones Keber, 7–24. Culver City, CA: Labyrinthos.

Crocker, Jon Christopher. 1985. *Vital Souls: Bororo Cosmology, Natural Symbolism, and Shamanism.* Tucson: University of Arizona Press.

Culbert, Patrick A. 1993. *The Ceramics of Tikal: Vessels from Burial, Caches, and Problematical Deposits*. Tikal Report 25. Philadelphia: University Museum, University of Pennsylvania.

Davies, Nigel. 1980. *The Toltec Heritage: From the Fall of Tula to the Rise of Tenochtitlán*. Norman: University of Oklahoma Press.

Day, Jane Stevenson. 1992. *Aztec: The World of Moctezuma*. Boulder, CO: Roberts Rinehart.

DeBoer, Warren R., and Donald W. Lathrap. 1979. "The Making and Breaking of Shipibo-Conibo Ceramics." In *Ethnoarchaeology: Implications of Ethnography for Archaeology*, ed. Carol Kramer, 102–38. New York: Columbia University Press.

de la Fuente, Beatriz, Silvia Trejo, and Nelly Gutiérrez Solana Rickards. 1988. *Escultura en Piedra de Tula: Catálogo*. Mexico City: Instituto de Investigaciones Estéticas, Universidad Nacional Autónoma de México.

Detienne, Marcel. 2000. *Comparere l'incomparable*. Paris: Seuil.

Devereux, George. 1941. "Mohave Beliefs Concerning Twins." *American Anthropologist* 43 (4): 573–92. http://dx.doi.org/10.1525/aa.1941.43.4.02a00060.

Díaz Balsera, Viviana. 2005. *The Pyramid under the Cross: Franciscan Discourses of Evangelization and the Nahua Christian Subject in Sixteenth-Century Mexico*. Tucson: University of Arizona Press.

Dibble, Charles E. 1971. "Writing in Central Mexico." In *Handbook of Middle American Indians* 10, book 1, ed. Robert Wauchope, 322–32. Austin: University of Texas Press.

Doesburg, Sebastián. 2001. *Códices cuicatecos: Porfirio Díaz y Fernández Leal*. Mexico City: Gobierno Constitucional del Estado de Oaxaca and Miguel Ángel Porrúa.

Doniger O'Flaherty, Wendy. 1980. *Women, Androgynes, and Other Mythical Beasts*. Chicago: University of Chicago Press.

Dumézil, Georges. 1974. *La religion romaine archaïque*. Paris: Payot.

Dumézil, Georges. 1994. *Le roman des jumeaux: Esquisses de mythologie*. Paris: Gallimard.

Durán, Fray Diego. 1967. *Historia de las indias de Nueva España e Islas de Tierra Firme*. 2 vols. Ed. Angel María Garibay K. Mexico City: Porrúa.

Durán, Fray Diego. 1971. *Book of the Gods and Rites and the Ancient Calendar*. Ed. and trans. Fernando Horcasitas and Doris Heyden. Norman: University of Oklahoma Press.

Durán, Fray Diego. 1994 [1581]. *History of the Indies of New Spain*. Trans. Doris Heyden. Norman: University of Oklahoma Press.

Durand-Forest, Jacqueline de. 1977. "Description des Divinités d'après les Textes en Nahuatl et leur Représsentation dans les Códices." *Journal de la Société des Americanistes* 64 (1): 9–17. http://dx.doi.org/10.3406/jsa.1977.2137.

Durand-Forest, Jacqueline de. 1998. "Del Simbolismo en el Tonalamatl del Códice Borbónico." In *The Symbolism in the Plastic and Pictorial Representations of Ancient Mexico*, ed. Jacqueline de Durand-Forest and Marc Eisinger, 285–318. BAS, vol. 21. Bonn: Bonner Amerikanistische Studien.

Durand-Forest, Jacqueline de, and Marc Eisinger, eds. 1998. *The Symbolism in the Plastic and Pictorial Representations of Ancient Mexico: A Symposium of the 46th International Congress of Americanists, Amsterdam 1988*. Bonner Amerikanistische Studien, vol. 21. Bonn, Germany: Bonner Amerikanistische Studien.

Durand-Forest, Jacqueline de, Françoise Rousseau, Madeleine Cucuel, and Sylvie Szpirglas. 2000. *Los elementos anexos del Códice Borbónico*. Trans. Edgar Samuel Morales Sales. Toluca, Mexico: Universidad Autónoma del Estado de México.

Egan, Martha J. 1993. *Relicarios: Devotional Miniatures from the Americas*. Santa Fe: University of New Mexico Press.

Eggebrecht, Arne, ed. 1987. *Les Aztèques: Trésors du Mexique ancien*. Hildesheim, Germany: Roemer-und Pelizaeus-Museum.

El Título de Totonicapán. 1983. Ed. and trans. Robert M. Carmack and James L. Mondloch. Mexico City: Universidad Nacional Autónoma de México, Instituto de Investigaciones Filológicas, and Centro de Estudios Mayas.

Eliade, Mircea. 1990 [1986]. *Tratado de historia de las religiones: Morfología y dialéctica de lo sagrado, ciroulo de lectores*. Trans. Tomás Segovia. Mexico City: Ediciones Era.

Elson, Christina M., and Michael E. Smith. 2001. "Archaeological Deposits from the Aztec New Fire Ceremony." *Ancient Mesoamerica* 12: 157–174. http://dx.doi.org/10.1017/S0956536101122078.

Escalante Gonzalbo, Pablo. 2002. "Cristo, su sangre y los indios: Exploraciones iconográficas sobre el arte mexicano del siglo XVI." In *Herencias indígenas, tradiciones europeas y la mirada europea: Actas del coloquio de la Asociación Carl Justi y del Instituto Cervantes de Bremen, Bremen, del 6 al 9 de abril de 2000*, ed. Helga von Kügelgen, in collaboration with Gabriele Schulz, 71–93. Ars Iberica et Americana 7. Frankfurt am Main: Vervuert; Madrid: Iberoamericana.

Fash, William F. 1991. *Scribes, Warriors and Kings*. London: Thames and Hudson.

Feest, Christian F. 1985. "Mexico and South America in the European Wunderkammer." In *The Origins of Museums: The Cabinets of Curiosities in Sixteenth- and Seventeenth-Century Europe*, ed. Oliver Impey and Arthur MacGregor, 237–44. Oxford: Oxford University Press.

Feest, Christian F. 1990. "Vienna's Mexican Treasures: Aztec, Mixtec, and Tarascan Works from 16th Century Austrian Collections." *Archiv für Völkerkunde* 45: 1–64.

Florentine Codex. 1979. *El manuscrito 218–220 de la colección Palatina de la Biblioteca Medicea Laurenziana*. Florence: Giunti Barbéra; Mexico City: Archivo General de la Nación.

Fox, James A., and John S. Justeson. 1978. "A Mayan Planetary Observation." *Contributions of the University of California Archaeological Research Facility* 36: 5–60.

Freedberg, David. 1989. *The Power of Images: Studies in the History and Theory of Response.* Chicago: University of Chicago Press.

Freidel, David, Linda Schele, and Joy Parker. 1993. *Maya Cosmos: Three Thousand Years on the Shaman's Path.* New York: William Morrow.

Galinier, Jacques. 1984. "L'Homme sans Pied: Métaphores de la Castration et Imaginaire en Mésoamerique." *L'Homme* 24 (2): 41–58. http://dx.doi.org/10.3406/hom.1984.368489.

Gallereta Negrón, Tomás, and Karl Taube. 2005. "Late Postclassic Occupation in the Ruinas de San Angel Region." In *Quintana Roo Archaeology*, ed. Justine M. Shaw and Jennifer P. Mathews, 87–111. Tuscon: University of Arizona Press.

Gamboa Cabezas, Luis. 2007. "El Palacio Quemado, Tula: Seis décadas de investigaciones." *Arqueología Mexicana* 85: 42–47.

García, Fray Gregorio. 1981 [1607]. *Origen de los indios de el Nuevo Mundo e Indias occidentales.* Mexico City: Fondo de Cultura Económica.

García Payón, José. 1936a. *La zona arqueológica de Tecaxic-Calixtlahuaca y los matlatzincas: Etnología y arqueología (primera parte).* Mexico City: Talleres Gráficas de la Nación.

García Payón, José. 1936b. *El mito de Quetzalcoatl.* Mexico City: Fondo de Cultura Económica.

García Payón, José. 1979. *La zona arqueológica de Tecaxic-Calixtlahuaca y los matlatzinca: Etnología y arqueología (textos de la segunda parte).* Ed. Wanda Tommasi de Magrelli and Leonardo Manrique Castañeda. Toluca, Mexico: Biblioteca Enciclopédica del Estado de México, vol. 30.

Gell, Alfred. 1992. "The Technology of Enchantment and the Enchantment of Technology." In *Anthropology, Art, and Aesthetics*, ed. Jeremy Coote and Anthony Shelton, 40–66. Oxford: Clarendon.

Glascock, Michael D., ed. 2002. *Geochemical Evidence for Long-Distance Exchange.* Westport, CT: Bergin and Garvey.

González Rul, Francisco. 1998. *Urbanismo y arquitectura en Tlatelolco.* Serie Arqueología, Colección Científica, vol. 346. Mexico City: Instituto Nacional de Antropología e Historia.

González Sobrino, Blanca Z., Carlos Serrano Sánchez, Zaid Lagunas Rodríguez, and Alejandro Terrazas Mata. 2001. "Rito y sacrificio humano en Teopanzolco, Morelos: Evidencias osteológicas y fuentes escritas." *Estudios de Antropología Biológica* 10: 519–532.

Gonzaléz Torres, Yólotl. 1979. "El panteón mexica." *Antropología e Historia* 25 (3): 9–19.

Graña-Behrens, Christian Prager, and Elizabeth Wagner. 1999. "The Hieroglyphic Inscription of the 'High Priest's Grave' at Chichén Itzá, Yucatán, Mexico." *Mexicon* 21: 1–66.

Gonzaléz Torres, Yólotl. 1995. "Dioses, diosas, y andróginos en la mitología mexica." In *Antropología simbólica*, ed. Marie Odile Marión, 45–52. Mexico City: Escuela Nacional de Antropología and Instituto Nacional de Antropología e Historia/Consejo Nacional de Ciencia y Technología.

Granados Vázquez, Daniel, Jorge Carrandi Ríos, Garbiel Lalo Jacinto, and Belem Zúñiga Arellano. 1993. "Apuntes sobre otros materiales arqueológicos procedentes de Tlapizáhuac." *Expresión Antropológica* 3 (11–12): 117–32.

Graulich, Michel. 1988. *Quetzalcóatl y el espejismo de Tollan*. Antwerpen: Instituut voor Amerikanistiek.

Graulich, Michel. 1992. "On the So-Called 'Cuauhxicalli of Motecuhzoma Ilhuicamina': The Sánchez-Nava Monolith." *Mexicon* 14 (1): 5–10.

Graulich, Michel. 1997. *Myths of Ancient Mexico*. Norman: University of Oklahoma Press.

Graulich, Michel. 1999. *Ritos aztecas: Las fiestas de las veintenas*. Mexico City: Instituto Nacional Indigenista.

Graulich, Michel. 2001. "El simbolismo del Templo Mayor de México y sus relaciones con Cacaxtla y Teotihuacan." *Anales del Instituto de Investigaciones Estéticas* 79: 5–28.

Griaule, Marcel, and Germaine Dieterlen. 1965. *Le renard pâle: Le mythe cosmogonique*. Paris: Institut d'Ethnologie.

Guggenheim Museum. 2004. *The Aztec Empire: Catalogue of the Exhibition*. New York: Guggenheim Museum Publications.

Gutiérrez Solana Rickards, Nelly. 1983. *Objetos ceremoniales en piedra de la cultura mexica*. Mexico City: Universidad Nacional Autónoma de México and Instituto de Investigaciones Estéticas.

Harrison, Peter D. 1999. *The Lords of Tikal: Rulers of an Ancient Maya City*. London: Thames and Hudson.

Hassig, Ross. 1988. *Aztec Warfare, Imperial Expansion and Political Control*. Norman: University of Oklahoma Press.

Healan, Dan M. 1989. *Tula of the Toltecs: Excavations and Survey*. Iowa City: University of Iowa Press.

Herdt, Gilbert. 1981. *Guardians of the Flutes: Idioms of Masculinity*. New York: McGraw Hill.

Hernández Sánchez, Gilda. 2005. *Vasijas para ceremonia: Iconografía de la cerámica tipo códice del estilo Mixteca-Puebla*. CNWS Publications. Leiden: Research School of Asian, African, and Amerindian Studies, Universiteit Leiden.

Heusch, Luc de. 1986. *Le sacrifice dans les religions africaines*. Paris: Gallimard.

Heyden, Doris. 1981. "Caves, Gods, and Myths: World-view and Planning in Teotihuacan." In *Mesoamerican Sites and World-Views*, ed. Elizabeth P. Benson, 1–40. Washington, DC: Dumbarton Oaks.

Heyden, Doris. 1988. "Black Magic: Obsidian in Symbolism and Metaphor." In *Smoke and Mist: Mesoamerican Studies in Memory of Thelma D. Sullivan*, ed. Kathryn J. Josserand and Karen Dakin, 217–36. British Archaeological Reports, International Series 402. Oxford: Oxford University Press.

Heyden, Doris. 1989. "Tezcatlipoca en el mundo náhuatl." *Estudios de Cultura Nahuatl* 19: 83–93.

Heyden, Doris. 1991. "Dryness before the Rains: Toxcatl and Tezcatlipoca." In *To Change Place: Aztec Ceremonial Landscapes*, ed. Davíd Carrasco, 188–202. Niwot: University Press of Colorado.

Heyden, Doris. 2005. "The Bodies of the Gods: As Seen in Cult Images Made of Wood in the Pictorial Codices." In *Painted Books and Indigenous Knowledge: Manuscript Studies in Honor of Mary Elizabeth Smith*, ed. Elizabeth H. Boone, 43–62. New Orleans: Middle American Research Institute, Tulane University.

Historia de los mexicanos por sus pinturas. 1941 [1543]. "Historia de los mexicanos por sus pinturas." In *Nueva colección de documentos para la historia de México*, ed. Joaquín García Icazbalceta, 209–40. Mexico City: Salvador Chavez Hayhoe.

Historia de los mexicanos por sus pinturas. 1973. "Historia de los Mexicanos por sus pinturas." In *Teogonía e historia de los mexicanos: Tres opúsculos del siglo XVI*, ed. Angel María Garibay K., 23–66. Mexico City: Editorial Porrúa.

Holien, Thomas, and Robert Pickering. 1978. "Analogues in a Chalchihuites Culture Sacrificial Burial to Late Mesoamerican Ceremonialism." In *Middle Classic Mesoamerica: AD 400–700*, ed. Esther Pasztory, 145–57. New York: Columbia University Press.

Hosler, Dorothy. 1994. *Sounds and Colors of Power: The Sacred Metallurgical Technology of Ancient West Mexico*. Cambridge, MA: MIT Press.

Houston, Stephen. 1993. *Hieroglyphs and History at Dos Pilas: Dynastic Politics of the Classic Maya*. Austin: University of Texas Press.

Houston, Stephen, and Tom Cummins. 2004. "Body, Presence, and Space in Andean and Mesoamerican Rulership." In *Palaces of the Ancient New World*, ed. Susan Toby Evans and Joanne Pillsbury, 359–98. Washington, DC: Dumbarton Oaks.

Houston, Stephen, and Karl Taube. 2000. "An Archaeology of the Senses: Perception and Cultural Expression in Ancient Mesoamerica." *Cambridge Archaeological Journal* 10 (2): 261–94. http://dx.doi.org/10.1017/S095977430000010X.

Hunt, Eva. 1977. *The Transformation of the Hummingbird: Cultural Roots of a Zinacantecan Mythical Poem*. Ithaca, NY: Cornell University Press.

Hvidtfeldt, Arild. 1958. *Teotl and Ixiptlatli: Some Central Conceptions in Ancient Mexican Religion, and a General Introduction on Cult and Myth*. Copenhagen: Munksgaard.

Ichon, Alain. 1969. *La religion des Totonaques de la Sierra*. Paris: Centre National de la Recherche Scientifique.

Jansen, Maarten. 1982. *Huisi Tacu, estudio interpretativo de un libro mixteco antiguo: Codex Vindobonensis Mexicanus I*. 2 vols. Amsterdam: Centre for Latin American Research and Documentation.

Jiménez García, Elizabeth. 1998. *Iconografía de Tula: El caso de la escultura*. Mexico City: Instituto Nacional de Antropología e Historia.

Jiménez Moreno, Wigberto. 1979. "De Tezcatlipoca a Huitzilopochtli." *Actes du 42nd Congreso International des Americanistas* 6: 27–34.

Jones, Christopher. 1969. "The Twin-Pyramid Group Pattern: A Classic Maya Architectural Assemblage at Tikal, Guatemala." PhD dissertation, University of Pennsylvania, Philadelphia.

Jones, Christopher, and Linton Satterthwaite. 1982. *The Monuments and Inscriptions of Tikal: The Carved Monuments*. Tikal Report 33, part A. Philadelphia: University Museum, University of Pennsylvania.

Justeson, John S. 1989. "The Ancient Maya Ethnoastronomy: An Overview of Hieroglyphic Sources." In *World Archaeoastronomy: Selected Papers from the 2nd Oxford International Conference on Archaeoastronomy*, ed. Anthony F. Aveni, 76–129. Cambridge, UK: Cambridge University Press.

Kaplan, Flora S. 2006. *The Post-Classic Figurines of Central Mexico*. Occasional Papers, vol. 11. Albany, NY: Institute for Mesoamerican Studies.

Karttunen, Frances. 1992 [1983]. *An Analytical Dictionary of Nahuatl*. Norman: University of Oklahoma Press.

Keleman, Pál. 1969. *Medieval American Art: Masterpieces of the New World before Columbus*. New York: Dover.

Kelley, David H. 1976. *Deciphering the Maya Script*. Austin: University of Texas Press.

Kempe, Margery. 1985. *The Book of Margery Kempe*. Trans. B. A. Windeatt. Harmondsworth, UK: Penguin; New York: Viking Penguin.

Kimbell Art Museum. 1987. *In Pursuit of Quality: The Kimbell Art Museum, an Illustrated History of the Art and Architecture*. Fort Worth, TX: Kimbell Art Museum.

Klein, Cecelia F. 1986. "Masking Empire: The Material Effects of Masks in Aztec Mexico." *Art History* 9 (2): 135–67.

Klein, Cecelia F. 1987. "The Ideology of Autosacrifice at the Templo Mayor." In *The Aztec Templo Mayor*, ed. Elizabeth H. Boone, 293–370. Washington, DC: Dumbarton Oaks.

Klein, Cecelia F. 1988. "Rethinking Cihuacoatl: Aztec Political Imagery of the Conquered Woman." In *Smoke and Mist: Mesoamerican Studies in Memory of Thelma D. Sullivan*, ed. Kathryn J. Josserand and Karen Dakin, 237–79. British Archaeological Reports, International Series 402. Oxford: Oxford University Press.

Klein, Cecelia F. 2000. "The Devil and the Skirt: An Iconographic Inquiry into the Pre-Hispanic Nature of the Tzitzimime." *Ancient Mesoamerica* 11 (1): 1–26. http://dx.doi.org/10.1017/S0956536100111010.

Klein, Cecelia F. 2001. "None of the Above: Gender Ambiguity in Nahua Ideology." In *Gender in Pre-Hispanic America*, ed. Cecelia F. Klein, 183–253. Washington, DC: Dumbarton Oaks.

Kollmann, Julius. 1895. "Flöten und Pfeifen aus Alt-Mexiko in der ethnographischen Sammlung der Universität Basel." In *Mitteilungen aus der ethnographischen Sammlung der Universität Basel* 1 (2): 45–81. Basel: Carl Sallmann.

Krickeberg, Walter. 1969. *Felsbilder Mexicos: Als Historische, Religiöse und Kunstdenkmäler*. Felsplastic und Felsbilder bei den Kulturvölkern Altamerika, vol. 2. Berlin: Dietrich Reimer Verlag.

Kristan-Graham, Cynthia B., and Jeff Karl Kowalski, eds. 2006. *Twin Tollans: Chichén Itzá, Tula, and the Epiclassic-Early Postclassic Mesoamerican World*. Washington, DC: Dumbarton Oaks.

Lacadena García-Gallo, Alfonso. 2005. "Los Jeroglíficos de Ek' Balam." *Arqueología Mexicana* 13 (76): 4–69.

Lagunas Rodríguez, Zaid, and Carlos Serrano Sánchez. 1972. "Decapitación y desmembramiento corporal en Teopanzolco, Morelos." In *Religión en Mesoamérica: XII Mesa Redonda*, ed. Jaime Litvak King and Noemí Castillo Tejero, 429–34. Mexico City: Sociedad Mexicana de Antropología.

Las Casas, Bartolomé de. 1967. *Apologética historia sumaria cuanto a las cualidades, dispusición, descripción, cielo y suelo destas tierras, y condiciones naturales, policías, repúblicas, manera de vivir e costumbres de las gentes destas Indias Occidentales y Meridionales, cuyo imperio soberano pertenece a los Reyes de Castilla*. Ed. Edmundo O'Gorman. Mexico City: Universidad Nacional Autónoma de México and Instituto de Investigaciones Históricas.

Lathrap, Donald W. 1976. "Shipibo Tourist Art." In *Ethnic and Tourist Arts*, ed. Nelson H.H. Graeburn, 197–210. Berkeley: University of California Press.

Lelegemann, Achim, ed. 2000. "Proyecto arqueológico Ciudadela de La Quemada, Zacatecas: Informe final." Report submitted to the Consejo de Arqueología, Instituto Nacional de Antropología e Historia, Mexico City.

León-Portilla, Miguel. 1958. "Ritos, sacerdotes y atavíos de los dioses." In *Fuentes Indígenas de la Cultura Náhuatl. Textos de los Informantes de Sahagún: 1*. Mexico City: Universidad Nacional Autónoma de México and Instituto de Investigaciones Históricas.

León-Portilla, Miguel. 1969. *Pre-Columbian Literatures of Mexico*. Norman: University of Oklahoma Press.

Lévi-Strauss, Claude. 1991. *Histoire de Lynx*. Paris: Plon.

Leyenda de los Soles. 1992a. *Codex Chimalpopoca: The Text in Nahuatl with a Glossary and Grammatical Notes*. Ed. John Bierhorst. Tucson: University of Arizona Press.

Leyenda de los Soles. 1992b. *History and Mythology of the Aztecs: The Codex Chimalpopoca*. Trans. John Bierhorst. Tucson: University of Arizona Press.

Linné, Sigvald. 1934. *Archaeological Researches at Teotihuacan, Mexico*, vol. 1. Stockholm: Ethnographic Museum of Sweden.

Loeb, Edwin M. 1958. "The Twin Cult in the Old and the New World." In *Miscellanea Paul Rivet*, ed. Pablo Martínez del Rio, 1: 151–74. 21st Congreso Internacional de Americanistas. Mexico City: Universidad Nacional Autónoma de México.

Looper, Mathew G. 2002. "Women-Men (and Men-Women): Classic Maya Rulers and the Third Gender." In *Ancient Maya Women*, ed. Traci Ardren, 171–202. Walnut Creek, CA: Altamira.

López Austin, Alfredo. 1973. *Hombre-Dios: Religion y Politica en el mundo Nahuatl*. Mexico City: Universidad Nacional Autónoma de México and Instituto de Investigaciones Históricas.

López Austin, Alfredo. 1982. "La sexualidad entre los antiguos nahuas." In *Familia y sexualidad en Nueva España*, 141–76. Memoria del Primer Simposio de Historia de las Mentalidades. Mexico City: Fondo de Cultura Económica and Secretaría de Educación Pública.

López Austin, Alfredo. 1988. *The Human Body and Ideology: Concepts of the Ancient Nahuas*. Trans. Thelma Ortiz de Montellano and Bernardo Ortiz de Montellano. Salt Lake City: University of Utah Press.

López Austin, Alfredo. 1990. *Los mitos del tlacuache: Caminos de la mitología mesoamericana*. Mexico City: Alianza Editorial Mexicana.

López Austin, Alfredo. 1994. "Homshuk: A Thematic Analysis of the Narrative." In *Chipping Away on Earth: Studies in Prehispanic and Colonial Mexico in Honor of Arthur J.O. Anderson and Charles E. Dibble*, ed. Eloise Quiñones Keber, 131–39. Lancaster, CA: Labyrinthos.

López Luján, Leonardo. 2005 [1994]. *The Offerings of the Templo Mayor of Tenochtitlan*. Rev. ed. Trans. Bernard R. Ortiz de Montellano and Thelma Ortiz de Montellano. Albuquerque: University of New Mexico Press.

López Luján, Leonardo. 2006. *La Casa de las Águilas: Un ejemplo de arquitectura religiosa de Tenochtitlan*. Mexico City: Fonda de Cultura Económica, Conaculta, and Instituto Nacional de Antropología e Historia.

López Luján, Leonardo, and Marie France Fauvet-Berthelot. 2005. *Aztèques: La collection des sculptures du Musée du quai Branly*. Paris: Musée du quai Branly.

Lorenzo, José Luis. 1957. *Las zonas arqueológicas de los volcanes Iztaccihuatl y Popocatepetl*. Dirección de Prehistoria, Serie Publicaciones, vol. 3. Mexico City: Instituto Nacional de Antropología e Historia.

Lounsbury, Floyd G. 1983. "The Base of the Venus Tables of the Dresden Codex, and Its Significance for the Calendar-Correlation Problem." In *Calendars in Mesoamerica and Peru: Native American Computations of Time*, ed. Anthony F. Aveni and Gordon Brotherston, 1–26. BAR International Series 174. Oxford: BAR.

Lounsbury, Floyd G. 1989. "A Palenque King and the Planet Jupiter." In *World Archaeoastronomy: Selected Papers from the 2nd Oxford International Conference on Archaeoastronomy Held at Merida, Yucatan, Mexico, 13–17 January 1986*, ed. Anthony F. Aveni, 246–59. Cambridge, UK: Cambridge University Press.

Love, Bruce. 1994. *The Paris Codex: A Handbook for a Maya Priest*. Austin: University of Texas Press.

Macri, Martha, and Matthew G. Looper. 2003. *The New Catalogue of Maya Hieroglyphs*, vol. 1. Norman: University of Oklahoma Press.

Maldonado Jiménez, Druzo. 2000. *Deidades y espacio ritual en Cuauhnáhuac y Huaxtepec: Tlalhuicas y Xochimilcas de Morelos (siglos XII–XVI)*. Mexico City: Instituto de Investigaciones Antropológicas and Universidad Nacional Autónoma de México.

Maldonado Jiménez, Druzo. 2004. "Cultos prehispánicos y coloniales de la región suroeste del Popocatépetl (Yecapixtla, Totolapan y Ocuituco, Morelos)." *Mirada Antropológica* (January–July): 61–74.

Maler, Theobert. 1908. *Explorations in the Department of Petén, Guatemala, and Adjacent Region: Topoxte, Yaxha, Benque Viejo, Naranjo*. Memoirs of the Peabody Museum of Archaeology and Ethnology, vol. 4, no. 2. Cambridge, MA: Harvard University.

Marcus, Joyce. 1992. *Mesoamerican Writing Systems: Propaganda, Myth, and History in Four Ancient Civilizations*. Princeton, NJ: Princeton University Press.

Marrow, James H. 1979. *Passion Iconography in Northern European Art of the Late Middle Ages and Early Renaissance: A Study of the Transformation of Sacred Metaphor into Descriptive Narrative*. Kortrijk, Belgium: Van Ghemmert.

Martí, Samuel. 1953. "Flautilla de la penitencia: Fiesta grande de Tezcatlipoca." *Cuadernos Americanos* 72: 148–157.

Martí, Samuel. 1968. *Instrumentos musicales precortesianos*. Mexico City: Instituto Nacional de Antropología e Historia.

Martin, Simon, and Nikolai Grube. 2000. *Chronicle of the Maya Kings and Queens: Deciphering the Dynasties of the Ancient Maya*. London: Thames and Hudson.

Mastache, Alba Guadalupe, Robert H. Cobean, and Dan M. Healan. 2002. *Ancient Tollan: Tula and the Toltec Heartland*. Boulder: University Press of Colorado.

Mathews, Thomas F. 1993. *The Clash of Gods: A Reinterpretation of Early Christian Art*. Princeton, NJ: Princeton University Press.

Matos Moctezuma, Eduardo. 1974. *Proyecto Tula (primera parte)*. Colección Científica, vol. 15. Mexico City: Instituto Nacional de Antropología e Historia.

Matos Moctezuma, Eduardo. 1982. *El templo mayor: Excavaciones y estudios*. Mexico City: Instituto Nacional de Antropología e Historia.

Matos Moctezuma, Eduardo. 1988. *The Great Temple of the Aztecs: Treasures of Tenochtitlan*. Trans. Doris Heyden. London: Thames and Hudson.

Matos Moctezuma, Eduardo. 1992. "Arqueología urbana en el centro de la Ciudad de México." *Estudios de Cultura Nahuatl* 22: 133–41.

Matos Moctezuma, Eduardo. 1995. *Life and Death in the Templo Mayor*. Trans. Bernard R. Ortiz de Montellano and Thelma Ortiz de Montellano. Boulder: University Press of Colorado.

Matos Moctezuma, Eduardo. 1996. "Arqueología y fuentes históricas: El caso del templo mayor de Tenochtitlan." In *Los arqueólogos frente a las fuentes*, ed. Rosa Brambila Paz and Jesús Monjarás-Ruiz, 105–28. Colección Científica, vol. 322. Mexico City: Instituto Nacional de Antropología e Historia.

Matos Moctezuma, Eduardo. 1997. "Tezcatlipoca, espejo que humea." In *Antiguo Palacio del Arzobispado*, 27–41. Mexico City: Museo de la Secretaría de Hacienda y Crédito Público and Espejo de Obsidiana Ediciones.

Matos Moctezuma, Eduardo, and Felipe R. Solís Olguín, eds. 2002. *Aztecs*. London: Royal Academy of Arts.

Meeks, Wayne A. 1974. "The Image of the Androgyne: Some Uses of a Symbol in Earliest Christianity." *History of Religions* 13 (3): 165–208. http://dx.doi.org/10.1086/462701.

Meeus, Jean. n.d. "Stations of Jupiter, Saturn, Venus, and Mars." Manuscript in possession of the author.

Mellinkoff, Ruth. 1993. *Outcasts: Signs of Otherness in Northern European Art of the Late Middle Ages*. 2 vols. Berkeley: University of California Press.

Mendieta, Gerónimo de. 1980 [1870]. *Historia eclesiástica indiana*. Ed. Joaquín García Icazbalceta. Mexico City: Porrúa.

Meslay, Olivier. 2001. "Murillo and 'Smoking Mirrors.'" *Burlington Magazine* 143 (1175): 73–79.

Métraux, Alfred. 1946. "Twin Heroes in South American Mythology." *Journal of American Folklore* 59 (232): 114–23. http://dx.doi.org/10.2307/536466.

Milbrath, Susan. 1995. "A New Interpretation of the Dresden Codex Venus Pages." In *Cantos de Mesoamérica: Metologías científicas en la búsqueda del conocimiento prehispánico*, ed. Daniel Flores, 257–92. Mexico City: Instituto de Astronomía, Facultad de Ciencias, and Universidad Nacional Autónoma de México.

Milbrath, Susan. 1997. "Decapitated Lunar Goddesses in Aztec Art, Myth, and Ritual." *Ancient Mesoamerica* 8 (2): 186–206. http://dx.doi.org/10.1017/S095653610000167X.

Milbrath, Susan. 1999. *Star Gods of the Maya: Astronomy in Art, Folklore, and Calendars*. Austin: University of Texas Press.

Milbrath, Susan. 2002. "The Planet of Kings: Jupiter in Maya Cosmology." In *Heart of Creation: The Mesoamerican World and the Legacy of Linda Schele*, ed. Andrea Stone, 118–42. Tuscaloosa: University of Alabama Press.

Milbrath, Susan. 2004. "The Maya Katun Cycle and the Retrograde Periods of Jupiter and Saturn." *Archaeoastronomy: The Journal of Astronomy in Culture* 17: 1–97.

Milbrath, Susan. 2005. "Jupiter in Classic and Postclassic Maya Art." In *Current Studies in Archaeoastronomy: Selected Papers from the Fifth Oxford International Conference at Santa Fe, 1996*, ed. John W. Fountain and Rolf M. Sinclair, 301–30. Durham, NC: Carolina Academic Press.

Milbrath, Susan. 2013. *Heaven and Earth in Ancient Mexico: Astronomy and Seasonal Cycles in the Codex Borgia*. Austin: University of Texas Press.

Milbrath, Susan, and Carlos Peraza Lope. 2003. "Revisiting Mayapán: Mexico's Last Maya Capital." *Ancient Mesoamerica* 14 (1): 1–46. http://dx.doi.org/10.1017/S0956536103132178.

Miller, Mary, Simon Martin, and Kathleen Berrin. 2004. *Courtly Art of the Ancient Maya*. San Francisco: Fine Arts Museum.

Miller, Mary, and Karl Taube. 1993. *The Gods and Symbols of Ancient Mexico and the Maya*. London: Thames and Hudson.

Miller, Virginia E. 1998. "Sacrifice, Skullracks, and Smoking Mirrors at Chichén Itzá: What the Aztecs Learned from the Maya." Paper presented at the Conference on Mayan Culture at the Millennium, SUNY Buffalo, New York.

Molina, Alonso de. 1970. *Vocabulario en lengua castellana y mexicana y mexicana y castellana*. Ed. Miguel León-Portilla. Mexico City: Porrúa.

Molina, Alonso de. 1977 [1571]. *Vocabulario en lengua castellana y mexicana y mexicana y castellana*. Ed. Miguel León-Portilla. Mexico City: Porrúa.

Muñoz Camargo, Diego. 1998. *Historia de Tlaxcala: Ms. 210 de la Biblioteca Nacional de París*. Ed. Luis Reyes García and Javier Lira Toledo. Mexico City: Gobierno del Estado de Tlaxcala, Centro de Investigación y Estudios Superiores en Antropología Social, and Universidad Autónoma de Tlaxcala.

Murphy, Yolanda, and Robert F. Murphy. 1985 [1974]. *Women of the Forest*. New York: Columbia University Press.

Nagao, Debra. 1985. "The Planting of Sustenance: Symbolism of the Two-Horned God in Offerings from the Templo Mayor." *Res: Anthropology and Aesthetics* 10: 5–27.

Nelson, Ben A. 1997. "Burial Excavations in Plaza 1 of Los Pilarillos, Zacatecas, México." Report to the Foundation for the Advancement of Mesoamerican Studies. http://www.famsi.org/reports/96075/index.html.

Neurath, Johannes. 2004. "El doble personaje del planeta Venus en las religiones indígenas del Gran Nayar: Mitología, ritual agrícola y sacrificio." *Journal de la Société des Américanistes* 90 (1): 93–118.

Nicholson, Henry B. 1954. "The Birth of the Smoking Mirror." *Archaeology* 7 (3): 164–70.

Nicholson, Henry B. 1958. "An Aztec Monument Dedicated to Tezcatlipoca." In *Miscellanea Paul Rivet, Octogenario Dicata*, ed. Pablo Martínez del Rio, 31st International

Congress of Americanists 1: 593–607. Mexico City: Universidad Nacional Autónoma de México.

Nicholson, Henry B. 1963. "An Aztec Stone Image of a Fertility Goddess." *Baessler-Archiv* 11 (1): 9–30.

Nicholson, Henry B. 1967. "A Fragment of an Aztec Relief Carving of the Earth Monster." *Journal de la Société de Americanistes de Paris* 56 (1): 81–94. http://dx.doi.org/10.3406/jsa.1967.2272.

Nicholson, Henry B. 1971. "Religion in Pre-Hispanic Central Mexico." In *Handbook of Middle American Indians, 10: Archaeology of Northern Mesoamerica, Part 1*, ed. Gordon. F. Ekholm and Ignacio I. Bernal, 395–446. Austin: University of Texas Press.

Nicholson, Henry B. 1973. "The Late Pre-Hispanic Central Mexican (Aztec) Iconographic System." In *The Iconography of Middle American Sculpture*, ed. Ignacio Bernal, 72–97. New York: Metropolitan Museum of Art.

Nicholson, Henry B. 1978. "The Deity 9 Wind 'Ehecatl-Quetzalcoatl' in the Mixteca Pictorials." *Journal of Latin American Lore* 4 (1): 61–92.

Nicholson, Henry B. 1979. "Ehecatl Quetzalcoatl vs. Topiltzin Quetzalcoatl of Tollan: A Problem in Mesoamerican Religion and History." *42ᵉ International Congress of Americanists (Paris 1976)* 6: 35–47.

Nicholson, Henry B. 1988. "The Iconography of the Deity Representations in Fray Bernardino de Sahagún's Primeros Memoriales: Huitzilopochtli and Chalchiuhtlicue." In *The Work of Bernardino de Sahagun, Pioneer Ethnographer of Sixteenth-Century Aztec Mexico*, ed. J. Jorge Klor de Alva, Henry B. Nicholson, and Eloise Quiñones Keber, 229–53. Albany: Institute for Mesoamerican Studies, State University of New York.

Nicholson, Henry B. 2001a. *The "Return of Quetzalcoatl": Did it Play a Role in the Conquest of Mexico?* Lancaster, CA: Labyrinthos.

Nicholson, Henry B. 2001b. *Topiltzin Quetzalcoatl: The Once and Future Lord of the Toltecs*. Niwot: University Press of Colorado.

Nicholson, Henry B., and Eloise Quiñones Keber. 1983. *Art of Aztec Mexico, Treasures of Tenochtitlan*. Washington, DC: National Gallery of Art.

Noguera, Eduardo. 1927. "Los altares del sacrificio de Tizatlán, Tlaxcala." In *Ruinas de Tizatlán*, ed. Agustín García Vega, 23–62. Publicaciones, vol. 15. Mexico City: Secretaría de Educación Pública.

Noguera, Eduardo. 1929a. "Los altares de sacrificio de Tizatlan, Tlaxcala." In *Ruinas de Tizatlan, Tlaxcala*, ed. Agustín García Vega, 25–64. Mexico City: Talleres Gráficos de la Nación.

Noguera, Eduardo. 1929b. "La pirámide de Tenayuca." *Mexican Folkways* 5: 50–57.

Nowotny, Karl Anton. 1976. "Commentary." In *Codex Borgia: Biblioteca Apostolica Vaticana*. Graz, Austria: Akademische Druck- u. Verlagsanstalt.

Olivera, Mercedes. 1979. "Huemitl de mayo en Citlala: ¿Ofrenda para Chicomecoatl o para la Santa Cruz?" In *Mesoamérica: Homenaje al Doctor Paul Kirchoff*, ed. Barbro Dahlgren, 143–58. Mexico City: Secretaría de Educación Pública and Instituto Nacional de Antropología e Historia.

Olivier, Guilhem. 1995. "Les paquets sacrés ou la mémoire cachée des Indiens du Mexique central (XVe-XVIe siècles)." *Journal de la Société des Americanistes* 81 (1): 105–33. http://dx.doi.org/10.3406/jsa.1995.1585.

Olivier, Guilhem. 1997. *Moqueries et métamorphoses d'un dieu aztèque: Tezcatlipoca, le "Seigneur au miroir fumant."* Paris: Institut d'Ethnologie, Musée de l'Homme, Centre d'Études Mexicaines et Centraméricaines.

Olivier, Guilhem. 1998. "Tepeyóllotl, 'Corazón de la montaña' y 'señor del eco': El dios jaguar de los antiguos mexicanos." *Estudios de Cultura Náhuatl* 28: 99–141.

Olivier, Guilhem. 2000. "¿Dios del maíz o dios del hielo? ¿Señor del pecado o señor de la justicia punitiva? Esbozo sobre la identidad de Itztlacoliuhqui, deidad del México prehispánico." In *Códices y Documentos sobre México, Tercer Simposio Internacional*, ed. Constanza Vega Sosa, 335–53. Mexico City: Instituto Nacional de Antropología e Historia .

Olivier, Guilhem. 2002. "The Hidden King and the Broken Flutes: Mythical and Royal Dimensions of the Feast of Tezcatlipoca in Toxcatl." In *Representing Aztec Ritual: Performance, Text, and Image in the Work of Sahagún*, ed. Eloise Quiñones Keber, 107–42. Boulder: University Press of Colorado.

Olivier, Guilhem. 2003. *Mockeries and Metamorphoses of an Aztec God: Tezcatlipoca, "Lord of the Smoking Mirror."* Trans. Michel Besson. Boulder: University Press of Colorado.

Olivier, Guilhem. 2004a. "Homosexualidad y prostitución entre los nahuas y otros pueblos del posclásico." In *Historia de la vida cotidiana en México*, tomo I: *Mesoamérica y los ámbitos indígenas de la Nueva España*, ed Pablo Escalante Gonzalbo, 301–38. Mexico City: El Colegio de México and Fondo de Cultura Económica.

Olivier, Guilhem. 2004b. *Tezcatlipoca: Burlas y metamorfosis de un dios azteca*. Mexico City: Fondo de Cultura Económica.

Olivier, Guilhem. 2006. "The Sacred Bundles and the Enthronement of the King in Tenochtitlan." In *Ancient America, Special Issue: Sacred Bindings of the Cosmos; Ritual Acts of Bundling and Wrapping in Ancient Mesoamerica*, ed. Julia Kappelman and F. Kent Reilly, 199–225. Barnardsville, NC: Boundary End Archaeology Research Center.

Olivier, Guilhem. 2007. "Las tres muertes del nuevo *tlatoani*: Una nueva interpretación de los ritos de entronización mexica." In *Símbolos de poder en Mesoamérica*, ed. Guilhem Olivier, 263–91. Mexico City: Universidad Nacional Autónoma de México, Instituto de Investigaciones Históricas, and Instituto de Investigaciones Antropológicas.

Olivier, Guilhem. 2010. "Gemelidad e historia cíclica. El 'dualismo inestable de los amerindios,' de Claude Lévi-Strauss en el espejo de los mitos mesoamericanos." In *Lévi-Strauss: Un siglo de reflexión*, ed. María Eugenia Olavarría, Saúl Millan, and Carlo Bonfiglioli, 143–83. Mexico City: Universidad Autónoma Metropolitana Unidad Iztapalapa, División de Ciencias Sociales y Humanidades.

Olmeda Vera, Bertina. 2002. *Los templos rojos del recinto sagrado de Tenochtitlan*. Colección Científica, vol. 439. Mexico City: Instituto Nacional de Antropología e Historia.

Olmo Frese, Laura del. 2003. "Conservación arqueológico en el edificio del Antiguo Arzobispado." In *Excavaciones del programa de arqueología urbana*, ed. Eduardo Matos Moctezuma, 215–26. Colección Científica, vol. 452. Mexico City: Instituto Nacional de Antropología e Historia.

Paddock, John. 1985. "Tezcatlipoca in Oaxaca." *Ethnohistory* 32 (4): 309–25. http://dx.doi.org/10.2307/481892.

Padilla, J., P. F. Sánchez-Nava, and Felipe Solís Olguín. 1989. "The Cuauhxicalli of Motecuhzoma Ilhuicamina." *Mexicon* 11 (2): 24–25.

Pagels, Elaine. 1989 [1979]. "God the Father/God the Mother." In *The Gnostic Gospels*, 48–69. New York: Vintage.

Pareyon Moreno, Eduardo. 1988. "Objetos maqueados." In *La Garrafa: Cuevas de La Garrafa, Chiapas; Estudio y conservación de algunos objetos arqueológicos*, ed. María Elena Landa A., Eduardo Pareyón Moreno, Alejandro Huerta C., Herrera G. Emma E., Rosa Lorena Román T., Martha Guajardo P., Josefina Cruz R., Sara Altamirano R., and Eva Rodríguez C., 183–209. Puebla: Gobierna del Estado de Puebla and Centro Regional de Puebla, Instituto Nacional de Antropología e Historia.

Pasztory, Esther. 1983. *Aztec Art*. New York: Abrams.

Pasztory, Esther. 1987. "Text, Archaeology, Art, and History in the Templo Mayor: Reflections." In *The Aztec Templo Mayor*, ed. Elizabeth Hill Boone, 451–62. Washington, DC: Dumbarton Oaks.

Pasztory, Esther. 1991. "The Problem of the Aesthetics of Abstraction for Pre-Columbian Art and Its Implications for Other Cultures." *RES* 19–20: 104–36.

Pérez-Castro, Guillermo, Pedro Francisco Sánchez Nava, María Estéfan, Judith Padilla y Yedra, and Antonio Gudiño Garfías. 1989. "El Cuauhxicalli de Moctezuma I." *Arqueología* 5: 132–51.

Peterson, Janette Favrot. 1988. "The *Florentine Codex* Imagery and the Colonial *Tlacuilo*." In *The Work of Bernardino de Sahagun, Pioneer Ethnographer of Sixteenth-Century Aztec Mexico*, ed. J. Jorge Klor de Alva, Henry B. Nicholson, and Eloise Quinones Keber, 273–93. Albany: Institute for Mesoamerican Studies, State University of New York.

Piho, Virve. 1972. "Tlacatecutli, Tlacochtecutli, Tlacatéccatl y Tlacochcálcatl." *Estudios de Cultura Náhuatl* 10: 315–28.

Pohl, John M.D. 1994. *The Politics of Symbolism in the Mixtec Codices*. Nashville, TN: Vanderbilt University.

Pomar, Juan Bautista de. 1964. *Romances de los Señores de la Nueva España Manuscrito de Juan Bautista de Pomar, Tezcoco, 1582*. Ed. Angel María Garibay K. Mexico City: Poesía Nahuatl 1 and Universidad Nacional Autónoma de México.

Pomar, Juan Bautista de. 1975. *Relación de Tezcoco*. Ed. Joaquín García Icazbalceta. Mexico City: Biblioteca Enciclopédica del Estado de México.

Pomar, Juan Bautista de. 1986. "Relación de Tezcoco." In *Relaciones geográficas del siglo XVI: México* 3, 23–113. Mexico City: Universidad Nacional Autónoma de México and IIA.

Popol Vuh. 1985. *Popol Vuh*. Ed. and trans. Dennis Tedlock. New York: Simon and Schuster.

Preuss, Konrad Theodor. 1998 [1925]. "El concepto de la Estrella de la Mañana según los textos regogidos entre los mexicaneros del estado de Durango, México." In *Fiestas, literatura y magia en el Nayarit: Ensayos sobre coras, huicholes y mexicaneros*, ed. and trans. Jesús Jáuregui and Johannes Neurath, 333–48. Mexico City: Instituto Nacional Indigenista and Centro Francés de Estudios Mexicanos y Centroamericanos.

Proskouriakoff, Tatiana. 1993. *Maya History*. Ed. Rosemary A. Joyce. Austin: University of Texas Press.

Quiñones Keber, Eloise. 1988a. "Deity Images and Texts in the *Primeros Memoriales* and *Florentine Codex*." In *The Work of Bernardino de Sahagun, Pioneer Ethnographer of Sixteenth-Century Aztec Mexico*, ed. J. Jorge Klor de Alva, Henry B. Nicholson, and Eloise Quiñones Keber, 255–72. Albany: Institute for Mesoamerican Studies, State University of New York.

Quiñones Keber, Eloise. 1988b. "Reading Images: The Making and Meaning of the Sahaguntine Illustrations." In *The Work of Bernardino de Sahagun, Pioneer Ethnographer of Sixteenth-Century Aztec Mexico*, ed. J. Jorge Klor de Alva, Henry B. Nicholson, and Eloise Quiñones Keber, 199–210. Albany: Institute for Mesoamerican Studies, State University of New York.

Quiñones Keber, Eloise. 1995. *Codex Telleriano-Remensis: Ritual, Divination, and History in a Pictorial Aztec Manuscript*. Austin: University of Texas Press.

Quiñones Keber, Eloise. 1997. "An Introduction to the Images, Artists, and Physical Features of the Primeros Memoriales." In *Primeros Memoriales by Fray Bernardino de Sahagún*, trans. Thelma D. Sullivan, 15–51. Norman: University of Oklahoma Press; Madrid: Patrimonial Nacional, Madrid, and Real Academia de la Historia.

Read, Kay A. 1994. "Sacred Commoners: The Motion of Cosmic Powers in Mexica Rulership." *History of Religions Journal* 34 (1): 39–69. http://dx.doi.org/10.1086/463381.

Reents-Budet, Dorie. 1994. *Painting the Maya Universe*. Durham, NC: Duke University Press.

Reichel-Dolmatoff, Gerardo. 1971 [1968]. *Amazonian Cosmos: The Sexual and Religious Symbolism of the Tukano Indians*. Chicago: University of Chicago Press.

Reichel-Dolmatoff, Gerardo. 1973. *Desana: Le symbolisme universel des Indiens Tukano du Vaupés*. Paris: Gallimard.

Robertson, Donald. 1959. *Mexican Manuscript Painting of the Early Colonial Period: The Metropolitan Schools*. New Haven, CT: Yale University Press.

Robertson, Janice Lynn. 2005. "Aztec Picture-Writing: A Critical Study Based on the Codex Mendoza's Place-Name Signs." PhD dissertation, Columbia University, New York City.

Robertson, Merle G. 1991. *The Sculpture of Palenque Vol. IV: The Cross Group, the North Group, the Olvidado, and Other Pieces*. Princeton, NJ: Princeton University Press.

Robicsek, Francis. 1978. *The Smoking Gods: Tobacco in Maya Art, History and Religion*. Norman: University of Oklahoma Press.

Robicsek, Francis. 1979. "The Mythical Identity of Kawil." In *Tercera Mesa Redonda de Palenque*, ed. Merle G. Robertson and Donnan Call Jeffers, 4: 111–28. Chiapas, Mexico: Pre-Columbian Art Research Center.

Rodríguez, Mariangela. 1991. *Hacia la estrella con la pasión y la ciudad a cuestas Semana Santa en Iztapalapa*. Mexico City: Centro de Investigaciones y Estudios Superiores en Antropología Social.

Roe, Peter G. 1998. "Paragon or Peril? The Jaguar in Amazonian Society." In *Icons of Power: Feline Symbolism in the Americas*, ed. Nicholas J. Saunders, 171–202. London: Routledge.

Roiz, Carlos Villa. 1997. *Popocatepetl: Mitos, Ciencia y Cultura*. Mexico City: Plaza y Valdés Editores.

Rojas, Gabriel de. 1985. "Relación geográfica de Cholula." In *Relaciones geográficas del siglo XVI: Tlaxcala,* ed. René Acuña, 2: 125–45. Mexico City: Universidad Nacional Autónoma de México and Instituto de Investigaciones Antropológicas.

Roskamp, Han. 2010. "God of Metals: Tlatlahuhqui Tezcatlipoca and the Sacred Symbolism of Metallurgy in Michoacan, West Mexico." *Ancient Mesoamerica* 21 (1): 69–78. http://dx.doi.org/10.1017/S0956536110000118.

Ruiz de Alarcón, Hernando. 1984. *Treatise on the Heathen Superstitions That Today Live among the Indians Natives to This New Spain, 1629*. Trans. and ed. Richard Andrews and Ross Hassig. Norman: University of Oklahoma Press.

Sahagún, Fray Bernardino de. 1950–82. *Florentine Codex: General History of the Things of New Spain*. 12 books. Trans. Arthur J.O. Anderson and Charles E. Dibble. Santa Fe, NM: School of America Research; Salt Lake City: University of Utah.

Sahagún, Fray Bernardino de. 1979 [1575–78]. *Códice florentino*. 3 vols. Facsimile edition. Florence: Biblioteca Medicea Laurenziana; Mexico City: Archivo General de la Nación and Secretaría de Gobernación.

Sahagún, Fray Bernardino de. 1969. *Historia general de la cosas de Nueva España*. Mexico City: Editorial Porrúa.

Sahagún, Fray Bernardino de. 1982 [1977]. *Historia general de la cosas de Nueva España*. Mexico City: Editorial Porrúa.

Sahagún, Fray Bernardino de. 1985. *Educación de los Antiguos Nahuas*. Trans. Alfredo López Austin. Mexico City: Secretaría de Educación Pública.

Sahagún, Fray Bernardino de. 1992. *Ritos, Sacerdotes y Atavíos de los dioses*. Ed. and trans. Miguel León-Portilla. Mexico City: Universidad Nacional Autónoma de México and Instituto de Investigaciones Históricas.

Sahagún, Fray Bernardino de. 1993 [1559–61]. *Primeros Memoriales by Fray Bernardino de Sahagún*. Facsimile edition, photographed by Ferdinand Anders. Norman: University of Oklahoma Press; Madrid: Patrimonial Nacional, Madrid, and Real Academia de la Historia.

Sahagún, Fray Bernardino de. 1997 [1559–61]. *Primeros Memoriales by Fray Bernardino de Sahagún*. Paleography of Nahuatl text and English translation by Thelma D. Sullivan. Norman: University of Oklahoma Press; Madrid: Patrimonial Nacional, Madrid, and Real Academia de la Historia.

Sahagún, Fray Bernardino de. 2000. *Historia general de las cosas de Nueva España*. 3 vols. Ed. Alfredo López Austin and Josefina García Quintana. Mexico City: Consejo Nacional para la Cultura y las Artes.

Saunders, Nicholas J. 1990. "Tezcatlipoca: Jaguar Metaphors and the Aztec Mirror of Nature." In *Signifying Animals: Human Meaning in the Natural World*, ed. R. G. Willis, 159–77. London: Unwin Hyman. http://dx.doi.org/10.4324/9780203169353_chapter_12.

Saunders, Nicholas J. 1991. "The Jaguars of Culture: Symbolizing Humanity in Pre-Columbian and Amerindian Societies." PhD thesis, University of Southampton, Southampton, England.

Saunders, Nicholas J. 1994. "At the Mouth of the Obsidian Cave: Deity and Place in Aztec Religion." In *Sacred Sites, Sacred Places*, ed. D. L. Carmichael, J. Hubert, B. Reeves, and O. Schanche, 172–83. London: Routledge.

Saunders, Nicholas J. 1997. "Obsidian Mirrors and Tezcatlipoca in Conquest and Post-Conquest México." Report to the Foundation for the Advancement of Mesoamerican Studies. http://www.famsi.org/reports/98056/. Accessed March 1, 2007.

Saunders, Nicholas J. 1998. "Stealers of Light, Traders in Brilliance: Amerindian Metaphysics in the Mirror of Conquest." *RES: Anthropology and Aesthetics* 33 (1): 225–52.

Saunders, Nicholas J. 2001. "A Dark Light: Reflections on Obsidian in Mesoamerica." *World Archaeology* 33 (2): 220–36. http://dx.doi.org/10.1080/00438240120079262.

Saunders, Nicholas J. 2004. "The Cosmic Earth: Materiality and Mineralogy in the Americas." In *Soil, Stones and Symbols: Cultural Perceptions of the Mineral World*, ed. N. Boivin and M. A. Owoc, 123–41. London: UCL Press.

Saunders, Nicholas J. In press. "Materialising Spirits: Smoke and Power in the Americas." In *The Art of Tobacco in Ancient America*, ed. C. Martinez and A. Llamazares Sarasola. Buenos Aires: CEPPA.

Saville, Marshall H. 1925. *The Wood-Carver's Art in Ancient Mexico*. Contributions, vol. 9. New York: Museum of the American Indian, Heye Foundation.

Saville, Marshall H. 1922. *Turquoise Mosaic Art in Ancient Mexico: Indian Notes and Monographs, no. 8, Museum of the American Indian*. New York: Heye Foundation.

Schele, Linda. 1976. "Accession Iconography of Chan-Bahlum in the Group of the Cross at Palenque." In *The Art, Iconography and Dynastic History of Palenque*, part 3 of *Proceedings of the Segunda Mesa Redonda of Palenque*, ed. Merle G. Robertson, 9–34. Pebble Beach, CA: Robert Louis Stevenson School.

Schele, Linda. 1984. "Some Suggested Readings of the Event and Office of Heir-Designate at Palenque." In *Phoneticism in Mayan Hieroglyphic Writing*, ed. John S. Justeson and Lyle Campbell, 287–306. Institute for Mesoamerican Studies, State University of New York at Albany, Publication 9. Albany: State University of New York.

Schele, Linda. 1992. *Workbook for the XVI Maya Hieroglyphic Workshop at Texas*. Austin: University of Texas, Department of Art History and Institute of Latin American Studies.

Schele, Linda, and David Freidel. 1990. *A Forest of Kings: The Untold Story of the Ancient Maya*. New York: William Morrow.

Schele, Linda, and Nikolai Grube. 1994. *The Proceedings of the Maya Hieroglyphic Workshop: Tlaloc-Venus Warfare, March 12–13, 1994*. Trans. and ed. Phil Wanyerka. Austin: University of Texas.

Schele, Linda, and Nikolai Grube. 1995. *The Proceedings of the Maya Hieroglyphic Workshop: Late Classic and Terminal Classic Warfare, March 11–12, 1995*. Trans. and ed. Phil Wanyerka. Austin: University of Texas.

Schele, Linda, and Peter Mathews. 1998. *The Code of Kings*. New York: Scribner.

Schele, Linda, and Jeffery H. Miller. 1983. *The Mirror, the Rabbit, and the Bundle: "Accession" Expressions from the Classic Maya Inscriptions*. In Studies in Pre-Columbian Art and Archaeology 25. Washington, DC: Dumbarton Oaks.

Schele, Linda, and Mary Miller. 1986. *The Blood of Kings: Dynasty and Ritual in Maya Art*. Fort Worth, TX: Kimbell Art Museum.

Scott, Joan Wallach. 1988. *Gender and the Politics of History*. New York: Columbia University Press.

The Selden Roll. 1955. Ed. Cottie A. Burland. Berlin: Verlag, Gebr, Mann.

Seler, Eduard. 1902–23. *Gesammelte Abhandlungen zur Amerikanischen Sprach- und Alterthumskunde*. 5 vols. Berlin: A. Ascher & Co. (vols. 1–2) and Behrend & Co. (vols. 3–5).

Seler, Eduard. 1904. "Ueber Steinkisten, Tepetlacalli, mit Opferdarstellungen und andere ahnliche Monumente." In *Gesammelte Abhandlungen zur Amerikanischen Sprach- und*

Altertumskunde, Vol. 2: *Berlin,* 717–66. (1961 edition, Graz: Akademische Druck- u. Verlagsanstalt.)

Seler, Eduard. 1960–61. *Gesammelte Abhandlungen zur Amerikanischen Sprach- und Altertumskunde.* Graz, Austria: Akademische Druck- u. Verlagsanstalt. (Reprinted from the 1902–3 edition, Berlin.)

Seler, Eduard. 1963. *Comentarios al Códice Borgia.* Mexico City: Fondo de Cultura Económica.

Seler, Eduard. 1990–98. *Collected Works in Mesoamerican Linguistics and Archaeology.* Trans. under supervision of Charles P. Bowditch, ed. Frank E. Comparato, J. Eric S. Thompson, and Francis B. Richardson. Culver City, CA: Labyrinthos.

Seler, Eduard. 1998 [1908]. "The Ruins of Chichen Itza in Yucatan." In *Collected Works in Mesoamerican Linguistics and Archaeology,* ed. Charles P. Bowditch 6, 41–165. Culver City, CA: Labyrinthos.

Serra Puche, Mari Carmen, and Felipe Solís Olguín, eds. 1994. *Cristales y obsidiana prehispánicos.* Mexico City: Siglo Veintiuno.

Siméon, Rémi. 1977 [1885]. *Diccionario de la lengua nahuatl o mexicano.* Trans. Josefina Oliva de Coll. Mexico City: Siglo Veintiuno.

Siméon, Rémi. 1988 [1885]. *Diccionario de la lengua Nahuatl o Mexicano.* Mexico City: Siglo XXI.

Sinopoli, Carla M. 1994. "The Archaeology of Empires." *Annual Review of Anthropology* 23 (1): 159–80. http://dx.doi.org/10.1146/annurev.an.23.100194.001111.

Smith, Michael E. 2002. "Domestic Ritual at Aztec Provincial Sites in Morelos." In *Domestic Ritual in Ancient Mesoamerica,* ed. Patricia Plunket, 93–114. Monograph 46. Los Angeles: Cotsen Institute of Archaeology, UCLA.

Smith, Michael E. 2003. "Comments on the Historicity of Topiltzin Quetzalcoatl, Tollan and the Toltecs." *Nahua Newsletter* 36: 31–36.

Smith, Michael E. 2004. "Aztec Materials in Museum Collections: Some Frustrations of a Field Archaeologist." *Nahua Newsletter* 38: 21–28.

Smith, Michael E. 2006. "Tula and Chichén Itzá: Are We Asking the Right Questions?" In *Twin Tollans: Chichén Itzá, Tula, and the Epiclassic-Early Postclassic Mesoamerican World,* ed. Cynthia Kristan-Graham and Jeff Karl Kowalski, 559–97. Washington, DC: Dumbarton Oaks.

Smith, Michael E. 2008. *Aztec City-State Capitals, Series: Ancient Cities of the New World.* Gainesville: University Press of Florida.

Smith, Michael E. 2011. "Aztecs." In *Oxford Handbook of the Archaeology of Ritual and Religion,* ed. Timothy Insoll, 556–70. Oxford: Oxford University Press. http://dx.doi.org/10.1093/oxfordhb/9780199232444.013.0036.

Smith, Michael E. n.d.a. "Archaeological Research at Aztec-Period Rural Sites in Morelos, Mexico," vol. 2: *Artifacts and Chronology* / Investigaciones Arqueológicas en Sitios Rurales de la Época Azteca en Morelos, tomo 2: *Artefactos y Cronología*. Oxford: BAR International Series.

Smith, Michael E. n.d.c. "Las bodegas de museos como fuente de información arqueológica: Las contribuciones de Felipe Solís Olguín." In *Homenaje al maestro Felipe Solís Olguín*, ed. Roberto García Moll and Rafael Fierro Padilla. Mexico City: Instituto Nacional de Antropología e Historia.

Smith, Michael E. n.d.c. *Residential Excavations in the Aztec-Period City of Yautepec, Morelos, Mexico* / *Excavaciones de casas en la ciudad azteca de Yautepec, Morelos, México*. Oxford: BAR International Series.

Smith, Michael E., and Frances F. Berdan, eds. 2003. *The Postclassic Mesoamerican World*. Salt Lake City: University of Utah Press.

Smith, Michael E., and Lisa Montiel. 2001. "The Archaeological Study of Empires and Imperialism in Prehispanic Central Mexico." *Journal of Anthropological Archaeology* 20 (3): 245–84. http://dx.doi.org/10.1006/jaar.2000.0372.

Smith, Michael E., Jennifer Wharton, and Melissa McCarron. 2003. "Las ofrendas de Calixtlahuaca." *Expresión Antropológica* 19: 35–53.

Smith, Michael E., Jennifer Wharton, and Jan Marie Olson. 2003. "Aztec Feasts, Rituals, and Markets: Political Uses of Ceramic Vessels in a Commercial Economy." In *The Archaeology and Politics of Food and Feasting in Early States and Empires*, ed. Tamara L. Bray, 235–68. New York: Kluwer. http://dx.doi.org/10.1007/978-0-306-48246-5_9.

Société des Américanistes. 1922. "La collection Géninau Musée d'Ethnographie du Trocadéro." *Journal de la Société des Américanistes* 14: 258–59.

Solís Olguín, Felipe R. 1976. *La escultura mexica del museo de Santa Cecilia Acatitlan, Estado de México*. Mexico City: Instituto Nacional de Antropología e Historia.

Solís Olguín, Felipe R. 1981. *Escultura del Castillo de Teayo, Veracruz, México: Catálogo*. Cuadernos de Historia del Arte, vol. 16. Mexico City: Universidad Nacional Autónoma de México and Instituto de Investigaciones Estéticas.

Solís Olguín, Felipe R. 1991. *Tesoros Artísticos del Museo Nacional de Antropología*. Mexico City: Aguilar.

Solís Olguín, Felipe R. 2004. *The Aztec Empire*. New York: Guggenheim Museum.

Solís Olguín, Felipe R., and Ted Leyenaar. 2002. *Art Treasures of Ancient Mexico: Journey to the Land of the Gods*. Amsterdam: Niewe Kerk.

Solís Olguín, Felipe R., and David A. Morales Gómez. 1991. *Rescate de un rescate: Colección de objetos arqueológicos de el Volador, ciudad de México*. Catálogo de las colecciones arqueológicas de Museo Nacional de Antropología. Mexico City: Instituto Nacional de Antropología e Historia.

Spranz, Bodo. 1964. *Los dioses en los códices mexicanos del grupo Borgia.* Mexico City: Fondo de Cultura Económica.

Stein, Gil J. 2002. "From Passive Periphery to Active Agents: Emerging Perspectives in the Archaeology of Interregional Interaction." *American Anthropologist* 104 (3): 903–16. http://dx.doi.org/10.1525/aa.2002.104.3.903.

Steinberg, Leo. 1996 (inc. reprint of *The Sexuality of Christ in Renaissance Art*, 1983). *The Sexuality of Christ in Renaissance Art and in Modern Oblivion.* Chicago: University of Chicago Press.

Sterpone, Osvaldo J. 2000–1. "La quimera de Tula." *Boletin de Antropologia Americana* 37: 141–204.

Stocker, Terry. 1992–93. "Contradictions in Religious Myths: Tezcatlipoca and His Existence at Tula, Hidalgo." *Notas Mesoamericanas* 14: 63–92.

Stuart, David. 1978. "Some Thoughts on Certain Occurrences of the T565 Glyph Element at Palenque." In *Tercera Mesa Redonda de Palenque*, vol. 4, ed. Merle G. Robertson and Donnan C. Jeffers, 167–72. San Francisco: Pre-Columbian Art Research Institute.

Stuart, David. 1987. *Phonetic Syllables.* Research Reports on Ancient Maya Writing 14. Washington, DC: Center for Maya Research.

Stuart, David, Stephen Houston, and John Robertson. 1999. *The Proceedings of the Maya Hieroglyphic Workshop: Classic Mayan Language and Classic Maya Gods, March 13–14, 1999.* Ed. Phil Wanyerka. Austin: University of Texas.

Sullivan, Thelma D. 1997. *Primeros Memoriale: Paleography of Nahuatl Text and English Translation.* Norman: University of Oklahoma Press.

Tait, Hugh. 1967. "The Devil's Looking-Glass: The Magical Speculum of Dr. John Dee." In *Horace Walpole, Writer, Politician, and Connoisseur: Essays on the 250th Anniversary of Walpole's Birth*, ed. W. H. Smith, 195–212. New Haven, CT: Yale University Press.

Tate, Carolyn E. 1992. *Yaxchilan: The Design of a Maya Ceremonial City.* Austin: University of Texas Press.

Tate, Carolyn E. 1999. "Writing on the Face of the Moon: Women's Products, Archetypes, and Power in Ancient Maya Civilization." In *Manifesting Power: Gender and the Interpretation of Power in Archaeology*, ed. Tracy L. Sweely, 81–102. London: Routledge.

Taube, Karl A. 1992a. *The Major Gods of Ancient Yucatan.* Studies in Pre-Columbian Art and Archaeology no. 32. Washington, DC: Dumbarton Oaks.

Taube, Karl A. 1992b. "The Iconography of Mirrors at Teotihuacan." In *Art, Ideology, and the City of Teotihuacan*, ed. Janet C. Berlo, 169–204. Washington, DC: Dumbarton Oaks.

Taube, Karl A. 1999. "The Iconography of Toltec Period Chichen Itza." In *Hidden among the Hills: Maya Archaeology of the Northwest Yucatan Peninsula*, ed. Hanns J. Prem, 212–46. Markt Schwaben: Verlag Anton Saurwein.

Taube, Karl A. n.d. "The Mirrors of Offerings 1 and 2 of Sala 2 in the Palacio Quemada at Tula: An Iconographic Interpretation." In *Ofrendas en un Palacio Tolteca: Turquesa y Concha en el Palacio Quemado de Tula, Hidalgo*, ed. Robert H. Cobean and Alba Guadelupe Mastache. Mexico City: Instituto Nacional de Antropología e Historia.

Taylor, Anne-Christine. 1993. "Remembering to Forget: Identity, Mourning and Memory among the Jivaro." *Man: Journal of the Royal Anthropological Institute* 28 (4): 653–78

Tedlock, Dennis. 1985. *Popol Vuh*. New York: Simon and Schuster.

Tena, Rafael. 1955. *The Selden Roll*. Ed. Cottie A. Burland. Berlin: Verlag. Gebr. Mann.

Tena, Rafael. 1987. *El calendario mexica y la cronografía*. Mexico City: Instituto Nacional de Antropología e Historia.

Thévet, André. 1905. "Histoyre du Mechique, manuscrit français inédit du XVIᵉ siècle." Ed. E. de Jonghe. *Journal de la Société des Américanistes*, nouvelle série, 2: 1–41.

Thompson, John Eric S. 1942. "Representations of Tezcatlipoca at Chichen Itza." *Carnegie Institution of Washington, Notes on Middle American Archaeology and Ethnology* 1 (12): 48–50.

Thompson, John Eric S. 1950. *Maya Hieroglyphic Writing: An Introduction*. Washington, DC: Carnegie Institution of Washington.

Thompson, John Eric S. 1960. *Maya Hieroglyphic Writing: An Introduction*. Norman: University of Oklahoma Press.

Thompson, John Eric S. 1970. *Maya History and Religion*. Norman: University of Oklahoma Press.

Thompson, John Eric S. 1972. *A Commentary on the Dresden Codex: A Maya Hieroglyphic Book*. Philadelphia: American Philosophical Society.

Tilley, Christopher, Webb Keene, Susanne Küchler, Mike Rowlands, and Patricia Spyer, eds. 2006. *Handbook of Material Culture*. London: Sage.

Torquemada, Fray Juan de. 1969/1975–83 [1613–15]. *Monarquía Indiana*. Ed. Miguel León-Portilla. Mexico City: Universidad Nacional Autónoma de México and Instituto de Investigaciones Históricas.

Torquemada, Fray Juan de. 1975. *Monarquía Indiana*. Ed. Miguel León-Portilla. Mexico City: Editorial Porrua.

Torriti, Piero, ed. 1977. *La Pinacoteca nazionale di Siena: I dipinti dal XII al XV secolo*. Genova: Sagep Editrice.

Tovalín Ahumada, Alejandro. 1998. *Desarrollo arquitectónico del sitio arqueológico de Tlalpizáhuac*. Colección Científica, vol. 348. Mexico City: Instituto Nacional de Antropología e Historia.

Townsend, Richard F. 1979. *State and Cosmos in the Art of Tenochtitlan*. Washington, DC: Dumbarton Oaks.

Townsend, Richard F. 1987. "Coronation at Tenochtitlan." In *The Aztec Templo Mayor*, ed. Elizabeth H. Boone, 371–410. Washington, DC: Dumbarton Oaks.

Townsend, Richard F. 1992. *The Aztecs*. London: Thames and Hudson.

Tozzer, Alfred M. 1941. *Landa's Relación de las cosas de Yucatán*. Papers of the Peabody Museum of American Archaeology and Ethnology, vol. 18. Cambridge, MA: Harvard University.

Tozzer, Alfred M. 1957. *Chichen Itza and Its Cenote of Sacrifice: A Comparative Study of Contemporaneous Maya and Toltec*. Cambridge, MA: Peabody Museum of Archaeology and Ethnology, Harvard University.

Trexler, Richard C. 1991. "Habiller et Déshabiller les Images: Esquisse d'une Analysis." In *L'Image et la Production du Sacré: Actes du Colloque de Strasbourg (20–21) Janvier 1988 Organisé par le Centre d'Histoire des Religions de l'Université de Strasbourg II: Group "Theorie et Pratique de l'Image Cultuelle,"* ed. Françoise Dunand, Jean-Michel Spieser, and Jean Wirth, 195–231. Paris: Méridiens Klincksieck.

Trexler, Richard C. 1993. "Gendering Jesus Crucified." In *Iconography at the Crossroads: Papers from the Colloquium Sponsored by the Index of Christian Art, Princeton University, 23–24 March 1990*, ed. Brendan Cassidy, 107–20. Princeton, NJ: Index of Christian Art, Department of Art and Archaeology.

Trexler, Richard C. 2003. *Reliving Golgotha: The Passion Play of Iztapalapa*. Cambridge, MA: Harvard University Press.

Tuckerman, Bryant. 1964. *Planetary, Lunar, and Solar Positions a.d. 2 to a.d. 1649*. Memoirs of the American Philosophical Society 59. Philadelphia: The American Philosophical Society.

Tudela, José. 1977. *Relacíon de las ceremonias y ritos y poblacíon y gobierno de los indios de la provincia de Michoacán (1541)*. Morelia, Mexico: Balsal Editores.

Umberger, Emily. 1981a. "Aztec Sculptures, Hieroglyphs, and History." PhD dissertation, Columbia University, New York City.

Umberger, Emily. 1981b. "The Structure of Aztec History." *Archaeoastronomy* 4 (4): 10–18.

Umberger, Emily. 1984. "El Trono de Moctezuma." *Estudios de Cultura Náhuatl* 17: 63–87.

Umberger, Emily. 1987a. "Events Commemorated by Date Plaques at the Templo Mayor: Reconsidering the Solar Metaphor." In *The Aztec Templo Mayor*, ed. Elizabeth Hill Boone, 411–49. Washington, DC: Dumbarton Oaks.

Umberger, Emily. 1987b. "Antiques, Revivals, and References to the Past in Aztec Art." *Res: Anthropology and Aesthetics* 13: 62–105.

Umberger, Emily. 1996a. "Appendix 3: Material Remains in the Central Provinces." In *Aztec Imperial Strategies*, by Frances F. Berdan, Richard E. Blanton, Elizabeth Hill Boone, Mary G. Hodge, Michael E. Smith, and Emily Umberger, 247–64. Washington, DC: Dumbarton Oaks.

Umberger, Emily. 1996b. "The *Monarchía Indiana* in Seventeenth-Century New Spain." In *Converging Cultures: Art and Identity in Spanish America*, ed. Diana Fane, 46–58. New York: Brooklyn Museum and Abrams.

Umberger, Emily. 1998. "New Blood from an Old Stone." *Estudios de Cultura Nahuatl* 28: 241–56.

Umberger, Emily. 1999. "The Reading of Hieroglyphs on Aztec Monuments." *Thule, Revista italiana di studi americanistici* 6–7: 77–102. Perugia, Italy.

Umberger, Emily. 2002. "Notions of Aztec History: The Case of the 1487 Great Temple Dedication." *Res: Anthropology and Aesthetics* 42: 86–108.

Umberger, Emily. 2005. "Tezcatlipoca and Huitzilopochtli in Aztec Images and Politics." Paper presented at the University of London Conference on Tezcatlipoca, London.

Umberger, Emily. 2007a. "Art History and the Aztec Empire: The Evidence of Sculptures." *Revista Española de Antropología Americana* 37 (2): 165–202.

Umberger, Emily. 2007b. "The Metaphorical Underpinnings of Aztec History: The Case of the 1473 Civil War." *Ancient Mesoamerica* 18 (1): 11–30. http://dx.doi.org/10.1017/S0956536107000016.

Umberger, Emily. 2008. "Ethnicity and Other Identities in the Sculptures of Tenochtitlan." In *Ethnic Identity in Nahua Mesoamerica: The View from Archaeology, Art History, Ethnohistory, and Contemporary Ethnography*, by Frances F. Berdan, John Chance, Alan Sandstrom, Barbara Stark, James Taggart, and Emily Umberger, 64–104. Salt Lake City: University of Utah Press.

Valencia Rivera, Rogelio. 2006. "Tezcatlipoca y K'awiill, algo mas que un parecido." *Anales del Museo de América* 14: 45–60.

Velázquez, V. Ricardo. 1975. "Miscelanea de barrio." In *Teotenango: El antiguo lugar de la muralla*, ed. Román Piña Chán, 2: 317–31. Mexico City: Gobierno del Estado de México.

Vernant, Jean-Pierre. 1974. *Mythe et société en Grèce ancienne*. Paris: Maspéro.

Vié-Wohrer, Anne-Marie. 1999. *Xipe Totec, notre seigneur l'écorché: Étude glyphique d'un dieu Aztèque*. Mexico City: Centre Français d'Études Mexicaines et Centraméricaines.

Villagra Caleti, Agustín. 1954. *Pinturas rupestres "Mateo A. Saldaña," Ixtapantongo, Estado de México*. Mexico City: Instituto Nacional de Antropología e Historia.

Viveiros de Castro, Eduardo. 1992. *From the Enemy's Point of View: Humanity and Divinity in an Amazonian Society*. Chicago: University of Chicago Press.

Wicke, Charles. 1975. "Once More around the Tizoc Stone: A Reconsideration." *Acts of the Forty-First International Congress of Americanists, Mexico, 1974* 2: 209–22.

Wicke, Charles, and Fernando Horcasitas. 1957. "Archaeological Investigations on Monte Tlaloc, Mexico." *Mesoamerican Notes* 5: 83–96.

Wilk, Richard R. 2004. "Miss Universe, the Olmec, and the Valley of Oaxaca." *Journal of Social Archaeology* 4 (1): 81–98. http://dx.doi.org/10.1177/1469605304039851.

Yasugi, Yoshiho, and Kenji Saito. 1991. "Glyph Y of the Maya Supplemental Series." In *Research Reports on Ancient Maya Writing* 34. Washington, DC: Center for Maya Research.

Zantwijk, Rudolf Van. 1976. "El Parentesco y la Afiliación Etnica de Huitzilopochtli." Paper delivered at the International Congress of Americanists, Paris, 1976. Paper in author's possession.

Zaragoza Ocaña, Diana. 2003. *Tamohi, su pintura mural*. Tamaulipas, Mexico: Gobierno del Estado de Tamaulipas.

Index

acculturation, Aztec deities and festivals in, 149–50
Acolhuacatl, *102*
agave, origins of, 73
agricultural cycle, and festivals, 149–50
atlatls, 95, 96, 104, 113, *117*, 130, 132
altars, momoztli, 9, 13, 23–27
Alta Vista, burial at, 31–32
androgyny, 136; of divinities and founding ancestors, 151, 156(n7); of Jesus Christ, *139, 140, 141, 142, 143, 152–54*, 155, 156(n6); of man-gods, 137–38
animals, 3, 64; as avatars, 170, 171. *See also by type*
arrows, 13, 132, 133
art history, focus of, 10–11
astrology, 172
astronomy, 3; events recorded at Tikal, 185–86; and Kawil, 192–94; Tezcatlipoca and Kawil's and, 172–75. *See also* planetary retrograde; planets; *various celestial bodies*
atl tlachinolli glyph, 4
auto-sacrifice, 4, 6, *101*
avatars: animal, 170, 171; astronomical, 172–73
Axayacatl, 95, 124
axes, smoking, 163, 164, *165–66, 168*
Azcapotzalco, 86

aztaxelli, 95, 104, *117*, 132
Aztec empire, 109(n3); influence of, 35–36
Aztezcatl, 14, *15*
Aztlan, migrants from, *15*

Baktun endings, at Tikal, 183
ballcourts, platforms associated with, 25
battlefields, smoke as symbolic of, 4
beauty, 67; of Jesus Christ, 138, *139,* 157(n8); of Toxcatl impersonator, 136–37, 148
bells, 2, *130*; gold, 116, 118; symbolism of, 120–29; warriors and, *117*, 131, 132
bisexuality: of divinities and founding ancestors, 151, 156(n7), 157(n15); of Tezcatlipoca impersonator, 142, 144
Black Tezcatlipoca, 70, 81(n15), *173*
blades, obsidian, 4–5
blood, in ezpitzal iconography, 41, 43–53, *55*, 56, 58; sacrifice of, 4–5
Bolon Dzacab, 166, 176
bone, smoking, 163
bracelets, gold, 116, 118
breast-plate, 41; butterfly, 98, *99, 100*
burials, 21; Chalchihuites culture, 31–32; Templo Mayor, 130–32
butterfly breast-plates, 98, *99, 100*

231

Calakmul, 178, 185
calendar names: Mixtec, 69, *70*; of Quetzalcoatl and Tezcatlipoca, 60, 61–*63*
calendars, 60, 73, *74*, 87, 89
calendrical cycles, 111(n16); katun endings in, 182–92; Mayan, 175–78, 179, 194–95(n3), 196(n9); Tezcatlipoca and Huitzilopochtli in, 102–3
Calixtlahuaca, 11, 13, 21, *26*; Tezcatlipoca imagery at, 33, *34*, 39(n9)
Cantares Mexicanos, 120
capes: eagle feather, 116; netted, 172
Capilco, 21
captives: symbols associated with, 95, 104; in Toxcatl rite, 135–37
Caracol, 178
Castillo de Teayo, 11
castration, 147
Catholic Church, feast days of, 149–50
caves, 4
Ce Acatl, 62, *63*
Ce Ehecatl, 61
celestial imagery, 167. See also astronomy; *various celestial bodies*
Centzon-Huitznahua, 94, 99, 101, 104
Ce Ocelotl, 66
Cerro de Estrella (Huixachtecatl), 148–49, 159(n31), 160(n33)
Cerro Tlaloc, 11
Chac, 170, 196(n9)
chalchihuatl, 56
Chalchihuites culture, 29, 31–32
Chalchiuhtlicue, 85, 89–90
Chalco, 62, 159(n28)
Chiapas, 33, *35*
Chichén Itzá, 29, *30*, *169*, 170, 171, 196(n9)
Chichimecs, depictions of, 104
Chilam Balam, 174
Chimalpahin Cuauhtlehuanitzin, Domingo de San Anton, 137
Chimayo, 161(n42), *Christ of Esquipulas*, 151, *154*
Cholula, 33; and Quetzalcoatl, 61, 69, 81(n11); Quetzalcoatl impersonators in, 62–63, 66–67
Christianity: and indigenous festivals, 149–50; Tezcatlipoca's relevance to, 9, 150–51
Christ of Esquipulas, 151, *154*
Christ of Ixquimilpan (Ibarra), 151, *153*, 160(n41)
cihuacoatl, office of, 71, 81(n15, n16)
Cipactonal, 73

cities, patron gods of, 86
Classic period, 163, 171, 172; katun endings, 182–83
Cleveland Museum of Art, 132
clothing, jaguar skin, 4
cloud riders, at Tikal, 188
Coatepetl (Serpent Mountain), 94, 99
Coatetelco, 25
Coatlicue, 70, 99
Codex Azcatitlan, obsidian mirrors in, 14, *15*
Codex Borbonicus, 46, 60, 70; ezpitzal in, 41, 44, 45, *46*, *47*, *48*
Codex Borgia, *15*, 81(n15); Tezcatlipoca in, 44–45, 64, 81(n15), *147*, 158(n20), 171, *173*
Codex Fejérváry-Mayer, 32, 64
Codex Laud, 74
Codex Madrid, Kawil in, 163, *167*
Codex Magliabechiano, *129*, *130*; pulque gods in, 56–*57*
Codex Matritense: ezpitzal in, 41–*42*; writing and layout in, 42–43
Codex Mendoza, 5, 136; tribute lists in, 124, *125*–*26*; obsidian mirrors illustrated in, 14, *15*
Codex Porfirio Díaz, *55*; ezpitzal in, 41, 58
Codex Ramírez, gold ornaments in, 116
Codex Ritos y Costumbres, 49, 57
Codex Telleriano-Remensis, 3, 129; butterfly breast-plates in, 98, *99*; date-deity associations in, 89–90; ezpitzal in, 41, 44, 50–*52*, 58; Tezcatlipoca in, *164*, 170
Codex Tudela (Codex of the Museum of America), 50, 60; ezpitzal in, 41, 44, 46, 48–*49*, 58; and pulque gods in, 56–57
Codex Vatican A (Rios), 61; ezpitzal in, 44, 50–*52*, 58
codices, 3, 12; as sources, 8–9. See also by name
Colloquios (Sahagún), 150, 160(n39)
Colonial period, 2, 14, 164; festival synchronization, 149–50; Tezcatlipoca in, 9, 57–58
colors, symbolism of, 56
Coltzin, *105*, 106–7
commoners, depictions of, 104
confrontations, between Quetzalcoatl and Tezcatlipoca, 73–74, 75
conquests: and patron gods, 99, 101, 104; scenes of, 86–87, *88*
Copan, 193; rulers at, 178, 181–82
Cordamex dictionary, 164
Cortés, Hernán, 76

INDEX

cosmic cycles, 74. *See also* calendrical cycles
costumes, 94; as political indicators, 107–8; Sahagún's depictions of, *91*, *92*
Coyolxauhqui, 114, 133; bells and, 120–*22*
coyote, Tezcatlipoca as, 51–*52*, 171
craft specialization, obsidian mirror manufacture, 19
creation myths, 60, 99; Quetzalcoatl and Tezcatlipoca in, 72–73; Tezcatlipoca's, 171–72; twins in, 69–72
cremations, 4, 130
Cross Group (Palenque), Kawil in, 166–67, *178*
crucifixion: and human sacrifice, 150–51; reenactment, 148, 149, 159(n31), 160(n35)
Cuexcomate, 21, 23
cups, with Tezcatlipoca imagery, 33
curing, domestic, 23

darts, 130; on Tizoc Stone depictions, 95, 96
days, dates, deities associated with, 87, *89*. *See also* calendrical cycles
Dee, Dr., obsidian mirror used by, 17, *18*
deities, 59, 83, 150, 160(n38); conquered, 103–5, 106–8; figurines, 23, 132; hierarchy of, *88*, 92–93; in Huitznahuac, 101–2; identifying, 28–29; in manuscripts, 87, 89–92; one-legged, 28, 29, 41; patron, 84–86; Pulque, 56–57, 58; on sculptures, 93–98; victorious, 98–99, 101–3; warrior, 113–19
destruction, 60, 61
divination, 23, 95, 172
divination books (tonalamatl), 87; date-deity associations in, 89–90, 103
domestic sphere, ritual, 22–23
Dos Pilas, 178, 195(n6); katun endings at, 184–85
Dresden Codex, 189; Venus in, 172–74, 180, 188, 192, 195(n7)
drums, 23, 68
drunkenness, Tezcatlipoca's, 75, *76*
Durán, Diego, 3, 7, 101, 116, 140; on Quetzalcoatl, 61, 68; on warfare, 123–24

Eagle warriors, 114
Early Classic period: katun endings, 183–84; Kawil in, 165–66
Early Postclassic period, 36; Tezcatlipoca imagery in, 29–32
earplugs, gold, 116, *117*, 124, 127, 132
earth, 4; creation of, 171

Ehecatl (Wind), 60, 66, 72
Ek' Balam, 177
elites, 4, 69. *See also* nobility; royalty
Epiclassic period, 36; Tezcatlipoca cult in, 29–32
Ex-Arzobispado Stone, 86–87, *88*
exchange, long-distance, 34–36
ezpitzal, *55*–56, 57–58; in codices, 41–43, 44–53; etymology of, 43–44

face paint, 56; black band of, 29, 114; on Tizoc Stone deities, 95, 96. *See also* starry sky masks
feasts, festivals: Holy Cross, 149–50; veintena, 66. *See also* Toxcatl festival/ritual
feather balls (yuiteteyo), 114
femurs, human, 13
fertility, symbols of, 4–5, 62, 120
fertility rites, 149–50; domestic, 23. *See also* Toxcatl festival/ritual
figurines, 23; gold, *117*, 132
fire drills, in K'an Chitam images, 184
flags (pantli), and warriors, 114, *117*, 132
flayed skin, 147, 158(n24, n25)
flint, 164; knives of, 116, *118*
Florentine Codex, *21*, 135; deities in, *54*–55, 90–93; ezpitzal in, 42, 44, 52, 58
flutes, 13, 32, 38(n6), 157–58(n18, n21); ceramic, 9, 20, 21–*23*, *24*, 158(n21); Tezcatlipoca impersonator's, 138, 140, *144*, 148; in Toxcatl festival, 68, *145*–46
foot (leg): missing, 28, 29, 41, 96, 97, 146, 158(n20, n21), 171; serpent-replaced, 163, *164*, 170
funerary bundles, gold artifacts in, 127, 129, *130*

García Payón, José, Calixtlahuaca excavations, 13–14
gender identity, 149, 155, 160(n38), 161(n43); of Christ, 151, 156(n6); of Toxcatl impersonator, 136, 142, *144*, 146, 147–48
God K, 163. *See also* Kawil
gods. *See* deities; *by name*
God the Father, as Tezcatlipoca, 150, 160(n39)
gold, 2, 130, 132; bells of, 120–29; as symbol of power and status, 113, 133; in Tezcatlipoca representation, 115–19
grackles, great-tailed, 164, 171
grave goods, Chalchuites, 31–32
Great Coyolxauhqui Stone, 103–4
Great Jaguar Cuauhxicalli, 99, 101

Great Temple of Texcoco, 101
green, symbolism of, 56
Gucumatz, 66

Hackmack Box, 3
hair, gendered styles of, 136, 156(n4)
hat, Xipe Totec's, 56, 57
headdresses, 96, 114; hummingbird, 95, 98, 108–9
hearts, 4; ezpitzal iconography, 41, 44–53, *55*
hero twins, 69–70, 82(n18)
hierarchy, of deities, 85–86, *88*, 92–93, 99
Hieroglyphic Stairs (Dos Pilas), katun endings on, 184–85
Historia de los mexicanos por sus pinturas, 60, 71, 73
Holy Cross, Feast of the, 160(n36, n37); fertility focus of, 149–50
Holy Week, 160(n38); and Huixachtecatl, 148–49
homosexuality, of Tezcatlipoca impersonator, 140, 142, 144
Huastecs (Huaxtecs), 33; warriors, 123–24
Huehuetoca, migrants from, *15*
Huemac, 77
Huexotzinca, Huexotzinco, 110(n9), 129
Huey tozoztli, 149–50
Huitzilihuitl, 71
Huitzilopochtli, 13, *54*, 58, 61, 64, 66, 70, 77, 78, 89, 104, 106, 110–11(n7, n9, n13, n16), 112(n18); bells and, 120, 122–23, 124; in calendrical cycles, 102–3; in Codex Matritense, *42*, 43; hierarchical place of, 92–93; hummingbird and, 95, 98; in political history, 84–87; rise to power, 94, 99, 101; on Tizoc Stone, *88*, 96–97, *105*, 107
Huitzilopochtli's Temple, offerings in, 130–32
Huitznahuac, 101; conquered gods in, 101–2
Huitznahuatl, 102
Huixachtecatl (Cerro de Estrella), 148–49, 159(n31), 160(n33)
human body, humans, 110(n7); as polity metaphor, 96–97; in Templo Mayor offerings, 130, 132
hummingbird: and Huitzilopochtli, 95, 98, 108–9; and Quetzalcoatl, 70, *71*
Hunahpu, 69
Hunbatz, 69
Hunchouen, 69

Hun Hunahpu, 69
hurricanes, Quetzalcoatl and, 61

Ibarra, José de, Christ of Ixquimilpan, 151, *153*, 160(n41)
iconography, 7, 9, 41, 83–84; of bells, 120–29; in Codex Matritense, 42–43; ezpitzal, 44, 45–55, 57–58; Kawil, 163–66, 196(n9); of Tezcatlipoca as warrior, 113–*15*, 116(table)
ihuitzitzinahual, 43
illnesses, Tezcatlipoca and, 60
imperialism, Aztec, 35–36
impersonators (ixiptla), 19, 20, 31, 83, 97; gender identity of, 147–48; Quetzalcoatl and Tezcatlipoca, 62–63, 66–68; Tezcatlipoca, *67*, *69*, 118, 124, 135–37, 139–40, 142, 144–47, 149, 155, 156(n5), 157(n11, n17), 159(n27)
Itztlacoliuhqui-Cinteotl, 172
Itztlacoliuhqui-Corn, 73, *74*
itzli. *See* obsidian
Ixbalamque, 69
ixiptla. *See* impersonators
Ixtapalapa, 135, 156(n2); and Huixachtecatl, 148–49
Ixtapaluca Viejo (Acozac), platforms, 25, *26*
Ixtapantongo, Tezcatlipoca imagery at, *30*, 31, 32
Iztapalapan, 135, 149, 156(n2), 159(n28)

jaguar (*Panthera onca*), 1, 3–4, *67*; Tezcatlipoca as, 64, *65*, 66, 171, 172, 194(n2)
Jasaw Chan K'awiil I (Ruler A), 185
Jesus Christ, 157(n8); androgyny of, 138, *139*, *140*, *141*, *142*, *143*, 152–54, 155, 156(n6), 161(n42); crucifixion reenactment, 148, 149, 159(n31), 160(n33); sacrifice of, 150–51
Jimbal, 188
Jupiter, 3, 113, 172; and katun endings, 182–83, 184, 185, 186–87(table), 188, 190–91(table); and Kawil, 174, 176–77; and Maya rulers, 178–82, 192–94, 195(n4); retrograde motion of, 175–76(table), 195(n7)

Kan B'alam II, 179, 180–81
K'an Chitam (K'an Ak), 184
katun endings, 193; Kawil and, 176–77, 179; planetary retrograde and, 175–76(table), 182–92
Kawil, 4, 8; astronomical associations of, 173–75, 176–77, 178–82, 192–93, 195(n7);

and iconography of, 163–66; katun endings, 182–92; multiple forms of, *166–67*; and Pakal II, 180, *181*; and rulership, 193–94
Kawil cult, 171
K'awinal, 181
kings, kingship, 71, 87. *See also* rulers, rulership
kinship, of gods, 59, 69–70
knives, flint, 116, *118*

La Garrafa, 33, *35*, 36
Landa, Diego de, on Kawil, 174, 176
Late Classic period: katun endings, 185–87; Kawil, *168*, 170
Late Postclassic period, 1, 2, 133; long-distance exchange, 34–36; Tezcatlipoca imagery in, *31*, 32–*34*, 37
leg (foot): missing, 28, 29, 41, 96, 97, 146, 158(n20, n21), 171; serpent-replaced, 163, *164*, 170
Libro de Figuras, 49, 57
life force (tonalli), 5
lightning and thunder, Kawil and, 164–65, 170, 194
lineages, Maya ruling, 165, 193–94
Linné, Sigvald, 17
lip plugs, gold, 127
Long Count calendar, Maya, 176, 177–78, 194
Lucifer, Tezcatlipoca as, 113

Machaquila Aguateca, Kawil and Jupiter at, 177
madness, of Tezcatlipoca, 44
magicians, obsidian mirrors, 172
Magliabechiano Group, 55; ezpitzal renderings in, 48–*50*, 58; Pulque gods in, 56–57
maize, 73, 172; and Kawil, 163–64, 167, *168*
malinalli, 56, 58
man-gods, depictions of, 137–38
manikins, Kawil, 166, 167, 170, 177, 179, 180
Mapuche shamans, 151
Mars, 178, 195(n5)
masks, starry sky, 95, 96
Matlatzincatl, *88*, 95, 96, 107
Matlatzincatl-Coltzin-Tezcatlipoca, *105*
Matlatzinco, Matlatzinca, patron god of, 106–7, 111–12(n17)
mat makers, 62
Maya, 4, 61, 69, 161(n43), 195(n4); etymology of k'awil, 164–65; katun endings, 182–92; Kawil iconography, 163–*64*; rulers, 178–82, 192–94, 193–95(n3)

Mayahuel, 73
Mayapan, 189
Mexica, 109(n3), 114; civil war, 102, 107; and Huitzilopochtli, 66, 86
Mexico, Valley of, 86, 94; Tezcatlipoca in, 37, 86, 171
Michoacán, obsidian from, 18, 20
Middle Postclassic, 32–33, 34, 37
military training, 114
Milky Way, 171, 180, 195(n4)
mirrors, 79. *See also* obsidian mirrors; smoking mirrors
Mixcoatepetl, 78
Mixtec: divine couple in, 69–70; sacred bundles, 64
momoztli altars, 9, 13; identifying, 23–27
monkeys, and Quetzalcoatl and Tezcatlipoca, 64, *65*
Monte Albán, 33, *35*
moon, 3, 60, 62, 74, 85, 172; and Kawil, 174–75
Moon Goddess, Kawil and, 180
Moquequeloa, 60
Moquihuix, 132
morals, Tezcatlipoca's, 75–*76*
Morelos, ceramic flutes from, 21, *24*
Morning Star, 180, 194–95(n3); Tezcatlipoca and Kawil as victims of, 173–74, 188, 192. *See also* Venus
mortals, as representatives of gods, 66
mortuary practices, Chalchuites cultures, 31–32
Motecuhzoma I, stones of the sun, 86
Motecuhzoma II, 76, 82(n19), 157(n17)
murals, *166*; Tizatlan, 33, *34*, 44, *45*
Musée du quai Branly, catalog of sculptures in, 11
Museo Nacional de Antropología, 12, 18
Museo Regional de Toluca, 13, 39(n9)
museum collections, documenting, 11–12
music, in Aztec ritual, 22, 68
musical instruments, 22–23, 38(n6), 68–69. *See also* drums; flutes; whistles
mutilation, ritual, 31

Nacxit, 69
Nacxitl Quetzalcoatl, 64
Nahua, origin myths, 71–72
Nahualac, 11
name glyphs, 97
names, of gods, 60–63
Nanahuatl, 75

Nappatecuhtli, 62
Naranjo, 177, 178, 195(n6)
Necoc Yaotl, 113
New Fire ceremony, 23, 62, 103; at Huixachtecatl, 148, 149, 159(n31)
New Year rituals, Bolon Dzacab's role, 176
Nezahualcoyotl, 101, 124, *128*
9 Wind, 70
9 Wind-Quetzalcoatl, sacred bundles, 64
nobility (pipiltin), 104, 119, 124, 165. *See also* royalty
noseplugs, gold, 124

Oaxaca: bone flute from, 23; Tezcatlipoca imagery at, 33, *35*
obsidian, 1, 3, 164, 171; sacrifice with, 4–5; sources of, 20, 38(n5)
obsidian mirrors, 9, 172; biomodal size distribution of, 18–20; characteristics of, 14–17; provenience of, 17–18; rulership and power, 2–3; symbolism of, 1–2; from Toluca area, 13–*14*
ocelopetlatl, oceloyotl. *See* warriors
ocelotl. *See* jaguar
Ocelotl (month), 3
Ocelotl warriors, 114
Ocotelulco, Tezcatlipoca imagery at, 33, *34*, 36
offerings, 28; on platforms, 25, 26–27; in Templo Mayor, 130–32
Omacatl (Ome Acatl), 62, *63*, 103
Omecihuatl (Woman 2), 70, 71
Ometecuhtli (Lord 2), 70, 71
Ometochtli, 73
1 Deer, 69, *70*
1 Flint, *89*, 92; deities associated with, 103, 110(n9)
1 Reed, 61, 62, *63*, 89–90
opossum (tlacuache), 64
ornaments: gold, 2, 116; warriors' use of, 127, *128*
Otomí, 146
Oxomohco, 73

Painal, 58, 106, 108, 109, 111(n14); in Codex Matritense, *42*, 43; as Huitzilopochtli imitator, 107, 112(n18); in *Primeros Memoriales*, 53–54, 95, *105*
Pakal II, as Kawil, 170, 180, *181*–82
Palenque: Kawil at, 166–67, *169*, 170, 176, 177, *178*; rulership and Jupiter at, 179–81, 184, 193
Palenque Triad, *178*

Panquetzaliztli, 66, 101
pantli, and warriors, 114, *117*, 132
Paris Codex: katun sequences in, 189, 191; Kawil in, *167*, 188–89
patron gods, 94, 110(n7, n9); conquered, 103–4, 106–8; hierarchical status of, 85–86; Tezcatlipoca and Huitzilopochtli as, 84–85, 86–87; on Tizoc Stone, 95–98; victorious, 98–99, 101–3
Peabody Museum of Natural History (Yale), 17
pectoral gorget (anahuatl), 114
pelts, jaguar, 4
pendants, obsidian, 17
penis, flute as, 146, 157–58(n18)
Peñón de los Baños (Tepetzinco), 87, *89*
Piedras Negras, 178
Pisom C'ac'al, 64
pipiltin, 104, 119, 124, 165. *See also* royalty
planetary retrograde, and katun endings, 174, 175–77, 182–92
planets, Kawil and, 174, 176–77, 193–94. *See also by name*
plants, and deities, 73
platforms: in Aztec urban settings, 24–25, 38(n7); momoztli, 9, 23, 25–27
political hierarchy, 101; calendar dates and, 89–90; and deity hierarchy, 85–86; traits associated with, 98–99; Valley of Mexico, 93–94
political history: depiction of, 108–9; of Texcoco and Tenochtitlan, 99, 101–2; Tezcatlipoca and Huitzilopochtli in, 84–87; Tizoc Stone and, 93–94, 98, 104–8
polities, human body metaphors for, 96–97
Pomar, Juan Bautista de, 68; Relación de Tezcoco, 116
Popocatepetl, 5
Popol Vuh, hero twins in, 69
Postclassic period: calendrical cycles in, 191–92; ceramic flutes, 21, 22; Kawil in, 163, *167*, 170; Tezcatlipoca imagery in, 29–34
power, 69, 85, 102, 113; depictions of, 108–9; obsidian mirror, 2–3; Tezcatlipoca cult and, 119–20; traits associated with, 98–101
precious stones, in Tezcatlipoca cult, 13
priests, and obsidian mirrors, 172
Primeros Memoriales (Sahagún), *42*, 43, 106; deity depictions in, *90*, 92, 95, *105*; ezpitzal in, 44, 52–54, 58

INDEX   237

prostitution, prostitutes, 75–76
publication, of museum collections and excavations, 12
Puebla, Tezcatlipoca imagery, 33, 37, 171
pulque, gods of, 56–57, 58, 73
pyramids, platforms associated with, 25

Quetzalcoatl, 8, 59, 68, 80(n4, n6), 81(n11), 82(n21), 111(n16), 156(n3); construction of name, 78, 79, 82(n21); creation in, 72–73; images of, 29, 30, *42*; names/aspects of, 60–63; representatives of, 66–68; sexual transgression, 75, 76–77; as Tezcatlipoca's twin, 59, 69–70, 71–72
Quiché, 64, 66
Quichea, 170

radial pyramids, Maya, 185, 187
rage, of Tezcatlipoca, 44, 57
rain, 5, 66, 120, 170; Feast of the Holy Cross/Toxcatl and, 149–50
rattles, 22
Red Tezcatlipoca, 70, 81(n15), 110(n9). *See also* Xipe Totec
reed mats, 62
regeneration, bells as symbols of, 120
Relación de Michoacán, gold bells in, 124
Relación de Tezcoco (Pomar), 116
religion, material culture of, 9–12
representatives. *See* impersonators
residences, ritual in, 22–23
ridicule, as characteristic, 60
Ritual of the Bacabs, 174
rock art, Ixtapantongo, *30*, 31
royal insignia, Kawil as marker of, 188–89
royalty, 4, 113, 124; Maya, 164–65; warriors as, 119–20
Ruiz de Alarcón, Hernando, on aspects of Quetzalcoatl, 60, 61
rulers, rulership, 71, 124, 132, 137; depicted as gods, 94, 95–98, 103–4, 180, *181*–82; Maya, 170, 178–82, 193–94, 195(n8); and obsidian mirror, 2–3; Tezcatlipoca cult and, 113, 119–20

sacred bundles (tlaquimilolli), 15, 63–64, *65*, 66
sacrifice(s), 2, 60, 79; of Christ, 150–51; costuming associated with, 95, 104, 114; in Huitznahuac, 101–2; human, 77–78; with obsidian blades, 4–5; of Quetzalcoatl impersonator, 62–63; of Tezcatlipoca impersonators, *69*, 135–39, 144–46, 148, 158(n22)
Sahagún, Bernardo de, 7, 110–11(n12, n13); *Colloquios*, 150; on ezpitzal, 41, *42*, 58; Florentine Codex, *91*, 92–93, 135; on obsidian mirror manufacture and sale, 14–15, 19; *Primeros Memoriales*, *90*, 106; on Tezcatlipoca, 2, 113, 118, 171–72; on Tlamatzincatl, 111–12(n17); on Toxcatl sacrifice, 135, 136, *137*, 144–*45*, 159(n27, n28)
San Angel (Yucatan), 171
sandals, obsidian, 171
San Nicolás Citlala, Feast of the Holy Cross/Toxcatl, 149, 160(n37)
Santa Cecilia Acatitlan, 11, 12
Santa Cruz (Holy Cross), Feast of, 149–50, 160(n37)
Santa Rita, calendrical cycles depicted in, 191–92
Santuario de Santo Sepulcro (Ixtapala), 149, 159(n32), 160(n33)
Sarcophagus Lid (Palenque), Kawil/Pakal II imagery on, 170, 180, *181*
Saturn: and katun endings, 182–83, 185, 186–87(table), 188, 189–90(table), 193; retrograde motion and, 175–76(table), 177, 179
Sayil, 170
scholarship, on Tezcatlipoca, 7–9
sculptures, 13, 102; art history approach to, 10–11; with bells, 120, *121*–22; deity depictions on, 89, 90, 92, 93–98; patron deities in, 86–87, *88*
seeing staff (tlachialoni), 95, 114, 116
Seibal, Kawil at, 167, *168*, 176, 177
self-sacrifice, 4, 66, *101*
Señor de la Cuevita, El, 149, 159(n32)
serpents: in Kawil iconography, 163, *165*, 170, 171, 174
sexual transgression: of prostitutes, 75–76; Quetzalcoatl's, 76–77
shamanism, 2, 3, 151
shields, *123*, 124, 129; Tezcatlipoca's, 13, 114, *115*, *117*, 132
shrines: at Ixtapalapa, 149; momoztli, 9, 23, 25–27
sky, creation mythology, 171
smoke, 4, 5
smoking mirrors, 37, 41, 95, 98, 114, *115*; images of, 28, 29, *30*–31, 99; and Kawil, 163–64, *165*–66, 167, *168*, 170

Solís Olguín, Felipe, 11, 12
sorcerers, 3, 61
sound, 2, 20; of bells, 118, 120–24
staffs (tlachialoni), 13, 114
star glyphs, on Mayan monuments, 185
starry sky mask, 95, 96, 106
stars, 85. *See also* Milky Way
stone objects, and momoztli shrines, 24
stones of the sun (cuauhxicalli; temalacatl), 86
Stormy Sky, 179, 194(n1)
sun, 60, 74, 85, 89, 172, 178
Sun God: Aztec, 103; Mayan, 166, 178
syntax, of images, 84

Tamoanchan, 75
Tamohi, Tezcatlipoca imagery at, 33, *35*, 36
Tarascan empire, 18, 19, 124
Teconal, 132
Tecuciztecatl-Moon, 62
Tecuilhuitl festival, *129*
Telpochcalli school, 114
Telpochtli, 114, 119
temples, 39(n10); in Tlapitzauayan, 135, 144–46, 148, 149, 156(n2), 157(n16), 158(n19), 159(n27)
Temple of the Warriors (Chichén Itzá), 29, *30*
Templo Mayor, 11, 93, 94, 129; archaeological research, 9, 37–38(n2); Coyolxauhqui depicted in, 120–21, *122*; offerings in, 130–32; Tezcatlipoca imagery at, 33, *34*, 103–4
Tenayuca platforms, 25
Tenenepango, Tlaloc vessels, 11
Tenochtitlan, 5, 25, *85*, *88*, 109(n3), 124, 135; and rise of Huitzilopochtli, 86–87; rise to domination of, 93–94, 99, 101; Tezcatlipoca cult in, 20, 33, 66
Teopanzolco, 12; platforms at, 25, *27*
Teotenango, broken flutes from, 21, 22, *23*
Teotihuacan, 17, 62, 171
Tepeyollotl (Heart of the Mountain), 3, 4, 48, *65*, 66, 194(n2)
Terminal Classic period, 196(n9); Maya, 163, 170, 171
Texcoco, 86, 119; conquest of, 99, 101, 102
Texcoco, Lake, 5
tezcachiuhqui, 19
Tezcacuitlapilli, 123
tezcanamacac, 15
Tezcatepec, 14

tezcatli. *See* obsidian mirrors; smoking mirrors
Tezcatlipoca: attributes of, 28–29; construction of name, 78, 79; names/aspects of, 60–63
Tezcatlipoca cult, 171; archaeological evidence of, 9–10, 27–28, 36–37; ceramic flutes in, 20–23; obsidian mirrors in, 13–20; royalty and, 119–20
Tezcatlipoca impersonator, in Toxcatl festival, *67*, 68, *69*, 118, 135–38, 140, 142, 144–46, 148
Tezcatlipoca-Itztlacoliuhqui, *55*, 75
thrones, jaguar-skin, 4
Tikal: katun monuments at, 183–84, *185*, 187–88, 193; Kawil images at, *165*, 166, 167, 170, 176, 177, 195(n6); rulers at, 4, 178, 179, 194(n1)
time, deities of, 73, *74*. *See also* calendrical cycles
Titlacahuan, 79, 103, *105*
Tizatlan murals, 33, *34*, 36, 44, *45*
Tizoc, 93, 124; depiction as deity, 97–98, 103, *105*, 107, 170
Tizoc-Huitzilopochtli, 103, *105*, 107; traits of, 95, 98
Tizoc Stone: conquered gods depicted on, 103, 104–8; ruler-gods/patron gods depicted on, *85*, 86, *88*, 93–98, *102*, 170
Tizoc-Tezcatlipoca, 96
tlachialoni (seeing staff), 95, 114, 116
Tlacopan, 101
tlacuache (opossum), 64
Tlahuizcalpantecuhtli-Venus, 74
Tlaloc, 11, 85, 110–11(n13)
Tlalteotl, 70, 71, 72, 73
Tlapitzahuac, 149
Tlapitzahuan, 149
Tlapitzauayan, 149, 156(n2), 158(n19); Toxcatl ritual and, 135, 144–46, 148, 157(n16), 159(n27)
tlaquimilolli (sacred bundles), 15, 63–64, *65*, 66
Tlatelolcatl, *88*, 96, 107, 108, 109
Tlatelolcatl-Huitzilopochtli, *105*, 108
Tlatelolco, Tlatelolca, 25, 86, 94, 96, 104, 106, 109(n3), 132
tlatoani, 69, 81(n15)
tlatocayotl, 96
Tlaxcala, 33, *34*, 37, 171
Tlazolteotl, 66
Tohil, 164–65, 170
tohueyo, 76–77
Tollan, 78; Quetzalcoatl in, 62, 75; Xochiquetzal at, 75–76, *77*

Toltecs, 75, 104; and butterfly breast-plates, 98, *100*; and Tezcatlipoca cult, 32, 37; Tezcatlipoca imagery, 29–31
Toluca, obsidian mirrors from, 13–14
Toluca Valley, 21; patron gods of, 106–7
Tonacatecuhtli, 89
tonalamatl (divination books), 87; date-deity associations in, 89–90, 103
tonalli, 5
tonalpohualli, 90, 92
Tonatiuh Ilhuicac, 120
Tonina, 178
Topiltzin, 76
toponyms, 14
torches, flaming, 163, *165*
Torquemada, Juan de, 61, 111–12(n17)
Totoltecatl, 56, *57*
Toxcatl festival/ritual, 66, 160(n38); ceramic flutes, 20, *21*; and Feast of the Holy Cross, 149–50, 160(n36); Tezcatlipoca impersonator in, *67*, 68, *69*, 118, 135–38, 140, 142, 144–46, 148
transexxual, Tezcatlipoca as, 144
tribute: Codex Mendoza lists, 124, *125–26*; gold as, 124, 129
trickster, Tezcatlipoca as, 172
Triple Alliance Empire, 101
Tula, 38(n7), 171; butterfly breast-plates in, 98, *100*; Quetzalcoatl at, 78, 80(n6); Tezcatlipoca imagery at, 29–31, 32, 64
Tulum, 166, 192
tun cycles, Postclassic interest in, 191–92
turkey, as Tezcatlipoca's avatar, 171
twin-ness, twins, 79–80, 81(n14), 82(n22, n23); mythic, 59, 69–72, 74, 78, 82(n18)
twin-pyramid complexes, Mayan, 185, 187
2 Reed, 61, 62, *63*
Tzotzil Maya, 146

Uaxactun, katun records at, 188
Ucareo obsidian source, 20
urban planning, Aztec, 24, 25
Ursa Major, 3, 172

vases, Tlaloc effigy, 11
veintenas, 66
Venus, 74, 82(n18), 196(n9); and Dresden Codex, 188, 192; and Kawil, 173–74, 180, 193, 195(n7); and Tezcatlipoca, 172–73. *See also* Morning Star
Veracruz, 18, 33
volador offerings, 12
volcanoes, 5
Vucub Hunahpu, 69

warfare, 61, 80(n4), 132–33; bells in, 2, 120–24; Tenochca-Tlatelolca, 102, 107; Tezcatlipoca as initiator, 113–14
warriors, 3–4, 61, 132, 148; bells and, *121*, 122–24, 130, 131; jewelry used by, 127, *128*; as royalty, 119–20; Tezcatlipoca as, 61, 113–*15*, *117*, *118*
weeks (trecenas), deities associated with, 87, 89–90
whistles, 22, 38(n6), 140, 146
wind, deities associated with, 60–61
worldview, 2, 5–6

Xipe Totec, 56–57, 58, 61, 147, 156(n5)
Xiuhcoac, 129
Xiuhtecuhtli, 32, 98, *99*
Xochiquetzal, 51, 73, 75–76, *77*
Xolotl, 72, *73*
Xultun, 188, 195(n8)

Yaotl, 61, 113, 114
Yaotzin, 113
Yautepec, flute pieces from, 21, *24*
Yaxchilan, 176, 177, 179, 182, 184, 193
Yaxkin Chaan Kawil (Ruler B), 185, 195(n7)
Yax Pac, 181
yearbearer, Kawil as, 176
Yohualli Ehecatl (Night Wind), 60–61, *62*
Yucatan, 171
yuiteteyo (feather balls), 114

Zacatecas, Chalchuites cultures in, 29, 31–32
Zinapecuaro obsidian source, 20